Praise for *Everything and Nothing*

'Tender, intimate, inspiring; Mitchell holds you in her warm embrace and carries you across time and space, offering wisdom, guidance and her own uniquely exquisite take on life. A must-read for all women and for those who love them.'

Suzie Miller

'Exquisite, glorious and gutsy, just like Heather. A rare precious gift of a book revealing the extraordinary people and experiences that shape a life. I couldn't put it down.'

Sam Mostyn

'I didn't realise how much I needed this book until it was over. It has inspired me in ways that will buoy my spirits and comfort me for years to come.'

Bruna Papandrea

'Reading Mitchell's memoir reminded me of how I felt when I first read *Tuesdays With Morrie*. A gentle collection of musings on an extraordinary life; unpretentious and honest, full of stoic wisdom.'

Tim Minchin

'Heather's perspective on life and love speaks straight to the soul. Is there anything she can't do?'

Toni Collette

'This is exquisitely written, with such courage and candour. I was profoundly shaken, shocked, and I often wept. But best of all, I laughed—Heather is very, very funny. Superb.'

Sam Neill

'A life lesson in the power of optimism and self-belief, *Everything and Nothing* is for anyone struggling with illness, the death of a loved one or simply needing to find a light in the dark. This book will illuminate your soul . . . One of the best books I have read in years and one that will stay with me for a very long time. Heather's searing honesty, incredible bravery and unique ability to utterly absorb the reader in whatever she is writing about are extraordinary. You literally feel transported to that place in time. This should and hopefully will become an Australian classic.'

Rebecca Gibney

'To read her memoir is to understand why Heather Mitchell is universally beloved across the world of Australian theatre, film and television. An extraordinary life told in tender detail, capturing triumph, love and tragedy with a beautiful humanity.'

Annabel Crabb

'This book is a joy. Mitchell has a brilliant actor's empathy for the full panoply of human experience, and an astonishing storyteller's gift—she takes you through love, death, birth, more love, near-death and everything in between with courage, insight, hilarity and astonishing generosity of spirit. *Everything and Nothing* will make you feel life more keenly.'

Anna Funder

HEATHER
Everything AND Nothing
MITCHELL

A MEMOIR

ALLEN&UNWIN
SYDNEY • MELBOURNE • AUCKLAND • LONDON

First published in 2023

Some names have been changed to protect the privacy of individuals and their families

Allen & Unwin
Cammeraygal Country
83 Alexander Street
Crows Nest NSW 2065
Australia
Phone:(61 2) 8425 0100
Email:info@allenandunwin.com
Web:www.allenandunwin.com

Allen & Unwin acknowledges the Traditional Owners of the Country on which we live and work. We pay our respects to all Aboriginal and Torres Strait Islander Elders, past and present.

NATIONAL LIBRARY OF AUSTRALIA

A catalogue record for this book is available from the National Library of Australia

ISBN 978 1 76106 730 3

Set in 12.25/18.25 pt Bembo MT Pro by Bookhouse, Sydney
Printed and bound in Australia by the Opus Group

10 9 8 7 6 5 4 3 2

FSC www.fsc.org MIX Paper from responsible sources FSC® C008194

The paper in this book is FSC® certified. FSC® promotes environmentally responsible, socially beneficial and economically viable management of the world's forests.

In my ten foot bamboo hut this spring
there is nothing,
there is everything.

Yamaguchi Sodo (1642–1716)

For Marty, Finn and Seamus.

And to all the women before me, with me and after me

Contents

Prologue

Snow Domes

My first snow dome was of the Sydney Harbour Bridge. The hard moulded plastic was shaped like a classic Volkswagen Beetle's rear window and surrounded the tiny objects inside, preventing them from flying away as the shaken snow fell gently. When I shone a torch onto its clear, shiny surface in the dark, I could create shadows and project the snow-covered bridge onto my wall. The small sailboat (or maybe it was a ferry?) flowed forwards and backwards as I rocked the dome. Tiny polystyrene snowflakes would become jammed into the tack from repeated storms, and the boat would then jerk slightly on its course as if pushing through sandbanks and over rocky outcrops. I could imagine orchestral music building, velvety tympani thundering, before gently rolling into a mellow hum as the calm returned and woodwind birds caught the reflected sun on their wings.

As a young girl, I began collecting snow domes. People brought them back from their travels as gifts and, when I began to travel myself, I discarded clothes to make room for my domes.

Every dome told a story. Although they were mass-produced, each one was slightly different and I would spend ages in souvenir shops choosing the perfect one. I knew people regarded them as kitsch but, to me, they were beautiful.

In all, I collected 200, each one a springboard for my imagination. They were my miniature cinemas, theatres and homes. I could choose a scenario, give the figurines names and encourage them to interact as they developed relationships and explored their tiny world which at any moment might be disturbed by a change in weather. The snow would settle and the next scene would begin. The tiny set, inside its proscenium arch, remained constant but I could change the lighting, dialogue and the moment the world was shaken, when it slowly settled and how life went on. I could steer, shape and resolve the drama. If I looked after the dome, I knew the world inside was safe.

Everything contained within the dome—the figures, liquid and artificial snow—was fragile. The plastic could crack, the water could leak, the snow could become mouldy and the figurines could snap. If the dome broke, the world was shattered. Without water, the snow couldn't fall, and without snow, the drama was empty space. But if I could get them to my shelf in their shop-bought state, I could preserve their perfection.

These little domes reminded me that I could keep my memories alive by the stories I created from them. If I replayed a story often enough, it magically became even more lifelike than the event itself.

And so I began to pay attention, particularly in moments of crisis and drama, to ensure I could recall them accurately in the future. By directing my characters, I made my memories live. I would encase a memory in a snow dome, then label it and store it on the shelf with the others, so I could refer to it when I needed it.

Needed it? Why would I ever *need* it? Why would I want to revisit a specific drama, trauma, nightmare or overwhelming fear? Why remind myself of troubling times? Was it because they contained precious insights, which I could draw on to prepare myself for the future, or simply to help me understand a current situation? Why is it so satisfying to revisit happy times? Are they proof that we're capable of happiness, even when we think it's no longer possible?

If I preserved life in a snow dome, then I could manage any situation, difficult or easy. I felt happy to be feeling things. I loved being alive.

These stories are my snow domes. Many of them sit shoved to the back of a shelf where the light doesn't reach. Some are always front and centre. Others I haven't looked at for more than fifty years. Some are leaking and broken and, while I barely recognise them, they store their own truths.

Part 1
Girl

1

Baby, I Love Your Way

HSC trials. That's exactly what they were, a trial. Unlike my brother, who excelled scholastically without effort, I studied hard and wanted to do well, especially for my mother, even though I knew she didn't regard marks as an indication of intelligence. My father had spent many hours at the dining-room table, trying to explain mythical mathematical equations to me. Occasionally something would click, but how to apply it to the next set of numbers eluded me. It was a language full of tricks. I knew there was a logic, but I simply couldn't find it.

My brother and sister had both moved out, leaving me in Camden to see the HSC through. I had plans to live in Sydney and was looking into art schools and short drama courses, an imagined future distracting me from my studies.

Camden is a picturesque village about 65 kilometres from the heart of Sydney on beautiful land belonging to the Gandangara, Darug and Tharawal peoples. It has churches and historical buildings as well as the Macarthur estate, famous for its wool. What I loved most were its flood plains, paddocks and the flowing Nepean River with its kingfishers, kookaburras, eels and massive trees. As you approached Camden from Narellan to the north, coming over the rise you were met with a magnificent expanse of green. Poplars and jacarandas lined the streets and the wooden planked bridge rumbled under the car wheels as it welcomed you into the township.

A great attraction in Camden, for busloads of visiting city folk, was the Rotalactor: a large revolving milking machine, a 1950s merry-go-round for milked-up happy cows. The cows stood facing the centre, chewing away. Sitting on the grass, I munched on my Sao crackers with Vegemite, watching the steaming creamy milk being rhythmically pumped through tubes into clear glass containers above each cow, contemplating that the following day at 2 p.m. my HSC trial exams would be over. I wondered what cows would make of exams, and whether they put pressure on themselves to produce milk each day or compared their output with other cows'. I doubted it, but it was fun to wonder.

The following morning, I woke with only my Geography exam ahead of me. It was not a strong subject. While I could identify a mesa, I preferred to go into elaborate descriptions than discuss its geological properties. Graphs made me sweat and trying to decipher a table of numbers made me almost pass out. We were encouraged to stay home to study and only arrive at the school hall half an hour before the exam.

I walked into my mother's room at about 8 a.m. She was lying in bed. Her room was mauve: mauve walls, a mauve dresser, mauve bedspread, mauve bedside lamps. My father had spent a weekend painting it for her and she had been delighted. Her nightie was a light lemon nylon that reached the knee. For the past couple of years, her bedroom had become the centre of our home. In that room, we talked, shared stories, played charades, did our homework and the ironing, ate meals, meditated and cuddled.

My mother was keeping a secret that she took to her grave. Seven years earlier, when I was twelve years old, I had arrived home from school just as she returned from a day in the city. She was lying on her bed, her long slender legs stretched out, her neatly set hair now soft and loose, and her apricot lipstick just a faint suggestion. I slid down the wall next to her door. Untying my shoes, I said, 'Mum, I'm on the debating team and I have to argue for the government that "Ignorance Is Bliss". What'll I say?'

I loved discussing assignments with Mum and hearing her perspective on different topics. We would get out the big hardback world atlas that, one evening after dinner, a suited door-to-door salesman had convinced my parents was a bargain, especially because it came with a non-stick frying pan. We would thumb through *National Geographic* magazines, draw ideas from animal behavioural studies and refer to philosophy books by Alan Watts, Karl Jaspers and Søren Kierkegaard. We turned each topic over, examining its pros and cons. There was a natural pause when I was scribbling notes.

Mum said, 'If someone you loved knew they were dying, would you want them to tell you?'

This was a question I hadn't considered. 'No,' I said, arguing for the government. 'No, you wouldn't want to know. You wouldn't want them to tell you. It would be better to be ignorant. If you knew someone was dying, it might change your relationship with them. You might become scared or even angry, and then maybe you'd fight and stuff.'

Mum said nothing. She was feeling a little tired and closed her eyes for a while. 'Could you be a darling and bring the clothes in from the line? Then we'll find something to eat.'

Leaving the room, I tossed my book and pen on the kitchen bench and walked down the back stairs pushing my way through the wall of thickened and newly sprouted bamboo, which separated the garden from the washing and its intimate apparel.

Lying on her bed, my mother was processing the past few hours. She had gone to Sydney to see a medical specialist. She and my father sat opposite the bespectacled man in his white coat, with framed certificates on his wall, as he told her that pernicious anaemia had resulted in her developing leukaemia. There was nothing that could be done for her. He told them to prepare themselves to have at most three years and, because there was no hope for a cure, she should just go home and enjoy her life the best she could.

Mum apparently saw my 'Ignorance Is Bliss' question as a sign. On the trip home from the specialist, her biggest dilemma was whether to tell her children and sisters about her illness and prognosis, or to shield us from it. My question about the debate had decided it for her. This was in 1970, when cancer and serious illnesses were rarely discussed. I remember hearing about a neighbour, a mother of five, who had died, leaving her husband and children to somehow 'get on with life'. That's how it was talked about. A tragedy had happened, which was best not discussed so the survivors could pull themselves together and make the most of a bad situation. It was breast cancer (something I had never heard of), the information accompanied by shaking heads as if she had succumbed to a shameful affliction.

At the age of forty-two, Mum had decided that her youngest child, a twelve-year-old girl, while discussing a debate topic, had given her permission not to tell anyone of her diagnosis. She and my father would keep it a secret and she made him promise never to say a word nor give any indication that he was unduly concerned about her.

The day of my Geography exam, at about 8 a.m., I brought her a cup of tea and settled in for a chat.

'I want you to go in early for your exam and study at school,' she said.

I was about to ask why but she was looking at me with gentle determination, so I thought the better of it. When someone who is usually so open and giving puts up the 'Closed' sign, it means no transactions are happening till further notice. I promised I would and kissed her cheek. I felt her long fingers rest momentarily on my shoulder, then slide down my arm and unfold onto the bed. I gathered my things, put the front door key under the rock outside, which everyone knew about, and headed to the front gate. As I lifted the latch and hooked the low metal swing gate with the toe of my shoe to open it, an inexplicable dread came over me. I knew I mustn't leave her alone.

That's when I saw Mark.

Mark was smart and handsome. He lived directly across the road, and used to sit on his red-brick fence smoking a cigarette every day before and after school. He had picked up the early-morning paper delivery run, and would fling rolled newspapers from the wound-down window of his old blue Volkswagen. He would finish his morning shift by deeply inhaling a ciggy on the fence. For a person who seemed so reserved and private, he had chosen a very public position, sitting on the curved section of the fence that straddled the Hume Highway to his left and Macquarie Avenue directly ahead. Our house, across Macquarie Avenue, mirrored his. Anyone travelling by car, bus, bicycle or foot would see him.

My curiosity was piqued. Mark was an only child with a reserved father and tired looking mother. Mark and I were in the same year at school, but had never spoken and certainly never made eye contact. His mother was a nurse, who worked long hours at the local hospital, and I knew Mark wanted to be a doctor. I also knew my girlfriend Patti Ann, who lived down a gently sloping hill to a smaller street that ran parallel to the highway, really 'liked' him. Patti Ann looked like Liza Minnelli and sang like her, too. She and I were close and spent many hours at each other's houses after school. Her parents were always welcoming to me; once after I had eaten dinner at their house, Patti Ann's mother Pauline had given me a nip of brandy or port, and sent me off to audition for a role in the local theatre company production of *Mame*. I belted out a song, acted my tits off and landed a lead role. I gave Pauline full credit for my success but didn't make her method of preparation a habit.

I usually avoided contact with Mark because (A) he was brainy and out of my league, and (B) it would be unkind to Patti Ann. The difficulty was that I fancied him, too, and because our houses faced each other, I would occasionally go into our front garden early in the morning and rake leaves, even in spring, or check for the mail, which was delivered in the afternoons. My attempts to be noticed were feeble and he never acknowledged me.

But on this particular day, I kicked that gate open, still flooded with dread about Mum, and compelled by a force as powerful as a gale, I crossed the road. I counted eleven steps across the bitumen, one over the gutter and four across the grass and path before I stopped in front of Mark, clutching my textbooks under my arm. He had watched me cross with the same lack of interest someone gives to a garbage truck reversing. You wait for it to stop beeping and then everything goes back to normal. I leaned back against the warming bricks beside his dangling lower legs, staring across Macquarie Avenue to our house and its dark windows.

'Could I study at your place?' I asked, looking at the camellia tree that shaded the side of our house.

Mark stubbed out his cigarette on the crusty bricks between us. The heat of its embers prickled my elbow. He flicked it into the low shrubs and slid off the fence, scraping the pockets of his jeans on the rough edges. He mumbled something as he brushed past me that I took to mean, 'Sure.'

Following him along the welcoming central path and up the wide stairs to his front door, which he pushed open, I stepped into the cool darkness of the house. A narrow table sat against the wall for keys and bags, and a long dark hallway stretched right and left. To the right were the living spaces and kitchen, and to the left were the bedrooms. I only knew this because the previous owner had once invited me in to see her bottles of preserved peaches and plums that had lined the kitchen shelves.

Mark turned left and I followed, wondering whether he was even aware I was there. We entered his bedroom, which was diagonally opposite a bathroom. The room was more spacious than my bedroom and had a bed against the wall behind the door, adjacent built-ins and a decent-sized desk, which sat snugly below a large rectangular window facing directly onto our living-room, kitchen and back-room windows. I wondered whether he ever thought about me as he looked across to our house. I sat on the edge of his bed and opened a book, pretending to read. He carefully removed a Peter Frampton record from its cardboard sleeve and placed its small round hole over the central post of a portable record player. He lifted and lowered the needle, then sat on the floor as the initial crackling smoothed out and a male voice began to sing his first lyrics as a live cheering crowd gradually settled, the odd whoops piercing their concentrated focus. Peter Frampton sang of shadows growing before his eyes, moving across the page, whatever that meant.

I felt uncomfortable sitting on Mark's bed, being higher than him, and so joined him on the smooth pile carpet, crossing my legs like I was in primary school, feeling like I was about to be asked to read aloud when I had no idea what page we were up to. I was staring at the black-and-white hieroglyphics on the page, regretting my decision to cross the road, when Mark leaned towards me and kissed me. I pulled back, startled by his unexpected advance, and his lips hit my teeth and scraped my chin. We looked at each other for the first time ever. His soft brown eyes were quite broadly spaced, with faint greenish circles under them. I guessed he didn't sleep much between studying to qualify for medicine and his paper run. He looked like an only child, whatever that's supposed to look like, but he did. He looked lonely but not needy.

I wondered whether we should try to kiss again—whether he wanted to or was waiting for me to decide. I often felt too straight for boys my age and assumed I was regarded as a bit aloof. Not reckless enough, not looking for excitement like other girls. No one had ever expressed this to me, but I wasn't a girl who boys felt immediately comfortable or matey with. Occasionally, I tried to have a boyfriend when a girlfriend told me someone was interested in me, but beyond a bit of kissing when playing spin the bottle, I wasn't taken with the idea and nor, it seemed, were the boys. I didn't have any male friends and wondered whether that was something I should work harder to cultivate.

The lyrics about how Peter Frampton loved my way became louder as we kissed roughly. I lay back on the carpet, fully clothed in my blue woollen school skirt to the knee, long-sleeved white shirt and blue pullover. Peter Frampton went 'Hey, hey, hey,' as our legs became entangled. He wanted to be with me night and day . . . and then I orgasmed.

I sat up, all a-jumble, smoothing my skirt. I could feel blood swishing in my head, my limbs tingling, a pressure pulsing in my groin and a shocking wetness. I struggled to regain my composure, unsure of what had happened.

Mark was kneeling, also fully clothed, facing me. I pushed to my feet and, stumbling slightly, steadied myself on the back of a chair. The desktop was littered with textbooks, folders and pens. Peter Frampton had just sung something about clouds chasing the sun when I looked out the large rectangular window.

Framed perfectly in the centre of its clear pane of glass, on the other side of the street, was a figure on a gurney being eased into the back of an ambulance. It was like watching a terrifying moment in a movie. Curtains hung either side of the cinema's proscenium, waiting for the drama to resolve so they could close and release the audience back to real life. The characters looked unsettlingly familiar, and I dared not anticipate where the stomach-churning scenario I was witnessing might take me. I wanted it to stop. I wanted everything to stop.

Mark was standing next to me, far too close. Fearing he might touch me, I pushed him away. I opened the bedroom door and walked swiftly down the hallway. I opened the front door and gulped the cold air. I ran down the stairs, tripping on the bottom step but catching myself before I fell. I crossed the path and bitumen and stood over the gurney.

Mum looked up at me. I was breathing hard and she was breathing weakly. She looked shocked to see me. Her eyes showed no pleasure, only disappointment. All her hard work and planning had been for nothing, she seemed to be saying. Could she see that I'd not only lied to her about going to school but was flushed from my first sexual experience?

Only then did I see how wasted her body was, how bruised and frail. Her hair was greying, her skin yellow and the whites of her eyes were jaundiced. In the half-light, her skin looked so transparent that I wondered whether her limbs had been bandaged in cling wrap. The ambulance doors closed without explanation. The vehicle did a U-turn and disappeared.

There was no siren, only the sound of Joan, our neighbour, sobbing near the gate. I wondered why she was there, what she knew and what gave her the right to cry. I pushed past her, catching my skirt on the gate's metal latch. I flipped the rock over and, snatching the key, forced it into the lock. I turned it and left the key there. Joan followed me into the house. I stripped off my clothes in the dining room and slammed the bathroom door behind me. I showered and encouraged the warm soapy water to trickle between my legs as I washed away the experience with Mark. I felt sick with a terrible mixture of terror and pleasure, a feeling that threatened to overwhelm me and suck me down the drain along with the suds and swirling water. Keeping my head under the force of the nozzle, I assured myself that I was still upright and drowned out the sobs coming from Joan in the kitchen.

I redressed in my school uniform and ran the mile to school. A stitch in my side forced me to stop outside the house of the two Miss Freestones. The elderly sisters lived with a household of cats. A tabby arched around my ankles and I grabbed at the soft flesh below my ribs. I resumed walking briskly, favouring one leg, and caught a breeze that cooled my sweat as I approached the hill below the impressive St John's Church. I descended into the township of Camden. Only a year earlier, the main street had been underwater because of a devastating flood. The old cow pasture bridge over the Nepean River had been so twisted by the floodwaters, it needed to be replaced. Passing the council chambers, I slowed, attempting to collect the pieces of me, which were scattered and resisted being corralled. I tried to coax them, but it was like attempting to catch wily spiders with an upturned glass.

I rounded the corner into the school grounds and saw my fellow geographers waiting before the heavy double doors. They looked confident and ready. It was cold; some wore gloves, warming their fingers in preparation for an intense period of writing. There was an air of anticipation and nervous energy.

I drank from a bubbler near the rose garden and entered the hall. Metal heaters were suspended high on the walls, angled down with dangling ropes that you pulled to switch them on and off with a click. I sat at a table in line with a heater. The desk had years of graffiti etched into it. An inked-in arrow pointed to a heart with 'J.B. loves C.M'. There was hardened chewing gum in clumps under the lip of the table, and a charred circle where someone might have stubbed out their cigarette. The clock started; I read through the multiple-choice questions and had a good stab at them. There were maps and graphs and far too much empty space for answers. The time passed.

'Pens down!' This broke the silence and the metal bar across the big wooden doors was pushed open. Sunlight created a bright square on the timber floor. We poured onto the white asphalt, released at last. At least for now.

A maths teacher, Mrs Evans, whose husband was a doctor at the local hospital (they were friends of my parents), grabbed my arm. 'Quickly, your mother is being moved to Sydney hospital. I'll drive you.'

Oh my God, I thought. *It's true. It's real. It was her; it did happen; I didn't imagine it. Oh God,* no.

I pushed past her, the third person I'd pushed away that day, and ran. The hill rising towards the church, which I had sped down only hours earlier, now felt steep. The footpath rose and fell with tree roots pushing up through the black tar, an uneven footfall for my already ineffectual legs. I stopped, hitched up my tights and pushed through the burning in the backs of my calves. I just had to pass Macarthur Park and I would be closer . . . then past the big established homes and I was almost there. An ambulance obscured my line of vision to the hospital's entrance. That's when I saw my father.

He was lifting himself into the back of the white ambulance and was settling himself next to my mother in the dark cramped space. They looked so small, so fragile. I hid behind a tree so as not to disturb them. I had upset my mother already today; the thought of disappointing her again frightened me. It was a private moment I had no place in, so I retreated.

I stood leaning against the rough, cool bark as the ambulance doors closed and it disappeared down the highway. Again, no siren. I walked towards home, unable to think of anywhere else to go. I stopped at the strip of six low-lying aged-care apartments next door to our place, sat on the thigh-high brick fence and watched the sun set over the western paddocks. It was a red sky and darkness came quickly. My textbooks were neatly stacked on the front doormat. I assumed Mark or his mother had kindly delivered them. The key was still jutting from the door. I turned it and went inside. Somehow, I slept.

The following morning, I woke in a panic. The house was silent. The milk delivery was on the front step, the paper was on the front lawn and the cats were meowing for food, but nothing else resembled the life I knew. Mark was not on the fence; I felt relieved.

I walked the block and a half to Tacy's, a small general store with wooden counters and a large glass cabinet full of open cardboard boxes illustrated with images of lollies and names like Clinkers, Musk Sticks, Rainbow Balls and All-Day Suckers. My favourites were Caramel Cobbers, which were dipped in hardened chocolate, and Choo Choo bars in their blue wrappings with a train on the smooth surface. Both sweets were teeth-pullers and the Choo Choo made your teeth black, but I loved how long they lasted.

I entered the store and a bell rang. Mr Tacy appeared behind the counter. 'What can I do you for?'

'A loaf of bread, please, Mr Tacy.'

'Here you go. And how about some Adora cream wafers?'

'Yes, please.'

Mr Tacy reached up for the square tin of wafers. The tin was red with yellow writing—the word 'famous' was above 'Adora', which made the remnants even more special. He lifted the lid and pulled out the crinkly greaseproof bag, which had once been neatly stacked like a game of Jenga with delicate vanilla, strawberry and chocolate finger wafers. It was now a forlorn crumpled sack, but at its bottom were the multicoloured crumbs. He poured these skilfully into a brown paper bag. With a flick of both wrists, he spun the bag and made bunny ears at the corners. He picked up his sharpened pencil, which was attached with string to an exercise book, noted the price of the bread under the date and drew a line across the column underneath. He added the previous day's purchases, neatly wrote the final figure and returned the pencil and book to the countertop. Once a week, Mr Tacy would give me a slip of paper with the amount owed, and Mum would tell me to get cash from her purse, walk it down and thank him.

I sat in the kitchen with one of the cats, eating a slice of fresh bread, hoping the phone mounted on the wall by the fridge would ring and my father would tell me that Mum was fine and they'd both be home soon. I was deliberating whether to toast the next slice when I remembered it was Thursday. There was an excursion to an ice-cream factory for those who had finished all their exams. I swallowed the doughy lump, brushed my teeth and stuffed my small purse with a few dollars into my skirt pocket.

The ice-cream factory resembled a large public bathroom. It was a celebration of concrete and tiles, rather like the pub on the corner of the main street, which was hosed down every Friday night after the locals had stumbled out into the dark.

A conveyor belt stretched from the entrance to the exit. White square plastic containers travelled at regular intervals past us as we stepped in single file, watching the creamy white mass ooze out of metal tubes above. Two women with plastic shower caps, gloves and aprons stood on the opposite side of the belt, ensuring that no ice-cream escaped and, if it did, wiping it away. They looked bored and unaware of us. There were so many questions I wanted to ask *them.*

Do you get free ice-cream?

How long have you been doing this for?

Do you like each other?

Are you allowed to speak to each other or to us?

I was having this very thought when the woman closest to the exit looked up and stared straight into my eyes. I flushed with embarrassment, wondering if she had heard my thoughts. She leaned forward slightly over the passing containers and with the kindest expression said, 'Oh love, what a shame.'

She paused. For the slightest moment as she took a breath, I froze, dreading what she might say next. Then she continued, 'If only you'd come on Wednesday. It's Neapolitan day.'

I felt sure she was speaking in code, telling me that my mother wouldn't be coming home. I was convinced that this woman, a complete stranger working on a factory line, knew me inside and out—my past, my present and my future. And that she knew about Mark.

After we exited, we were all given a vanilla ice-cream for the bus ride. It looked so pale in its crisp yellow cone. As I accepted mine, my Geography teacher asked me how my mother was. I think I said she was fine. If a cow had appeared from around the corner and asked me how she was, I wouldn't have been surprised. She was all I could think of. I don't remember what happened between that moment and arriving back at the school except that, when we stopped for pupils to alight, I remained alone on the bus. We lived not far from the bus depot and, depending on the driver, I was welcome to enjoy a free ride for the extra distance.

Passing through the town's main shopping area, right outside Fossey's Haberdashery, I saw my brother Steven. He was wearing his purple flares and a green-and-gold paisley shirt. He hadn't been home for many weeks and yet there he was, questioning someone in a school uniform. The person he was talking to pointed up to me on the bus. I watched my brother walk to his car and follow the bus all the way to our place.

Steven was seven years older than me. Although I loved him and was proud of how smart he was, he had a difficult relationship with our mother.

I turned the key and walked into our darkened living room. The curtains were all closed, which surprised me. I hadn't noticed how dark the room had been when I left that morning. Now it felt foreboding as I stepped in from the bright light. Steven had beaten me by minutes, and was standing in the gloomy space between the dining table and living-room sofa. I couldn't see his face clearly, but his arms were folded.

'Hey, I've been looking for you.'

'I know,' I said. 'I saw you from the bus.' My heart was pounding.

'She's dead. Get your things, we're going to Aunty Rosemary's.'

We drove the hour and a half to Strathfield in little clumps of silence and small talk. Occasionally, Steven would mention something about the people he was sharing a house with in Surry Hills, which had a large mural saying 'SIREN' on its outer wall. One of his female flatmates had scored a job in a shoe shop in Centrepoint Tower; Steven said I should go in and see her and maybe 'get a discount'. His life in the city seemed so far from mine—the thought of going into a shoe shop and knowing the assistant kind of excited me. On his last visit home, he had brought me a T-shirt from the House of Merivale with Marilyn Monroe's face on the front in glitter; it was my favourite piece of clothing simply because Steven had thought of me.

We parked outside Aunty Rosemary's. I squeaked the low gate open, breathed in the scent of the jonquils lining the path, listened to her unlatching locks and let her hug me firmly. Her house was warm from baking, yet it had a chill that made me shudder. Everything looked half-done, not quite real. I could recognise the exterior surfaces of every object in her house, yet I suspected their interiors were as raw and unrealised as a bowl of batter. I felt myself slip and grabbed for the kitchen table with its thick clear plastic, which had protected the pretty patterned cotton cloth beneath it for years. I wanted to run again. I wanted to kick something to test my strength and check I was still there. I fought the urge, turned into my aunt's small cream-and-gold dining room with its lace tablecloth laden with cakes, and fell straight into the arms of my cousin Sue.

That night, I slept in my aunt's spare room. My sister Rosemary was given another room off the kitchen. Both rooms had neat, hard single beds. On the end of my bed, an envelope rested on a mohair rug with my name written on it in my mother's cursive. Inside was a piece of good writing paper, the kind you kept for special messages to accept an invitation or thank people for a party they'd held. I sat on the bed, placed the envelope on the rug and opened the neatly folded paper. I looked down at her handwriting. There didn't seem to be enough words on the page to express whatever it was she would say. I steeled myself to read beyond 'My dearest Heather', in case it just said goodbye and nothing more. I dared myself to continue. The curve of her writing nearly undid me, and I had to blink many times to clear my vision.

In the letter, she expressed how much she loved me, what a gift I'd been to her, and tried to assure me that I should be happy for her to rest because she'd been so very tired for so long. And then she thanked me for giving her permission to keep her six-year illness a secret from me. She was glad she had chosen not to tell.

My heart split. The ache was unbearable. I was responsible for her secrecy. I didn't know whether I felt grateful or angry. I didn't know whether I wanted to live or die. I didn't know how I would live without her. I felt frightened—for her, but mainly for me.

Where was she? How could she be gone?

I slept. Sometime later, I woke with a quiet mind, but the edges of my peace were being tugged by reality.

I heard birds and focused on their songs. One cry was like the beginning of a laugh that faded into a sigh, as if the thought of merriment was way too taxing. I lay with the letter on the pillow next to me. My tears had gone; my body felt heavy. In my mind, I traced the outline of my limbs lying on the sheet. It occurred to me that I may have died and was yet to accept it. Maybe death was as gentle and simple as being aware and unaware at once. Maybe I would remain like this forever and no one would ever enter the room, yet they would know I was gone and mourn me from other parts of the house as we had done last night for Mum. Maybe she was lying on her bed back at home, and we didn't know because we weren't there to see her.

I knew my thoughts were nonsense, but they allowed me to think of her without feeling frightened. I could see her face, not from when I last saw her in the ambulance, but from when she was younger, in a photo I had seen of her in an album. It was a black-and-white photo—she was leaning against a jeep, her long wavy hair blowing in all directions, partly obscuring her smiling face. I felt an unbearable pain. I knew she could never really leave me; it was up to me to keep her alive. She had been too tired to do it but now I could do it for her. As long as I felt her presence, I would be okay.

I read the letter again and saw a sentence I had missed, or maybe hadn't registered the night before.

She had written: 'I so want to be with you until you finish your exams, and I will do everything I can to see this happen.'

I replayed and pulled apart the morning of the day before. Mum had woken early on the day of my last exam, knowing that she was dying. She had organised the ambulance, with Joan I suspect, and sent me away to spare me the anguish. But I had stayed. And then I had gone across the road to Mark.

Her plan had not gone smoothly, and she must have been disappointed. But although the expression on her face was one I will always carry with me, it did not reflect her last feelings for me. I am certain that, as she neared death, she thought of me with unconditional love. That's who she was: loving. Our last moment of connection was one of fear and I needed to put it in perspective.

She must have fought so hard to stay alive. Each exam I did, she must have marked off as another milestone, another day won.

I failed Geography in the trials and also the final exams. The Board of Studies offered me a pass in the subject due to my circumstances, but I declined. I wanted my mark to reflect my experience. I hadn't failed. I had been focused on a different landscape, where the horizon was limitless and no words written on a page could describe its properties or importance.

2

Still, She Longed for Company

I was sure I had met my mother in a previous life. Shirley was always familiar to me. I know it's ridiculous to think I can recall this feeling of familiarity from my earliest months as a newborn, but I do. I have a blurred but vivid image of my mother's face looking down at me, her brown hair falling across her cheeks and onto her teeth. I can see sunlight falling on her and I'm sure I can feel it landing on me and warming me. Of course, this memory is probably from when I was older, but I attach it to being very young, because it gives me more time with her. It lets me believe we shared more time together than we did.

When I was still a young child, I remember having the thought: *Oh right, so I gotta do all this again? Well, I've come this far, so here I go.* I really did believe we had lived a life together before.

Reincarnation or not, I think Mum needed me, and I was happy to be with her in this life. My dad, on the other hand, was entirely new to me and my siblings were completely unrecognisable.

Shirley was fun. She was practical and smart, but mostly she was fun. She loved adventure; as a child, she had daydreamed of saving people from shipwrecks, mountain avalanches and all manner of disasters.

In 1945, as a young woman of twenty-one, having completed her schooling at Sydney Girls' High in Randwick, and armed with high scores in typing and shorthand, she flew to Chungking (now Chongqing) in southwestern China to work as secretary to the Australian Liaison Officer with UNRRA (United Nations Relief and Rehabilitation Administration). She told me she'd just had to go, and although she cried at times and felt guilty for leaving her family, to whom she wrote daily, she felt real happiness and purpose there. Later, working in Shanghai, Shirley met Arthur Mitchell, a red-headed American who went by the name 'Red'. They fell in love. Leaving China on the last plane out before it fell to the Communists, they flew to Hawaii and were married there in 1949.

Twenty years later, back in Australia with a husband and three children, Shirley spent the late 1960s and 1970s in pursuits that were 'aggressively nonviolent' (my father's words). She satisfied her social conscience by becoming secretary of the moratorium committee against Australia's involvement in the Vietnam War. With others, she marched peacefully against the war, for equal rights for women, and for the safety and protection of children. She would return home from a march or a small silent vigil, kick off her shoes, quoting the anthropologist Margaret Meade, 'Never doubt that a small group of thoughtful committed citizens can change the world: indeed it is the only thing that ever has', play Joan Baez, Pete Seeger and Bob Dylan records, and begin preparing dinner.

My brother Steven was in the Vietnam War draw, and I clearly remember my mother awaiting the news. He missed out by one number; I wondered what she would have done had he been drafted. I imagine pretty much anything. I recall her staying up through the night sewing fabric toys for my primary school fête, then spending fête day handing out leaflets for the new 'Australia Party' while we kids ate ice-creams and threw old fruit at a bucket of water. The Party's ideology was anti-conscription and pro-social liberalism. They didn't win any seats but directed their preferences to the Australian Labor Party, which in 1972 helped the ALP win government for the first time since 1949.

Both my parents had strong views about not actively influencing their children with their beliefs; neither involved us in politics unless we were genuinely interested and understood the concepts. I think they considered that the world was full of paradoxes, that nearly any statement could be countered by its opposite, and that any authority could be discounted or explained away. It was up to the individual to make their own sense of the world. While my father neither engaged in nor spoke of politics or politicians, my mother believed that social change could not happen without political intervention. But they both agreed that lasting change began with the individual. For the individual to have any real effect, you needed to be in touch with your own sense of purpose fuelled by a desire to help others.

My parents both sought a quality of life that went beyond owning houses and other possessions. They didn't particularly want to be wage earners and 'owe our soul to the company store'. They desired the freedom to travel with their three children to different cultures, learning from them, enjoying them, and offering environmental and humanitarian support. But life, with all its amazing and messy surprises, steered them in other directions. They ended up finding contentment wherever they were; Shirley eventually experienced deep happiness when confined to her bed in a rented suburban house with bamboo scraping the window pane.

Our family of five lived happily in wonderful homes that our parents created for us. I was born in Seoul, Korea, in 1958 where my father was doing reforestation and erosion-control work and my mother was looking after three children under seven and a foster son named Inchil.

After three years in Seoul we travelled via Japan to America and Hawaii to spend time with my father's family and eventually to Sydney, to visit my mother's family. Red was offered work in Jamaica and so began two glorious years in Jamaica's largest city, Kingston. Jamaica, was a paradise. Memories of its soft white sand, turquoise waters and pungent smells of tropical fruits mingled with the sweet frangipani, jasmine and the deep-red hibiscus and poinsettia are still vividly alive in me. After two carefree years we returned to Australia, where our brief stopover in Camden stretched to seventeen years.

Depending on how you looked at it, Camden was heaven or hell. It was white, conservative and rural. We arrived there from Jamaica, so the contrast was extreme. Mum had never articulated it, but while she and Dad travelled the world with us, I assume she felt uneasy about abandoning her parents, Rose and Harold, who were getting older in Sydney. She doted on them and decided Sydney should be our home for a while. Camden was a midpoint between the city, where her parents and sisters lived, and the catchment areas of the Nepean, Nattai and Warragamba Dams, where Dad's new job in soil conservation took him. He and Mum felt welcome anywhere in the world, and Mum's free spirit was eager to accept any option presented to her

Being the youngest child, I adapted quickly, making lifelong friends and loving the long walks through the paddocks. I felt that Camden was only a phase and would never be my home, but it was a phase I was happy to enjoy. Rosemary, I think, struggled with the lack of diversity and Camden's conservative leanings. Dad made the best of it, as he did with everything. There was always a sense that, as lovely as it was, Camden was a big compromise. Mum and Dad had imagined a life of travel; they may have said as much to Steven when he was young, and he probably resented the move to Camden more than any of us.

The house in Camden came with Dad's job. It was an unimaginative, three-bedroom, square, red-brick dwelling surrounded by concrete paths and patches of grass, on the corner of the Hume Highway and Macquarie Avenue. For years, Red laboured on the garden every weekend. When we eventually left, it was a magical jungle. Mum and Dad drew on all their travels to create Japanese gardens with maple and cherry blossoms, pebble gardens and sorrowful willows draping over ponds with large goldfish and lily pads. There were frangipani, hibiscus, gardenia and hyacinth from Hawaii; a gingko from China; bamboo from Jamaica; and Virginia creeper, which changed colour with the seasons. There was also a tall red cedar, red waratah and banksia from Australia.

During a free session at school, my teacher once said, 'Let's have an excursion. Where shall we go? We have forty-five minutes.'

Someone piped up: 'Let's go see if we can find Heather's house!'

The garden was lush. It provided solace, shade, colour and a habitat for animals both domesticated and wild. After frightening bushfires, Dad would bring home terrified creatures: an echidna, a carpet python, rabbits, ducks, guinea pigs and turtles. We would keep them and love them until they were ready to be released. My sister and I adored cats. We would dress them up and wheel them around in prams, or lie them on their backs in pretty frocks, and they never protested. Velvet, my favourite, escaped from the pram while we were on holiday down the South Coast. She was wearing a loose smock, which I felt confident she could walk out of. After days of desperate searching and taping notices to windows and poles, we had to leave. I was heartbroken. Months later, while I was watering the garden, a sticky sickly black cat with bulging sides brushed against my ankles. It was Velvet. Pregnant and emaciated, she had found her way back to me. She gave birth to five kittens in my bedroom cupboard on a pile of my shoes. We found Topaz, our little ginger stray, dangling by the neck between the palings of a fence—as a result, he could only walk downstairs backwards.

Rosemary's cat Smokey, a big silver Persian with a disdainful nature, disappeared one day. Our mother spied her lying in the gutter on the highway. Mum headed along the path to check if Smokey had been hit, when a street sweeper coming in the opposite direction sucked her up. Mum had to break the news to Rosemary, who was distressed, not only about the circumstances but because she had been weaving a wall hanging and was collecting the cat's moulted fur for her artwork, which she spun and fed through a large needle.

I was in awe of my big sister. She never wavered from being true to herself. Without ever offending anyone, she quietly maintained her unique perspective on life, and she translated what she saw and felt into remarkable creations. She sculpted intricate worlds in clay and massive wall-sized weavings of imagined emotional landscapes. She was careful with objects and all living things. Small creatures delighted her, and her light touch and soft voice soothed even the smallest mouse.

At the bottom of the garden, there was a row of tiny graves adorned with forget-me-nots. These small profusions of dainty blue blooms were self-seeding and replenished themselves annually, representing remembrance and true love.

Mum loved people. She collected them. While she enjoyed solitude, even after a group of guests had left, I think she still longed for company. She would seek out anyone new in town, especially if they had chosen Camden after arriving from another country, and invite them to our home. Many times a year, a busload of tourists would stop at our house for tea on their way to visit the nearby Warragamba or Nepean dams or Wollongong Beach. Mum had befriended a woman who coordinated these trips, convincing her that Camden was the perfect halfway stop and that everyone would be welcome at our place. We'd begin baking early, and then, just before the visitors' designated arrival, she whisked a brush through her above-shoulder-length wavy hair, applied some lipstick and lit up. She sought out people who were 'outsiders', who kept her connected to the wider world.

She began a discussion group, attracting the most wonderful people who became her closest friends and support. Many of them were teachers: the Wrigleys, Ahmads, Bakers, Evans, Stuckys, Sinclairs and Lehmans. I loved sitting in the kitchen listening to their discussions in the lounge room, which ranged through philosophy, politics, art and the sciences. They all sounded so thoughtful as they listened to each other's ideas. They generally seemed to avoid opinion; instead, they were inquiring and engaged. When someone did voice a strong opinion, it would be countered and usually followed by much laughter.

A box of books would arrive in preparation for each discussion night. I was always desperate to see what the topic would be. One night, when I was about thirteen, Mum opened a box of twentieth-century American playwrights—Miller, Synge, O'Neill, Wilder, Williams and Albee. I began with a play called *Picnic,* written by William Inge in 1953. Its hard cover was rough and sat well in my hands. I had never seen a book written with character names, settings and directions, with acts, scenes and the word 'curtain' on the final page. The format of play scripts freed me from my fear of reading fluently due to (unrecognised) dyslexia, because each line and groups of lines were clearly separated and had their own meaning, and because they carried direct speech rather than lengthy descriptions. Characters spoke, and from their conversations I could imagine everything I needed.

Mum and I would lie on her bed or the patio lounges and read. I would read a play and she often read poetry. Then she would rise to take care of some household chore. I could hear her wandering the house, quoting phrases and stanzas to herself throughout the day like spoken mantras.

'In the room the women come and go / Talking of Michelangelo . . .'

'I wandered lonely as a cloud . . .'

'Loveliest of trees, the cherry now . . .'

Shirley was a brilliant sewer, who made my sister and me clothes years after I longed for shop-bought ones. Other girls wore clothes with 'labels' attached and I wondered whether garments that were store bought gave the wearer more credibility and sophistication. I bought a pair of grey, high-waisted wide-flared pants and a cheesecloth embroidered top and wore them twice before acknowledging to myself and my mother that her skills and taste far outweighed the rag trade's attempts to get me hooked. When I was young and we were living in Jamaica, Mum's sisters sent her tea towels made of the finest Australian linen. She enthusiastically turned them into shifts stitched at the top corners and up along both sides, leaving room for my arms to slip though. I loved the prints of koalas, kangaroos, kookaburras and yellow wattle; or the map of Australia with its separate states defined by dotted lines, all in different colours, with tiny images of items unique to each state. An emu in Western Australia, the Sydney Harbour Bridge in New South Wales, wine in South Australia and beautiful Uluru in the Red Centre. And how practical these fine Australian linen dresses proved to be, when I was soaked after a dash under the hose on a muggy tropical day.

Beach towels she turned into funky over-the-head fringe-trimmed ponchos. As we got older, she made us pretty dresses from polished cottons printed with tiny donkeys or checks with sashes and removable collars called 'dickies', which could be whisked away and, with one deft pull unsnapping the press studs, turn a practical day dress into chic evening attire. She even made our bedspread covers, finishing them with piping trim and matching them with the gathered curtains.

Shirley approached cooking as an extension of her longed-for travel experiences. She could make a sensational Indian curry with an array of condiments, a Korean bulgogi served in its traditional pot or slow-cooked Japanese sukiyaki. But when it came to the drudgery of an Australian evening meal, she might easily be caught ripping open a packet of Deb Instant Mashed Potato, plucking a few chokos from the backyard vine and throwing them together with an overcooked chop. We loved baking and would hide pitted dates inside cocoons of shortbread, or empty tins of condensed milk into mounds of desiccated coconut. My favourite was our juicy pineapple upside-down cake, which had a glacé cherry in the centre of each circular tinned pineapple slice.

After dinner, we often played 'Animal, Vegetable, Mineral'. One person thinks of an Animal, Vegetable or Mineral, and the others ask questions with only a 'Yes' or 'No' answer allowed.

Are you famous? No.

Do you eat flies? No.

Do you live in a house? Yes.

Are you useful? Yes.

Can you fit in a bread box? No.

On and on it would go, until someone correctly guessed a thermometer or a quail or Robert Redford. We'd play round after round, until we pleaded to be let go from the table.

In the evenings, we played records, often Joan Baez, Pete Seeger, Don McLean or orchestral symphonies, while we washed and dried the dishes and placed them into cupboards. Then homework began, and shoes were shone, lunches made and we went to our bedrooms for some quiet time before sleep settled all sounds and the town was silent.

The TV was kept in a cupboard in our parents' bedroom, unplugged. For a while, it sat in the living room but I assume Shirley and Red decided it wasn't conducive to enjoying family time all together. We only watched it if we all agreed on a program together on a Friday night, when fish and chips was on the menu. Instead, I regularly pleaded to have slide nights. My father would bring out the heavy teal-green metal slide cases, carefully marked with dates and places. The screen would go up, the projector tilted into place by a pile of books on the coffee table and I would relive the part of my childhood spent in Korea and Jamaica. These captured images never failed to excite me. They would appear as fuzzy images on a sheet and, with a turn of a dial, zoom into sharp focus reminding me that I belonged, was loved and that life was an adventure. Perhaps I felt that the best of my childhood had happened before we moved to Camden, and that in a sense my childhood was now over.

My parents didn't drink; the only alcohol in our house was a bottle of Marsala on the top shelf of the linen cupboard behind the vases. Shirley said it was for cooking, but I never saw her use it. I suspect she had read in a recipe book to keep a bottle of Marsala handy, though she had no idea what for. The most daring thing she ever did in the kitchen was make a French Bombe Alaska. She lit it with a match and we excitedly watched it explode into flame. I thought, *Ah, she's used the Marsala at last.* Once, I saw an amber bottle of beer behind the reserve bottle of shampoo. I asked Mum what it was for. 'Oh darling, it's marvellous! It gives my hair a fabulous shine in the final rinse!'

We would often visit our best friends, Jean and John Hart, who lived in Wentworth Falls in the Blue Mountains. After dinner, the adults would sit facing the large window, discussing philosophy, art and politics. We kids would be at the far end of the room, on couches next to a roaring fire, watching *Mr McGoo* and *Top Cat* while we munched on Jean's homemade Anzac biscuits, smuggled from the top of the kitchen shelves. I would angle myself on the couch so I could keep an eye on the grown-ups. They arranged themselves in a semicircle, the expansive window before them and faint lights tinkling in the gully below, holding miniature crystal glasses of sherry. 'Sweet or dry?' John enquired. Red's glass remained full while Shirley's was sipped so slowly a thimbleful lasted her a couple of hours. Even so, she began to giggle and the next day she'd always say, 'It makes me silly as a wheel. I really shouldn't do it.'

Everyone commented on Shirley's zest for life. Even in the months before her death, people said, 'Shirley and Red have the best fun.' One day when I was about seven years old, my parents popped into the neighbours' place, leaving my sister and me alone in the house. It was late afternoon and Rosemary, who was three and a half years older than me, was in her room playing with her pet mice, which had won her a first prize at the Camden Local Show. I found a black felt-tip pen by the telephone, and proceeded to write prices on every piece of furniture and object in the living room. I wrote directly onto each item, leaving bold black markings on polished timber, book covers, upholstery fabric and shiny brass surfaces: $250 for a sideboard, $38.22 for a bookcase, $1 for a record. Imaginary people queued to inspect the sought-after displays, and I talked them through the pros and cons of each item until they decided on a purchase. Having sneaked some coins from my mother's handbag, I offered bargains and gave customers change. People were impressed with the quality of my stock, assuring me they would recommend me to friends. I wrapped smaller purchases in newspaper and encouraged the buyers to visit the library, which I also managed two doors down. I had written a version of the Dewey Decimal System on the spines of all the books, so people could find what they were looking for. Excusing myself from the shop, I'd arrive seconds later, unflustered, in the library to stamp people's library cards, warn them of late fines and wish them happy reading.

The back door opened and closed. I heard the metal kettle being filled and plonked onto the stove, and my mother saying something like, 'Oh well, she's certainly going to need some help . . .' as she entered the living room.

She stopped abruptly, sensing something wasn't quite right. As her eyes travelled around the room, I could see just how large the figures were that I had written, and just how black. My expert sales skills evaporated; the potential permanent damage I had done made my stomach clamp.

Mum stepped over to the dining-room table, a mid-century timber six-seater with hidden extensions. With one hand on her hip, she licked the thumb of her free hand and tried to rub the large, black offending dollar sign from the corner.

It didn't budge. I saw horror in her eyes. Fear even. Shock, definitely.

She dropped both her hands. Her shoulders slightly drooping, she sank onto an olive-green padded dining chair also decorated with its signature black markings, and looked directly into my eyes.

'Whatever am I going to do?' she said. 'I can't possibly afford any of this!'

Then she rose and put on a $4,000 Harry Belafonte record. 'Daylight come and I wanna go home' filled the kitchen as we peeled potatoes.

She loved dreaming up brilliant plans and getting Red to execute them. She would lie back on her chaise longue in the garden of our rented house, sipping tea and directing him as he laboured with large rocks and bags of soil. He adored her and loved seeing her happy. Together, they created a wonderland for us to live in wherever we were.

Red never rushed anyone. Whatever needed dealing with was worth spending time on. He calmed situations by just being there and not imposing his views. He must have felt compromised when his and Mum's ideas of what was best for their children differed, but he found a balance so as not to disappoint either mother or child. The only time I recall him getting angry was when Steven once called Mum 'a silly old cow'. Mum was in bed, her belly swollen from medications, her thin legs bruised and her hair thinning. I can only imagine that she and Steven had disagreed about something. He had spoken those words from the foot of her bed while looking down at her.

Red lost it. He stormed down the hallway after my brother. Steven slammed his bedroom door behind him. Dad pounded on it until he forced it open against Steven's pushing. I'd never seen my father angry. It was fearsome.

One of my parents' solutions to domestic conflict was a cardboard Suggestion Box, which sat on the plastic laundry basket at the end of the hall between our bedrooms. The idea was that whenever you experienced something annoying, unfair or downright rude and frustrating, you wrote it on a piece of paper and pushed it through the slot of the Suggestion Box, rather than take it out on another family member. It was like squeezing anger into a tight space and letting it fall into the future. Once a week after dinner, Dad would open the box and read out each anonymous suggestion or complaint, allowing for discussion. The messages were supposed to be anonymous, but it was obvious whose objection was whose. They often led to hilarity, sometimes to animated discussion, but most often to dismay that it had ever been a problem.

Of course, the system became abused over time, and ridiculous criticisms and suggestions defeated its purpose. I really admired one of Steven's, which was: 'Next time Heather wants to borrow my leather jacket, she should go to the fish shop.'

Steven was very handsome. He wore his hair to his shoulders in soft waves and had glasses that matched his extreme intelligence. While all his cohort were drinking and experimenting with hallucinatory drugs, Steven was heard saying, 'I studied up on drugs when I was fourteen—the pros and cons—and I agreed with our science teacher, who told us that we didn't need drugs to get the kicks out of life. So when I go to a party where there might be drugs, I bring my own Coke and peanuts.'

He told my parents that he refused to attend any more school, citing there were only two teachers he respected enough to teach him. My parents' response was to send him to board at the Friends' Quaker School in Hobart, Tasmania, but within months he returned to Camden and resumed some classes for his final year.

He'd made an agreement with his friend Eric, who was his academic rival, that neither of them would study because it felt like cheating. Instead, Steven spent his study periods playing his guitar and reading *Mad* magazines. Nevertheless, he and Eric both topped the year, each receiving a cash prize to buy books. Steven spent his on comics, which were presented to him on graduation night.

Red and Shirley used to sit up late into the night with Steven playing gin rummy and poker as a way to connect with him, and Dad sculpted and polished him a chess set to match his bright and unconventional ways. The kings and queens were hippies in flares and long dresses, and the pawns were straight out of the musical *Hair.*

While I loved my brother, I hated his tricky relationship with Mum. Years later, his wife Judy asked me, 'What the hell did your mother do to Steven?' My hackles rose in Mum's defence, but I had no answer. I couldn't understand their relationship. Had eldest child Steven, born in Scone on a property with neither electricity nor running water, where he spent long days with Mum, developed such a closeness with her that the arrival of two girls created jealousy? Did he feel Mum couldn't match his IQ? Did he blame her for returning to Australia and taking us away from a life of travel? Was he angry that she became ill? Did he see it as a failing and want to punish her?

Yet I knew he loved her. I saw how proud he felt in 1964 when Mum's cousin, the entrepreneur Kenn Brodziack, brought the Beatles to Australia. We were invited to the Sheraton Hotel in Kings Cross to meet them. Being only six, I was more impressed by the elevator, but Steven looked proud, particularly of Mum.

My parents made our Camden house a haven, but even though we lived there for seventeen years, it was never really home. Home for them was adventure and new people and places. Mum's diagnosis of leukaemia in 1970 put an end to any hope of travel. I assume that was when Steven unconsciously began blaming her for trapping Dad, whose love for her outweighed his desire to be free. Red never complained or expressed frustration, but I think maybe Steven resented Mum on Dad's behalf. Acceptance is so often the difference between feeling calm and anxious, and Shirley and Red both developed a lasting relationship with acceptance. By her bedside, Mum kept the quote: 'Grant me the serenity to accept the things I cannot change, the courage to change those I can and the wisdom to know the difference.'

When her energy began to fail, I practised calligraphy so I could pen Japanese haikus and stick them to her walls to remind her of the simplicity of life and its natural cycle.

'In my ten-foot bamboo hut this spring, there is nothing, there is everything.'

'Don't weep insects—lovers, stars themselves must part.'

At first, her illness was just a series of suspicious sojourns in bed. Such a vibrant, fun-loving and active woman lying down all day seemed odd to me, but never frightening. Her bedroom had become 'every room' for me. It was where we talked and read and laughed and even ate. I didn't question it. It was normal. It was how we lived.

As she weakened, she became a practising Zen Buddhist and found inspiration in the writings of Alan Watts, D.T. Suzuki and Abraham Maslow. She expressed to me many times that she had all she wanted in life, although she never referenced it in terms of her failing health.

It seems incredible to me now that I could have watched the woman I loved more than anything decreasing in size, her eyes turning yellow, her skin thinning, her stomach bloating and her legs ulcerating, while never being frightened by or even mentioning it. But her quotes like 'True freedom consists of accepting and loving the inevitable' stuck in my consciousness. I didn't question her disappearances to 'see someone in Sydney'. Her expressions of 'Don't ask,' and 'Give me a moment and I'll be with you,' kept me from dwelling on the pain she was in. Every morning, Shirley did the cryptic crossword. Then she read the obituary notices and circled her favourites. She would read these, giggling, to me. 'The cremation will take place at the family's convenience.' 'Our mother will now be able to purchase the mink coat that Dad always denied her.' 'She is survived by her son A.J., who loved and cared for her; her daughter Gloria, who betrayed her trust; and son Paul, who broke her heart.' 'Dear Flo was often woe betide, her frame was tall as it was wide, She rarely laughed and often cried. Methinks it's best that she has died.' We composed some of our own for fun, never acknowledging the dark reality lying beneath.

My role was to make her happy, massage her and keep the house tidy, and make her frothy eggnogs. I willingly joined in her conspiracy: to welcome people into the house, help her dress and pop on some lippy, sit on the couch, and pretend all was well. And I got brilliant at it. I became more entertaining to cover any silences when she was uncomfortable. I brought out my gregarious side—my slightly too loud, too helpful, too interested side—when we had guests. I acted my way through these visits to distract guests from the thinly veiled truth.

Shirley insisted that Red keep the secret between them and he doggedly agreed. Neither predicted the burden or gifts of such a secret. Red vowed to continue to live as normal; he went to work, on field trips and short bus journeys to the snow fields.

He did anything he could to avoid arousing suspicion, because this was her wish. And then he built the shed.

The shed was constructed of discarded timber, corrugated iron and square panes of glass with waist-high benches and old bathroom cupboards. At first, he began sculpting with lumps of clay and progressed to making moulds and casting and polishing. He moved his easel from the house to the shed, and the smell of turps, which I loved, went with it. He bought a sanding machine and increased his tool collection. He rigged up a light so he could work after the sun had set, and the shed and the sculptures became his peace and the place that took him away from her. Their secret demanded it; the shed gave him respite from the constant reminder that the love of his life was slowly leaving him.

My father wrote a letter to my mother's doctors to let them know she'd died. In it, he thanked them for the care they had given her for six and a half years. He told them that she realised her life span would be severely limited; therefore, her attitude was to fully experience and enjoy every precious moment, prepare her two daughters to become less dependent upon her, and ready herself to accept death when it came.

On the first two points, she succeeded remarkably and on the last, she tried hard. Unable to accept the traditional Jewish or Christian concepts of God, she studied Eastern concepts of one's unity with nature, the world and the universe, particularly through Taoism and Zen Buddhism. My father believed she had reached this stage not only through her intellect but through personal experience. The doctors told Red to expect her to slip into a coma and peacefully pass away. But moments before she died, after a long period of apparent unconsciousness, her strength returned. She tried to sit up with her eyes wide open. Dad lifted a sprig of wattle that my sister had picked and held it to her nose. She said, 'Yes, I smell it,' and then extending both arms, called out, 'Help me, help me, God help me! I don't want to die, I love living. Red, oh Red, I don't want to die, come with me!'

Her breathing was hard and her eyes, though yellow, were still bright. A doctor said she was disturbing the other patients and asked Red to leave. Throughout Red's protests of 'Don't do anything, don't help her. She's worked so hard for this, please just let her die,' the doctor injected her with a sedative. Although she relaxed and said nothing more, her imploring expression did not change.

Her breathing became slower and, a few moments later, ceased.

Red wrote the letter because he felt she had been deprived of her last self-expression, her last chance to gain full acceptance of her fate. She might not have reached it, but the sedative cut off her fight. Red had been waiting six and a half years for acceptance and peace to come; instead, he was left with an expression of desperate imploring and doubt. In the letter, he suggested that doctors might treat each case differently and that the last moments of life, even though they involved pain, might be sacred for the person experiencing them. He stated that this was, of course, his own personal reaction but it had so disturbed him that he wanted to bring it to the doctors' attention, or to the attention of any doctor who might be interested. Then he thanked them again for the years of care. He wrote the letter in beautiful handwriting, folded it, smoothed it into a blank envelope and put it away . . . never to be sent.

The day of Mum's funeral, I looked at my clothes, confused. How do you dress to say goodbye? Nothing felt right. I settled on a simple olive-green dress with knee-high patent leather boots. Rosemary and I picked nasturtium leaves from the garden and sipped dew from their veined pads. We made a wreath using Mum's favourite plants, which looked more like a mangle of seaweed than a floral arrangement, and set off with Red to the crematorium.

It was awful. The impersonal room with upright chairs facing the front was unwelcoming. The sea of black was unsettling and the exaggeration of flowers overpowered our simple offering, which sat limply on the shiny coffin. Nothing reminded me of Mum. When the man pressed a button and the curtains began to close, I clenched the seat of my chair so as not to hurl myself forward screaming in protest. Never should a curtain be used like that. Never should the show end without applause.

The funeral was so much worse than the death itself. Death felt less final. Death had the potential to be anything. There must be some reason those religions and beliefs had continued for so long. One of them must know something the others didn't. Death was a common circumstance. It felt real. But that curtain and its finality—its arrogance—pretending it wasn't just a gathering of heavy velvet but had some extra powers, was affronting, insulting and shitty.

If a show was worthy of it, the curtain call got multiple returns, but a life, even a brilliant and exceptional one like Shirley's, didn't stand a chance. Had they opened it again and closed it and opened it and closed it like in the theatre, I would have stood and applauded and cheered, feeling satisfied. *Use the fucking thing properly or cut it*, was all I could think.

We held another service for her at the synagogue. Her pharmacist, who had provided her medications over the years, also invited us to join him in a Catholic service where prayers for the faithful were read out and her name was among them. I knew this was his mark of respect for her and I valued his invitation, but I couldn't fathom how no one wanted to really make a fuss of her. I wanted everyone to be affected. I wanted everyone to mourn and celebrate her, not just continue on with life as normal. I found it bizarre that her loss didn't create more of a tremor. While I was grateful for the respectful privacy her friends all gave us, I was also dumbfounded that the world continued. I guess the death of someone who holds your heart defies explanation or expression. Artists, thank goodness, will forever grapple with articulating the depth and breadth of losing someone you love; not just the person but the intangible quality of love itself.

3

Deeper than Human Hands or Hearts Can Reach

My mother, Shirley Pat, had two elder sisters, Audree Kathleen Daphne and Rosemary Rae. They were the third generation of girls named after flowers. Shirley's cousins were Myrtle, Iris, Rose, Lily, Laurel and Violet. She was very proud of having broken the floral mould until she stumbled on the perennial 'Shirley' poppy. There was no escaping it.

The three sisters grew up in a Jewish household with their mother Rose and their father Harold, who both had Polish ancestry. They lived in a comfortable house above Coogee Beach in Sydney, and rode the tram each day to Sydney Girls High School.

My grandmother Rose, who died when I was twelve, was known as a trickster. She was strict and proper, but also mischievous. She would remove her false teeth before dinner and hide them, and then, as she raised her fork to her mouth, she would exclaim, 'Oh no, my teeth! Where's my teeth?' I would scrape my chair back and search behind cushions and bric-a-brac until they were found. She would pop them in and glare at me with an expression of *Is there a problem?* Before delicately masticating her food.

Rose had a unique sense of humour. One evening in the 1930s, she and Harold invited Rose's niece Laurel to dinner, so they could check out her fiancé Clarrie. 'I want him to know what sort of family he is marrying into,' Rose had said. She opened the door wearing Harold's oversized First World War uniform, holding a silver platter displaying an assortment of tin cans, including creamed corn and Spam, and a simple can opener. Before Laurel could even introduce Clarrie, Rose said, 'I'm so glad you've arrived, dinner is ready. Please take whichever tin of food you'd like. The opener is there.'

The three daughters were very close and they all adored Harold, or Papa. I remember him sitting in a rosewood armchair with the paper, his shiny bald head, big nose and broad smile available to everyone. The grandfather clock ticked beside him, competing with the tennis balls being hit on the public courts directly outside their small apartment in Strathfield. Harold was born in Sydney in 1884, the fifth son of parents who kept an open house on the Shabbat, when as many as thirty people would attend unannounced to eat fried fish and celebrate together. Harold had been with the 7th Light Horse Regiment at the landing at Gallipoli, wounded in the leg at Bullecourt on the Western Front, and blown up in the trenches. He suffered from pain and insomnia his entire life, yet everyone regarded him as the sweetest, most loving man, the best dad any daughter could have.

While the sisters were close to their parents, they did not inherit their religious faith. Shirley wed a Quaker and became a Buddhist, Rosemary wed a Jew and became a Christian Scientist, and Audree and her husband Ron remained agnostic. For all that, the sisters remained tight. My mother called her sisters every day. She would lie on her bed, holding the receiver to her ear and twisting the coiled phone cord in her left hand. Spontaneous laughter would erupt after bouts of silence, and the bedroom door would be pushed shut with an extended foot when the tone became hushed. I wondered how they could possibly have so much to talk about when so little seemed to be happening in their lives.

Audree and Ron lived at number 18 Boden Avenue, Strathfield, and Aunty Rosemary and Alan lived at number 4. For 40 years, the two sisters raised their children and spent their lives seven doors apart. At one end of the street, the golf course sprawled, and at the other end, the reliable 414 bus route stopped beneath a camphor laurel tree; in between were the two sisters' houses.

When we visited Sydney, I pleaded with my parents to be allowed to stay with Audree and Ron. 'Please, can we stay at number 18? *Please?*'

I loved crunching up the red gravel drive, which ended abruptly at the forest-green garage door. To its right was the front door. I would ring the bell and listen for Audree's bare feet padding across the carpet. Audree always opened the door with the enthusiasm of a winning contestant, enveloping me with the scent of powder, hairspray and perfume as she swooped me up, kissing my neck with her full pink lips. She always greeted my sister and me with small jars of tiny striped multicoloured boiled sweets from Darrell Lea, and although they tasted crap, we loved them.

Beyond her, a record player would be spinning 'Diamonds Are Forever' or 'What's New Pussycat?' and we knew we were in for some fun. She must have greeted my sister just as warmly, because Rosemary and I would always gently compete over which of us loved her more. She possessed glamour, while Ron, with his tall frame, slicked-back dark hair, moustache and cravat, was truly dapper.

There were occasionally square dances at Audree and Ron's, which my parents instigated. Red and Shirley had been introduced to square dancing in California; my father would 'call' the dances to songs like 'Won't You Be My Honey', 'Dream Lover' and 'The Ring of Fire'. The caller prompts the dancers through a sequence of steps, which are in time with the music, and the dancers have to remain alert so they maintain the correct steps. Rather than remember set routines, the dancers are taught basic core steps, which can be called in any order. All the living-room furniture would be cleared and eight dancers would sashay, promenade, swing on the gate and travel the wrong way grande. They swapped partners, allemanded left then right, and found their way home. Home was being reunited with your partner, and if you did make it home, it was always followed by cheering and laughter and more punch or wine being served. The bursts of laughter were so riotous that, now and again, someone would pee their pants or flop onto a chair begging for a break before being hauled up again for another round.

Audree regularly abandoned the other dancers mid 'do-si-do' to check on my sister and me. On one occasion, she perched on the edge of the cold bathtub to rub my back and ease a bout of stomach cramps I was having. Kicking off her flat ballet-like shoes by the door, she sat on the hard enamel with her full circular skirt draped across her long, crossed legs and falling onto the gold-and-black tiled floor, stared into my eyes.

'Are you real?' Audree asked me, her perfect powdered nose touching the tip of mine. Her long false eyelashes fluttered beyond her turquoise eyelids, our eyelashes meeting and mingling like butterflies kissing and dancing. 'Are you real?'

There was no answer required. This rhetorical question conveyed: *You're special, there's no one else like you, you are beyond real.*

Muffled laughter and voices were heard on the other side of the closed door, but they were not a distraction. We were alone, together, connected. She could step into a child's world as easily as slipping into warm water.

Audree loved me. Audree loved everyone. She had no filter when it came to love. If no one else had ever loved me in my whole life, I knew I had been loved by Audree. And that would have been enough.

Audree had that real glamour that doesn't cost much and isn't precious or vain. Effortlessly, it made everyone else feel rich. In summer, she wore polished cotton patterned shorts zippered at the side seam with matching midriff-baring crop tops edged with pompoms. Wide-brimmed hats and large dark sunglasses were always within reach and earrings were a must. In winter, she wore stretch ski pants and loose woollen jumpers with rollneck collars, matched with rings, eyeshadow, lashes, lipstick and nail polish. Her deep auburn hair was always elegantly teased into a bouffant and swept to one side.

Ron and Audree's house was dark-red brick, its front lawn edged with roses and a low red-brick fence. Bay windows, framed by deep-green timber, fronted the single-storey dwelling. Over time, the rooms beyond the façade transformed from 1930s floral carpet with heavy furniture to soft cream pile and a mid-century Parker couch and armchairs, scattered with golden and blue rough silk cushions. Brass birds and turquoise-and-gold-trimmed lamps adorned small tables. Bookcases flanked the fireplace opposite the turquoise-covered lounge. Sliding doors opened to a dining room with turquoise-covered chairs, a record player, a sideboard and oil paintings that my father had done. A large poster of Shirley Bassey was on the wall, before an even larger poster of Mahatma Gandhi took its place.

This dining room was where Christmas dinners were eaten, twenty-first birthday parties were celebrated and Audree's famous pavlovas were eaten down to the last crispy, sticky or fluffy skerrick. Sometimes, a sewing machine sat on the table beside the pavlova. Later, the dining room was where they nursed my grandmother Rose as she was dying.

Audree and Ron's bedroom was also turquoise and gold. Her dressing table was a fascination to me; she let me play at it for hours. Her daughter Suzanne would twist and tease and pile my hair high with pins and lacquer as I arranged Audree's make-up, false eyelashes and earrings into neat formations in the compartments of the plastic tray in her vanity drawer.

The backyard was large. Over the years, the flower beds and swing sets gave way to an in-ground pool and fish pond at the rear of the garden, which my father made especially for Audree to sit by and enjoy. This pond was more than a decorative addition to a suburban backyard; it reached into the future and was a symbol of hope. It reflected the sky, which stretched across oceans to the faraway places where my parents had travelled. Audree kept the aerograms and postcards they'd sent from those places where she had never been and longed to go.

My parents kept those places alive by growing plants associated with each climate and culture. My father had dug, cemented and filled this pond with fish, and surrounded it with rocks and greenery, to give Audree hope, space and beauty. He wanted her to feel tranquillity and peace. Although it was never said aloud, the pond was never going to work.

On the open grassed area of the backyard facing the garden, folding aluminium-framed nylon-webbed reclining chairs sat beneath a large, fringed umbrella. Shirley and Audree talked here for hours, their husbands bringing them tea and date-nut slices or shortbreads, which Audree had prepared the day before. Audree shelled peas into a colander while they watched the pale orange and pink poppies open. They thought this was the most fun anyone could have. They fell into paroxysms of laughter, completely aware of their connected humour. Their sister Rosemary often joined them, placing herself neatly on an upright chair in her waisted pleated frock and stockinged legs with low-heeled shoes. Rosemary, the eldest, wore a girdle until she was in her seventies, so lounging was neither appropriate nor comfortable for her. The three of them spent hours talking over one another, yet could follow and remember each other's conversations. The men always tutted and shook their heads, flummoxed by so much happening simultaneously.

Audree was genuinely anguished by other people's pain. If she could find a way to alleviate suffering, she would do everything she could. Joan Brassil was an unofficially adopted sister to the girls; she had been in Aunty Rosemary's year at school and had bonded with Audree. Joan was included in all our family gatherings. Joan's husband had died before I was born, and she brought up her two sons alone. She was an art teacher and when the boys finished school, she became a professional artist. Her work was astonishing. Her concepts merged sound and light with electronics, printed poems, water and nature. Her installations were masterpieces in sensory dreaming. She transported you from the Earth's core to the stars and beyond. Before Joan could begin her journey into art, however, she had to find a way to survive. With her husband gone, no prospect of income and a broken heart, she found financial support in Audree and Ron. I shall never forget the day Joan's son was killed on a motorbike. Joan arrived at Audree's and the three sisters enveloped her. I observed that nothing can remove pain altogether, but the arms and hearts of genuine friends can make life seem bearable.

One warm afternoon, the three sisters were chatting while Tchaikovsky played in the background. My mother jumped up, followed by Audree. They went into the spare room and tore the white nylon curtains from their rails, threw off their clothes, swathed themselves in tuille, came back outside and danced among the poppies like woodland nymphs. Rosemary borrowed a long, white nightie and joined them as a more demure member of the 'Three Graces'. I have no idea whether my father had anything in common with their husbands, Ron and Alan, but I didn't care. Being in Strathfield was all about the three sisters, who celebrated each other and gave each other a place in history.

In my naivete, I believed that they shared everything, that nothing was too much for them to deal with, and that together they had the answers to all life's unspoken riddles. I had no idea then of the secrecy, the unspoken, deep longings and fears they all shared: their mutual fear of the truth.

I began to join Audree in her living room doing calisthenic exercises on her carpeted floor. She would ask me to take her through the relaxation exercise I had learned at a drama summer camp at the National Art School in Darlinghurst. She lay on her turquoise bedspread and I sat on her dressing-table stool. With her eyes closed, I guided her through a rotation of the body, encouraging her to breathe into each limb and organ. I recorded it onto a tape so she could play it when I wasn't there. I think she tried, but a restlessness within her made it difficult without human contact.

Ron worked hard. When his and Audree's two children, who were academically brilliant and beautiful, met partners and moved out of the family home, Audree's focus shifted. This was when the whispering began. I heard the words 'menopause' and 'worry' mentioned in the same sentence. And then I heard the term 'shock treatment'. Why was 'menopause' being followed by 'shock treatment'? What happened in menopause that warranted such a thing? How could menopause cause depression or anxiety or whatever she was going through? I held my breath as I pressed my ear to the wall, trying to hear the adults' indistinct murmurings in the living room. Trips to number 18 became quieter; the garden chairs sat empty. Doors were closed and scrambled eggs replaced lavish dinners.

It was arranged for Audree to come and stay with us in Camden for a few days. It was school holidays, and I had a job in the local pharmacy keeping the shelves tidy, occasionally using the till and even counting pills. I turned from dusting a bottle of Charlie perfume and there was Audree—a vision between the oral stand and the disinfectants, an oddity in Camden, a town of sensible attire. Her white silk belted pantsuit with generous organza ruffled collar, her dyed jet-black hair swept to the side, her bright full lips and huge lashes . . . for a moment, I mistook her for a life-sized cardboard cut-out advertising perfection in cosmetics and style.

She saw me, beamed and stepped towards me. That's when I realised the world was tilted and that everything would change from this moment. The earlier time was over. We could never go back. It felt dangerous and I was scared. She picked up a tube of mascara and asked me to tell her about it. Her hands were trembling and her jaw was clamped. She was biting down hard on her back teeth and breathing through her nose. She was focused on holding the silver tube, concentrating with all her energy to not drop it, willing herself to control the shaking, not mistaking it for something else, just getting it right. Her false lashes were angled obtusely, creating a sadness to her expression, and her eyes had dark smudges underneath. One eyelid was a deeper shade of blue, her rouge was far too bright and her pink bottom lip too full on one side.

'How did you get here?' I asked.

'I walked,' she said. 'I wanted to see you at work. It's so lovely.'

I had no idea whether she walked the mile from our house, but I doubted it. I have no memory of how she got home, or indeed how I did. My heart was broken and I was certain hers was, too.

Mum kept a stylish, black-and-white, 1950s make-up carry-on bag next to her bed. It was square with a solid frame and was the size of a large shoebox. It accompanied her on all our trips, every aeroplane and taxi ride. It had always been out of bounds to me. It had pale pink satin lining with elastic satin compartments for make-up and hair products. My mother rarely wore make-up. When guests were coming over, she would throw a few hot rollers, which had been boiled on the stove, into her hair but never left them long enough to really take effect. She brushed her auburn hair into a loose wave, applied brown pencil lightly to her eyebrows and dashed on a bit of lippy. Once a fortnight, she visited the hairdressers and had a 'do', but this carefree look suited her so much more and made her more accessible and real.

This vanity bag or make-up case, which had travelled so far, now sat on her bedside table. I could hear her riffling through it at night when the house was still, before closing it again. It had the tiniest gold key and she began locking it.

While Audree was staying with us, she found the key. I walked into Mum's room with a cup of tea to find Audree staring at the case. Audree opened the case. Audree closed the case. She was scribbling, with a shaking hand, the names on the tiny bottles.

I gently closed the door, listening to it scrape across the carpet, praying that I hadn't been seen. Audree's concentration on the task was so intent, it prevented her from noticing me.

Audree's audacity in opening the locked make-up case somehow released an unspoken truth into the house. Nothing would ever be the same. My mother was spending increasing amounts of time in bed. All of us were now on a precipice. Somehow, I connected this change with Audree unlocking Mum's case.

Only a year before, Audree and I had done a 'practice-pack' together. We threw open her golden wardrobe and across the turquoise bedspread laid outfits suitable for locations she imagined she would be visiting. She produced brochures from her dressing table and opened them to images of glorious white sand beaches and glamorous hotels with views of the tropics. Her raw silk black-and-deep-green striped evening dress needed matching shoes, so we spread newspaper on the kitchen bench and, dipping a small foam brush into tiny circular bottles, we painted her shoes emerald-green. She didn't care that the job was far from professional, nor did she fret when the toes of one pair stuck together as they dried, ripping off all the paint like a layer of skin peeling after sunburn. She showed no irritation when the dried shoes cracked like parched earth. Audree thought it was all such fun; she squeezed my hand as though I'd intentionally caused damage to entertain her.

Audree was never cross with us. Once, my sister stepped onto a pair of Uncle Ron's prescription glasses while getting off the top bunk bed. Audree waved it away with a smile that opened our hearts. I often wondered where all her love came from.

To the sound of Shirley Bassey's 'Goldfinger' on the record player, we mixed and matched outfits with complementary accessories, making allowances for warm mornings and cool evenings. When we were satisfied, we neatly folded all the precious items. With great pride and a wonderful sense of completion, we snapped the case shut, placing it by the wall between the wardrobe and the window. We were packed and she was ready.

It didn't seem sad to me that, weekends later, I helped Audree lift her untravelled case onto the bed, unpacked all the neatly folded clothes, which now looked less flash, and re-hung everything. We never discussed why the trips didn't happen, or whether any actual trips had been planned. I assumed it wasn't important. Maybe it was simply a game we liked playing: the packing was the thing. That was the fun part. That was where the promise lay. The excitement. I don't even know whether she was doing it just for me because I enjoyed it so much, or if it was to keep herself busy. Either way, it didn't stop us from performing the ritual many times, always enjoying the promise of adventure.

The games were over now. The truth was being dug up, and she was determined.

My father tried to introduce Audree to meditation. Like my mother, she struggled with it. I assume she found the silence deafening, the stillness only amplifying her agitation. Despair is sometimes deeper than human hands or hearts can reach.

I didn't ask questions, obeying my parents' warning glances not to do anything that might discomfort her. I tried my best to be just the same, and to be good.

We received the call in late May. Mum had dressed that night because an old school friend had come to dinner. I was pushing asparagus around my plate when the phone rang. My father excused himself to answer it. He returned moments later, asking Shirley to come with him. To our guest, he said, 'I'm sorry, would you please stay with the girls?'

They closed the bedroom door. I shivered. Then the door reopened, and Rosemary and I were invited in. Shirley sat on the edge of the bed. Her thin legs hung over the edge, her feet lightly touching the floor.

'Darlings, Audree's gone.'

I looked at my mother, trying to comprehend the words and how she could have uttered them so effortlessly. She looked beaten, but not surprised. She was not crying. She was looking at her hands resting in her lap, then up at my sister and me. Rosemary was in the corner of the room. I dared not look at her. I had no idea how to react. I had rehearsed this scene in my bedroom but now that it was happening, I felt nothing I could identify. I observed myself from above, taking note of every detail in the room. I wanted to ask *How?* but knew the answer would sever the silence, and terrible unthinkable pictures would begin to form and probably never leave my mind. I knew the 'how' would never be spoken of.

Many years later, the incomprehensible was said out loud. Audree had taken her own life and was found by Ron in her beautiful bedroom. Depression had overwhelmed her. The most joyous woman in the world had had depression. Why had I not been told? How could this have happened? Why had no one fixed her?

Red drove us to Strathfield, to Aunty Rosemary's at number 4. The whole trip, I watched my mother. Her hand was resting on my father's leg as he drove but neither of them spoke. I pretended to sleep with my head angled towards the passenger door. I looked out at passing telegraph poles with wires stretching from town to town, carrying communication between people. The news of Audree's death had come along these wires, which linked houses to poles, and now they led us back to where the news originated. The news of her death had travelled so fast, yet the car ride seemed to be taking forever. How many messages were being carried along those wires right now as we sped by, changing people's lives forever?

We entered Aunty Rosemary's house. We slowly stepped into the lino kitchen, which was heavy with an almost sickly sweet smell of freshly baked cakes. Rosemary must have been baking since she'd heard. I imagined her beating butter and sugar in the glass bowl she kept in the sideboard. She had opened the door and hugged me like it was my birthday rather than a day of mourning. Her upbeat behaviour and smiling eyes confused me. We turned right into the compact dining room with its dark mahogany timber-framed window and mantle, the table with its lace tablecloth groaning with sweet offerings. I beheld the distraught face of my cousin Sue, Audree's daughter. I sat next to Sue in front of the small, recessed fireplace. We gripped hands, speechless, wondering what was supposed to happen now. Aunty Rosemary put the kettle on the back gas ring, and after agonising minutes, the whistle pierced the silence.

We sat not speaking for the longest time, while murmurs came from the spare room across the kitchen. I assumed Red, Shirley and Aunty Rosemary were talking with an undertaker. When I'd crept to the bathroom earlier, I'd seen leaflets depicting sunlit coffins on the kitchen table.

One month later, on 1 July 1976, Mum died. This time I was in a car with my brother, driving in silence down the same highway from Camden to Sydney. We parked outside number 4. We entered through the same door, walked down the short hallway to the kitchen, and turned right into the dining room. Once more, I sat next to Sue, who was there with her back to the fireplace. Again I held her hand, stared at the cakes and teacups, listened to murmurs in a far room and felt the earth swallow me up.

4

God You Can Lose

In 1931, at the age of fourteen, my mother's eldest sister Rosemary wrote a letter to her parents on behalf of herself, Shirley and Audree, who had all been sent to their room.

> *We wish to state that we are decidedly unhappy and tired of such unpleasant surroundings, and we are distressed that circumstances make it essential to inform you of this colossal grievance. We find it unbearable, and can endure it no longer. It is a grave offence to our natural welfare to be deprived of freedom and beg you to take immediate steps into the matter. Regretting the necessity to perform this disturbing duty. Unless you decide to satisfy us in an appropriate manner, we will be obliged to make our own arrangements.*
>
> *Signed Rosemary Price.*

I have no idea whether the letter had an impact but I'm sure that, if her terms weren't met, she would have found another approach until they were. She was fiercely loyal and protective of her younger sisters, and she maintained this commitment throughout their lives. When they died, she effortlessly transferred her boundless love and loyalty to her sisters' children, and for the following thirty years she doted on us all.

As a child, I thought it unlikely that I'd ever become close to my Aunty Rosemary. She had too many rules, too many things I couldn't touch, too many words I couldn't say and, strange as it sounds, she was too happy. She became known to us as 'Aunty' Rosemary to differentiate herself from my sister, who was named, I assumed, after her. Early on, it was agreed that titles such as 'big and small' Rosemary, or 'old and young' Rosemary, were neither appropriate nor kind, so she went by 'Aunty Rosemary'.

'This is my Aunty Rosemary,' I would announce. 'Have you met my Aunty Rosemary?' I forgot she had a surname, and everyone who ever met her referred to her as 'your Aunty Rosemary'.

It puzzled me that Aunty Rosemary was always smiling. Her eyes would disappear into multiple creases as her naturally pink cheeks rose high in her Botticelli face. I couldn't understand why her constant cheerfulness made me uncomfortable. Wasn't it good to be happy?

Her husband Alan, who called her Cherub, died unexpectedly in his sleep lying next to her at the age of sixty-six. That night, she had read poetry to him. Even as she told the story, remembering those last sweet moments, she smiled.

When both of her sisters died tragically a month apart, she smiled throughout everyone else's heartache. When her son went overseas to live, she smiled through her feelings of loss.

When the unthinkable happened and her young grandson lost his life, she still smiled.

Her smiling was a comfort, offering reassurance that everything would turn out for the best, but I didn't think it possible or genuine that she could always feel happy. Sometimes it felt inappropriate and sometimes downright weird.

What I didn't understand, and only later came to not only admire but gain direct benefit from, was her belief in the power of prayer. Though she never spoke of it, she had become a Christian Scientist. As a Christian Scientist, Rosemary rarely, if ever, took medications. I came to realise that her smiling was not artifice but a form of waking prayer that she practised. Her smile was a genuine result of her devotion to life and the people she loved. She prayed for all the family and her friends, and her regular practice of prayer helped maintain her health, because I never witnessed or heard of her taking medications or being hospitalised.

After my mother's death, in a mutual desire to 'check in on each other' over the following thirty years, we developed an unexpected bond that made my heart open with every encounter, and ache when she finally left me.

Aunty Rosemary phoned me daily. On the first of every month, she'd wake me with 'Happy new month, darling'. Every Monday, it was 'Happy new week'.

Each visit I made was a 'red letter day' and I was always a 'boon' to her. I never understood the red letter idea until someone pointed out the red markings on a calendar, days of celebration and respect. Originally, the red-marked days were religious days; eventually, they broadened to include the Queen's

Birthday, Labour Day and New Year's Day. For Aunty Rosemary, my visits ranked equally with those days.

Every goodbye involved prolonged hugs with her standing on the footpath waving and waving until I was completely out of sight. Each phone call ended with 'Love you, Heather darling, love you. You are so special. I love you for being you. Take care, darling. Love you. Bye. Love you. Bye. Love you, Byyyyyeeeee . . .' until her voice faded as the receiver was replaced.

When I was little, Aunty Rosemary looked just like photos I'd seen of Queen Elizabeth II. She sat straight-backed on a chair, aided by a girdle and 'steppings', which she endured until years later when fashions relaxed their hard-line approach to gravity. With her stockinged legs neatly pressed together, the hemline of her frock was protectively draped over her knees, as if knees with their smooth rounded forms might offend or excite. Her dresses with high, round necklines and belted waists were made of polished cotton. Skirts flared gently but not provocatively, and fine-wool 'twin-sets' (a matching sweater and cardigan worn together) were finished with a simple pearl necklace and matching earrings. She also wore a wig, which more than faintly resembled Queen Elizabeth's 'do'. I never knew whether the wig was a link to Aunty Rosemary's Jewish ancestry, or whether she reacted badly to detergents. 'Detergents don't agree with me,' she often commented, 'and neither do vegetables.'

In my second year at NIDA, when we were about to do a 'friends and family' performance, a fellow actor came into the rehearsal room. 'Ya gotta see this,' he said. 'There's a woman out here who looks just like the Queen.'

There was Aunty Rosemary sitting outside on a wobbly bench under a massive fig tree, in her cornflower blue, fine-wool twin-set and cream pearls, with her wig freshly set and a neat handbag, her hands lightly clasped and resting on her lap, looking for all the world like she was about to address the nation.

On another occasion, she came to see me in a production of Chekhov's *The Cherry Orchard*, directed by the brilliant Rodney Fisher at the Sydney Opera House. I played Varya, the plain loveless housekeeper. I invited Aunty Rosemary to meet me in the Green Room between shows for some light refreshment. I was sitting with the cast at the far end of the vast room, where the floor-to-ceiling windows look out over the side forecourt and across the harbour to the smiling mouth of Luna Park. Rosemary had been given access to the lift from the underpass near the stage door, which brought her directly into the 'artists only' Green Room. She appeared near the cafeteria wearing a fur coat, her handbag looped through the crook of her elbow. In her gloved hand was her small black Instamatic camera. She stopped, taking in the wondrous view of dancers, opera singers, musicians and crew members. She moved respectfully towards small groups and, asking permission, took photos of them eating their dinner, slipping coins into drink machines or lounging on couches. I watched her travelling among them, entrancing them. They all responded so positively to her, so graciously, so acceptingly. She offered her gloved hand as if she was on a Royal Tour and told them how beautiful they were, what pleasure they gave, how much the world needed their talent. I swear I saw a ballerina curtsy to her, confirming her royal status. And then she saw me. I waved and she lit up.

She approached my group of resting thespians and immediately asked if she might take a photo.

'Oh, I know who you are. You're Hugo Weaving,' she reminded him, as if it may have slipped his mind. 'I just saw you on stage, you were wonderful. You were all wonderful.' Then: 'May I please capture this? One with Heather in the middle, please.' Everyone happily obliged and introduced themselves.

Afterwards, we sat together. She leaned into me, smiling beatifically and resting her gloved hand on my knee, patting it like a sleeping kitten.

'Never mind,' she said. 'Everyone else was very good.'

I know she wasn't being mean! She didn't know how to be mean. She simply thought that my character didn't suit me, didn't do me justice—she thought a prettier or more elegant role would have been better.

When we were young, she generously offered to take my sister and me to see movies in the city: age-appropriate films such as *Chitty Chitty Bang Bang, The Railway Children* and *Mary Poppins.* We were encouraged to wear dresses and told we could choose one thing to eat at the movie. We should spend the 30-minute train trip to the cinema deciding what that would be, so as not to waste time when we arrived. She'd neatly cut out the movie times from the newspaper's entertainment section and leave them on the dining-room table for us to look at while she powdered her nose. Displaying the printed movie ads was part of the whole process. This was the entrée for the movie. The actual 'fillum', as she pronounced it, was the main course, while the dessert was the carefully chosen ice-cream or fairy floss. She monitored our reactions throughout the movie to ensure we were getting maximum benefit from the selected entertainment. When Truly Scrumptious kissed Caractacus Potts in *Chitty Chitty Bang Bang*, she shifted in her seat and kept her eyes on me, smiling like she was witnessing my introduction into womanhood and loving every moment of it. I always felt I had to try that little bit harder than felt natural to show my pleasure—the effort to please her kept me from fully enjoying myself.

Above the fireplace in her dining room was a framed retouched studio photograph of a pretty young girl with shoulder-length golden wavy hair and a bow securing the left side of her locks. She wore a pale-blue embroidered dress with short puffy sleeves, and held both hands against her cheek in a sideways prayer position. It was a lovely photograph and Aunty Rosemary liked it very much. I always assumed she was just a little girl. When I was six years old, I asked my mother who the girl in the photo was. She had gently shaken her head.

One afternoon, while standing by Aunty Rosemary's bedroom door, I watched her wrap a large, almost life-size doll in a clear cellophane-fronted box.

'Who is that doll for?' I pried.

'A girl in Newcastle,' she answered softly, tangling her fingers in sticky tape and shaking her hand in vain to release it.

I thought it was pretty rich that some stranger in Newcastle was getting a doll for apparently no reason. Anyway, who did she know in Newcastle? She didn't even go visiting friends' houses, only family and neighbours. I felt shut out and shut down.

Years later, while sitting at her table facing the fireplace, it dawned on me that the girl in the photo above the fireplace might be the girl in Newcastle. I was right: she was Aunty Rosemary's and Alan's firstborn child.

'She had a difficult birth,' was how my mother eventually explained her to me.

'So, is she okay?' I asked her. 'Did she remain a young child and that's why she likes dolls?'

My mother was not forthcoming. I sensed she wanted to be, but without permission she would not discuss it. Aunty Rosemary regularly made the almost eight-hour return train trip to Newcastle laden with gifts, She never allowed me to accompany her and she always returned exhausted but happy.

For all the love in our family, so many questions were out of bounds. It was the kind of loving silence designed to protect children from upsetting information. There seemed to be a hard-and-fast rule that, until something was spoken about, it didn't exist. Aunty Rosemary had not given permission for her daughter to be discussed. Final.

Aunty Rosemary received all information in confidence, whether the teller had asked for it or not. She never gossiped and would never share anyone's news without their blessing. Once given approval, however, she gushed forth and her enthusiasm couldn't be outdone. She spread the word via any means accessible to her: letter writing, phone calls, chatting with strangers on the bus, the taxi driver, the usher and the mail man, elevating each of her extended family to positions of superhuman excellence. She did this with great pride and personal satisfaction. Amazingly, she never sounded like she was boasting—she spoke of others' achievements with such warmth and enthusiasm that the person receiving the news felt included and bizarrely special.

My sister, my cousin and Aunty Rosemary's daughter-in-law all individually shared with her the news that they were pregnant with their first child. Each time, she kept her lips tightly sealed. When the three heavily pregnant women were invited to Aunty Rosemary's for tea one day, they discovered to their amazement that they were all due within a day of each other and that the day was imminent.

The only time Aunty Rosemary betrayed herself was the day I introduced her to Marty, my boyfriend and future husband. We met at the Sydney Theatre Company (STC) Wharf for lunch. When I excused myself to use the bathroom, she told Marty that I had been school captain not once but twice, in both primary and high school, voted unanimously by both students and teachers. Marty was the only boyfriend I had introduced her to, so she saw this as an opportunity to subtly warn him that I wasn't a pushover; I was my own person and I had plenty of allies ready to take him on if he didn't treat me well. Although Aunty Rosemary looked and dressed like Queen Elizabeth, and although she always smiled and had been a doting wife and devoted stay-at-home mother, she had a formidable inner strength and the conviction of the Queen herself.

Alighting from the bus, I was taken by how calm her suburban world seemed. The streets were wide and quiet, the houses neat and silent, the scent of seasonal flowers in bloom, and magpies and currawongs calling. Aunty Rosemary's front garden had a squeaky green metal gate bolted on each side to a thigh-high cream-brick fence. To one side was an inbuilt letterbox with a green metal flap, which clanged when mail was pushed through. The house was a warm, cream-brick art-deco building that said, *Approach, I'm here waiting for you.* A short green-painted cement path led at a slight angle to a flyscreen door protecting a dark timber front door with a brass knob, which you twisted to activate the bell, and a tiny peephole at a grown-up's eye height. Hydrangeas softened the exterior façade, gardenias flourished beside the path and the grass was kept short and neat.

After her husband Alan's death in 1972, and with her son Jon having already married and moved abroad, Aunty Rosemary was suddenly alone. I remember hearing conversations about security, followed by the appearance of a matching deep-green metal-framed screen door that was fixed into the brickwork. This of course meant a more modern bell was needed and a small, rectangular, white plastic buzzer was attached to the right-hand wall as you stood on the small porch at the top of the two shallow steps. I thought this buzzer looked cheap and I missed the brass bell and the tinny noise it made inside.

Pressing the buzzer created activity inside, as if a stick had disturbed an insects' nest. A faint but excited voice would call out, 'Coming . . . coming . . .' I could hear her low-heeled shoes crossing the kitchen lino or tapping on the tiled bathroom floor before being silenced by the pale-blue wool pile carpet as she neared the front door. I imagined her taking a right turn into her bedroom, still reassuring me with 'Coming . . . hold on, coming . . .' I pictured her riffling through her handbag to find the key then, snapping it closed, returning it to its place on the bed or dressing table and heading back to the door.

The security chain was scraped across its track, unhooked and let fall; next, a small sliding knob was pushed to the right; and lastly, the key was inserted into the narrow jagged crevice of the lock and turned. The door opened inward and sunlight illuminated her vibrant smile, high cheekbones and eyes creased from decades of smiling.

But we were only halfway there. The meshed screen door stood sentinel, allowing only a fractured and hazy image of one another. 'Wait a minute, I'll get the key,' she said. She turned away and took four steps past the serene living room to her right and lamp-lit bedroom on her left to the floor-to-ceiling mahogany timber linen cupboard, which included a cleverly designed telephone table and heavy square seat that housed the White and Yellow Pages telephone directories. She kept the screen door key on this table. Turning back and beaming, she stopped with an intake of breath as if caught off guard by a scene of immense beauty.

'I'll just get my camera.'

'Why don't I come in first?' I suggested.

'No, you look so beautiful standing there. I'll just take a photo, I want to remember this. Don't move!'

I waited, my arms tingling in their crooked position balancing cakes and flowers, but enjoying her excitement. She retraced her steps towards the dining room, which led off from halfway through the light-filled kitchen, before reappearing with the camera. Slipping the little strap around her wrist and checking the batteries, she said, 'Hold still.'

She aimed and . . . pressed.

'Did that press? I didn't hear the click. Did you hear the click?'

'I'm sure it clicked,' I said.

'I'll take one more to be sure,' she said. And then: 'Beautiful,' or rather, 'Bootiful', as that was how she said it.

'Bootiful! You are so bootiful! Now, I'll just take one more.'

'Why don't you open the screen door first?' I asked. 'You'll get a better picture.'

'No, this is bootiful. Just step back a little more so you're in the sunlight . . .' *Click*. 'There!'

With her camera dangling from her wrist, it now dawned on her. 'Oh, bother!'

When she picked up the camera, she had put the key on the dining table. Now she retraced her steps, returning with the screen-door key sans camera. As expertly as she could, she dealt with the screen-door locks by pushing a tiny lever under the handle into an 'up' position, slipping the long silver key into the keyhole and turning it, releasing the handle down and pushing the screen out towards me.

You may imagine that this ritual, which sometimes took up to 20 minutes, might dampen her enthusiasm, but it did not. She'd hug me for longer than was comfortable, her firm body and tight grip causing me to gasp for air. With my arms still loaded with flowers and shopping bags, it was impossible to reciprocate, but I tried, breathing deeply to keep my neck from snapping, and waiting for the release.

Hugging her was always particularly awkward because she proceeded it with a warning: 'Careful of my bosom'. The word 'bosom' would make me laugh. She liked to comment on women's bosoms, saying, 'Doesn't she have a lovely bosom,' or 'My, your bosoms have grown'. When I was pregnant with my first son, she loved admiring the size of them and said, 'Let's hope you keep your shapely bosom.' And nothing delighted her more than me putting on weight. The first thing she'd say as she searched for the key to let me in was, 'Oh goody, you're fatter in the face.' I felt like Gretel being appraised by the witch, ready to feed me gingerbread. I hated being told I had a fat face, and although I groaned every time she said it, she continued as if one day I would thank her for it. She also invariably commented, 'How much lovelier you'd look in dresses.'

I visited Aunty Rosemary at least once a week and always brought the same three things: a flan, flowers and Jonathan apples. Later, when I visited by car, I used to stop at Red Rooster and buy a roast dinner for her. 'Only the breast meat please, and no vegetables.'

Directly opposite Aunty Rosemary's house was Mrs Mandel's. Mrs Mandel, or Camille, was Hungarian and lived alone. I heard she had lost most of her family in the Holocaust and she rarely had visitors. My radar switched on as the gate creaked open; Mrs Mandel was starting her countdown. She gave Rosemary and me sufficient time to settle and pop the kettle on before she came padding across the street to say 'Hello'. She was probably no more than four-and-a-half feet tall with a strong, kind, tanned, lined face. Her intention was never to interfere, but she wanted me to know she was happy to see me and her neighbour, who lived alone, spending time alone together. She wanted us to know how happy she was for us . . . to be alone.

So she stood at the screen door pressing the little buzzer, waiting. Rosemary, though never cruel, lifted her eyes skyward and muttered.

'I'll go,' I said. 'I'll say "Hello" and tell her I'll pop over later.'

On one visit, Camille didn't buzz. Rosemary told me she'd been unwell and not to disturb her. 'Probably best to leave her to rest.'

Camille's house had a large, dark living room and on every surface were *tchotchkes*, or knickknacks. She looked so diminutive in her surroundings. Sitting on her couch with her little legs barely reaching the floor, she was like a knickknack herself. We didn't speak a great deal because she seemed to prefer just to look at me, smiling and absorbing the company.

One day, just as Aunty Rosemary and I settled before a piping-hot cup of tea and a peach and custard flan, Camille rang the bell. Rosemary sighed. 'Leave it. Pretend we're in the backyard and haven't heard it.'

We sat motionless until the ringing stopped and the front gate latch fell. A couple of hours later, as we sat in the living room right next to the door, she buzzed again. Rosemary rose, removed the chain and snib latches, and turned the handle. There was Camille beaming up at her. She had her hand on the screen-door knob. Rosemary hesitated before saying, 'Camille, Heather's leaving soon so I only have a few more moments with her.'

'Oh,' I heard Camille say. 'I have something for her.'

'Wait a minute while I get the key.'

Aunty Rosemary turned to the telephone table, found the key, undid the lock and snib, and released the screen just enough for a child's foot to squeeze through.

I stepped around Rosemary and looked down at Mrs Mandel's deeply creased face, her large strong nose and tiny hazel eyes. She resembled a small brown marsupial standing behind the screen, a grainy sepia photograph taken at a zoo. Her hands were behind her back. She was waiting for me to give her permission to speak.

'Mrs Mandel, how are you?'

My words seemed to release her. From her hiding place, she produced a small white porcelain vase no taller than a child's toothbrush. It had a rose painted on one side of it, and extending from the narrow lip was a single nylon rose. Its petals were dusty, but it might just have been dust on the tiny holes of the flyscreen door, which filtered everything on the other side.

I opened the door and leaned down towards her. No, the petals were definitely dusty. She offered the vase to me. As my hands made contact with it, she covered my hands and gripped them tightly.

With tears in her eyes and looking more like a possum than a person, she said, 'Your talisman. This is your talisman. Remember, God you can lose but rubbish never leaves you.'

And with that she smiled, turned and, carefully navigating the two shallow steps, headed down the path past the gardenias. She opened the green gate, closed it and, ensuring the latch had dropped, slowly walked across the road to her home. I never saw her again.

Aunty Rosemary's dining room was off the kitchen, which was in a direct line with the front door. It was beyond her bedroom and a spare room, which had a single bed laden with gifts, either given to her or to give to others, as well as wrapping paper and ribbons. The dining room was a pleasant rectangular room with two windows with sheer curtains and a small inbuilt cream-brick fireplace angled in the corner nearest the mahogany door leading to the kitchen. Taking up most of the room was a beautiful honey-coloured art-deco table with smooth curved corners. Matching chairs with padded fabric-covered seats could be pushed out only so far—should you choose to sit on the far side, you would have little chance of being asked to bring things from the kitchen without everyone having to stand and push their chairs in.

'I'll pop the kettle on,' were always the first words Aunty Rosemary spoke once I'd crossed the threshold and the screen door had been relocked, the key put back and the front door closed tight. Two heavy timber-framed glass doors led to the bright kitchen, a happy room with a window above the sink overlooking a large backyard. Above the sink was a circular battery-operated wall clock. Periodically, the clock's batteries died and the little black hands shuddered to a stop.

'When do you think Martin might next be visiting?' she asked. 'I really need the batteries replaced.'

I offered to change them myself but she staunchly refused, saying, 'That's a man's job. A lady wouldn't be safe standing on a stool.'

No amount of assuring her that I changed my own light bulbs and batteries at home would convince her. And so she spent weeks with blown lights and time standing still until a man arrived to save her.

One small step down from the kitchen was a little mud room where you left your dirty shoes and umbrellas. Hanging from a hook in this little alcove was a canary in a cage. Aunty Rosemary told me that, when her husband Alan was alive, the canary sang the moment he alighted from the bus at the top of the street. A small window in the mud room looked out to the garden where daffodil bulbs, planted in memory of Alan, sprouted each spring.

Popping the kettle on was a multi-step process. She filled the kettle with no more than an inch of water, lit the gas stove, placed the kettle always on the back burner 'so as any small children could not be burned,' and ushered me to sit down at the table, which was always covered with a plastic and then a lace tablecloth. No sooner had we sat down than the kettle whistled. She rose, extinguished the flame, removed the lid and poured the inch of boiled water into the teapot, popped on its lid and covered it in a knitted tea cosy. The kettle was refilled with another inch of water. Then she relit the gas, rested the metal whistle on the kettle, and returned to sit with me. A good 20 minutes passed before the teapot arrived at the table, then another six minutes passed to allow the tea to steep.

There were always cakes, tiny sandwiches, homemade shortbread, coconut macaroons and rum balls. For a woman who hadn't tasted alcohol in her entire life, she had a loose wrist and made a mean and potent rum ball. After one visit, I remember her loading me up with a Tupperware full of uneaten rum balls. I met my friend Robyn in the city to see the French film *La Grande Bouffe*, about a cook, a pilot and a film director who rent a villa in the countryside and hire prostitutes with the intention of eating themselves to death. Robyn and I ate the entire container, felt pleasantly drunk and threw up when we got home.

Aunty Rosemary loved sweets. In the last years of her life, although Meals on Wheels delivered to her daily, the meals mounted up in her fridge as she delighted herself with chocolate Magnums for breakfast, lunch and dinner, reassuring me that 'the doctor said dairy was good for me'.

When she was young, Aunty Rosemary's ambition was to be a journalist. She had finished school and, while studying at Business College, took a position as assistant to the aviator Nancy Bird when she was compiling a book of her adventures. She then worked at the Czech Consulate in Sydney due to her knowledge of English, French, German and Latin, but the outbreak of the war put an end to that and marked the beginning of her life as a wife, mother and homemaker. For twenty-three years, she volunteered at International House on the edge of the Sydney University campus. International House provided accommodation and activities for students from abroad; its mission was to provide global understanding and friendship. Rosemary fitted in perfectly. Given a small office, she photographed the students and kept notes on their arrivals, departures and what subjects they were studying.

Seeing her in this environment, I realised she saw her life as being in service to other people. She became a mother figure to all the students. She listened to their life stories and they told her their problems. Many were dealing with loss and loneliness, being away from their homes and their parents, and often their partners and children. She kept their secrets and prayed for them and they trusted her. Her presence became invaluable. I recognised her pure emotional understanding of pain; her smiling made complete sense to me. She hadn't endured pain, she worked with pain and accepted it as a gift. It had shown her how to experience true empathy and compassion. Her camera, her little companion, was always loaded and ready to aim, capturing moments of joy for the students to keep as a reminder that they were happy.

Aunty Rosemary spent thousands of dollars on taxi rides to and from her voluntary job, and kept the local one-hour photo lab in work, producing hundreds and hundreds of duplicate photographs for everyone, copies for students to keep and copies to send home to their families.

She must have been in her seventies when she asked me to photograph her without her wig. She was sitting in her living room on her pale-blue couch, her glorious below-waist-length caramel mane with wisps of grey cascading down around her shoulders. She was breathtaking, radiant, smiling at the camera as if to say, 'Remember me?'

And I saw her. The young girl who wrote the letter to her parents. The hopeful bride, the mother-to-be and nurturer of everyone she was yet to meet. There she was, smiling. She had endured great losses, felt excruciating pain, known that life wasn't fixed but constantly in flux, yet she had chosen to smile through it all. At first, it may have been to cover the pain she felt in private, but as the years passed and she discovered prayer, the smile became her gift to others: a smile for a stranger, student, gardener, neighbour, shop assistant or her family. When she smiled, someone benefited. After her death, I was told how people who had come into contact with her, even only fleetingly, felt loved.

We walked to the bedroom, where she removed her 'good dress' and hung it on a padded hanger in the free-standing Edwardian wardrobe. She placed her shoes in a box, squeezing some paper padding into the toes and, turning the soft floral nylon bedspread down so as not to crease it, she sat down in her slip on the now-revealed gold-and-blue checked woollen blanket. She swivelled sideways and asked me if I would like to brush her hair. Then we both braided it, twisting it across the top of her head and pinning it just like Heidi wore it in the movie. Aunty Rosemary was a young girl, sitting there smiling up at me, smoothing the hollow of the mattress where she had slept for more than fifty years.

I sat in the hollow next to her. She swung her stockinged feet a little as she spoke of meeting Alan, the poetry they had read to each other every night in that very bed, and how he called her Cherub. She talked of childbirth and her daughter, and how alone and desperate she had felt. I was overcome by such a wave of love for her and her gentle and generous life.

It was not until she succumbed to dementia that she let her hair fly, and although it was greyed and thinning, I never got over the beauty of it.

She was the lifeline connecting me with my mother and Audree, and keeping the extended family together. Every time I left her home was wrenching, and every farewell was indeed a sweet sorrow.

5

Red

I always felt enormous pride when introducing my father to people. He was a man of great humility and humour. Although named Arthur Lyon Mitchell, he was only ever referred to as 'Red'. His red mane, lengthened and shortened over the years, often accompanied by a beard, was his most beautiful and defining feature. He wore thick wire-rimmed glasses, which he only took off to sleep, shower or remove splinters. Even his swimming goggles had prescription lenses. He maintained his trim muscular physique through his love of hiking, skiing, rowing, snorkelling and swinging from ropes into rushing rivers, and his rough capable hands were always warm and extended, either to help someone or soothe their pain. He played guitar to lull my sister and me to sleep each night, and he massaged our feet when our hearts were heavy.

The year after my mother's death, at the end of my first year at art school, my father invited me to travel to Hawaii with him. He considered Hawaii his spiritual home and had spent the years 1942–46 on the islands of Maui and Oahu, when he had been assigned to the Civilian Public Service as a conscientious objector to the Second World War.

Red was born in 1916 into a Quaker family at La Crosse, Kansas, in the USA. In the 1930s, after years of devastating and prolonged drought, Kansas experienced violent dust storms that savaged the land. The skies were choked and darkened with 'Black Blizzards', and children suffered from black lung pneumonia. The topsoil erosion was devastating and dust travelled across the country; it could even be seen in New York. Shortly before this, in 1927, Red's parents Eugene and Hattie had moved the family of three children—David, Red and young Helen—east to Millbrook, Poughkeepsie, in upstate New York. I imagine that Red's passion for soil conservation, which he developed in the arid plains of China's provinces after the Second World War, was driven by his early vivid experience and knowledge of these dust blizzards.

Red's parents had met on a farm in La Crosse. Eugene, one of the USA's first chiropractors, had assisted his brother Charlie, a surveyor, on the construction of the Panama Canal. A resourceful farm hand, Eugene fell in love with Hattie Schaumberg and they married in 1913. In 1922, Hattie completed her Master's degree in science and became a teacher, but was unable to teach in Millbrook where they lived, because working married women were frowned upon. She travelled many miles every day to neighbouring towns to fulfil her desire to teach.

Their house in Millbrook was simple and without water, so Red, his brother and their father dug a trench one mile long and three feet deep to connect them to the nearest spring. The winters were freezing, but Red loved skiing and spent long days travelling cross-country.

Red became fond of his uncle Charlie, Eugene's brother, who lived on a nearby property in what became known as 'Mitchell Castle' or 'The Flying Elephant' because its roof resembled two elephant ears. Charlie was an engineer who loved using cement. His cement castle stood on a hill surrounded by orchards, which had been inspired by his trips to Europe. He travelled around Europe with two dollars in his pocket, sleeping rough and soaking up the Italian and French countryside, being seduced by the olive groves and vineyards. Around his own castle, he grew orange groves and grape vines while his second wife Helen, a small wiry woman, reportedly did all the picking and hard labour, lugging crates that strong men could barely lift, and selling their produce on the side of the road.

Charlie had met his first wife Lillian, a Cuban singer, in the Florida Keys, although he reported to the local paper that he met her in Cuba. He fell for her immediately and promised her a castle in upstate New York with Roman columns and extensive vineyards. She was dubious, but Charlie went home, built his cement castle and returned to Florida to collect her. Three years had passed. Although she was shocked to see him again, she admired his determination and was won over. The marriage was short-lived, because not only was the castle primitive, the land arid and the town devoid of nightlife, Charlie and Lillian were completely incompatible. Charlie collected cars, which he drove into the ground and, rather than repair them, he parked them in his garage. As each garage filled, he built another, then sheds around them, until extensions to house old cars littered his land. He purchased a fire engine and, when first gear failed, he used second and third until, eventually, all the gears failed apart from reverse. He drove that old fire truck backwards, manoeuvring her around the trees on his estate, along winding roads and eventually onto the main road and into town and back again.

Champion wrestlers, Charlie and Eugene taught Red to wrestle, which he loved. Eugene had been taught his profession in the early 1900s by the founders of chiropractic treatment, D.D. Palmer and J.B. Palmer, in Wichita, Kansas. The original chiropractic practice, which literally means 'to do with the hands', was hands-on wrestling; it did not use force but gentle manoeuvring of the body and muscles. The idea was that if you could manipulate another person's body through wrestling and chiropractic, then you could manipulate out-of-place joints into proper alignment.

When the family moved from Kansas to New York, Red and his brother David were enrolled in a public school. The other boys in class wanted to test the new kids in town, challenging them to fights. David and Red had to prove themselves by wrestling every single one of them. Using their skills in chiropractics, the brothers made quick work of them. After that, they were readily accepted and no longer needed to prove anything.

When Uncle Charlie's horse died, he asked Red to help him bury her. Red told me they dug for ages until Charlie said, 'Enough, that's it. That'll do just fine.' The two of them dragged the horse back-first into the hole, covered her body with dirt and, and with her four stiff legs sticking skywards, placed a timber plank on top of her hoofs, drew up two chairs and ate lunch.

In 1936, at the age of twenty, after graduating in silviculture—which means 'forest growing'—at Michigan State University, Red loaded up his loud Harley-Davidson Red Indian motorbike with a change of clothes; frying pan; billy; cup, knife and fork; bedroll; and what would become his lifelong essentials—a guitar, fishing rod, pocketknife, sketchpad and paints. He headed across the country and then sold the bike for a passage to Hawaii.

Hawaii was warm and sunny, as well as geologically exciting and novel. He loved the multicultural island where people of Polynesian, Japanese, Chinese, Korean, Portuguese, South American and northern European ancestry lived side by side. The first settlers of Polynesian origin were followed by Japanese, Chinese and Korean immigrants; then English people set up cattle ranches and pineapple plantations, and brought in workers from South America. People of Portuguese and Indian origin brought with them banjos, ukuleles and guitars, as well as a style of 'slack key' playing that morphed into the traditional Hawaiian music we recognise today.

Red wandered the islands learning from the Hawaiians how to make throw-nets for fishing, deep-sea dive for crayfish, and catch and cook goat, rabbit and wild boar in the traditional Hawaiian manner. He explored the islands barefoot, sleeping under the stars, painting and writing poems. One of his poems went:

> Yes, perhaps I am a bum. But is being a bum so very bad?
>
> I do not actually ask people to give me things, I only linger by the fireside when the feast is on.
>
> All morning I wander by the shore picking up stones and shells and seeds of plants. And in the evening I throw them all into the sea.
>
> And when I see the black stone-crab I watch how silently he glides along sideways across the rocks.
>
> Then I smile to the fisherman sitting by his line and bid him luck when the tide comes in.
>
> A campfire glows as the stars come out, and quietly I drift within the sound of the ukuleles.
>
> Someone is sure to find me there, and then I, too, will join the feast.
>
> As we sing and laugh, I am glad that I am only a bum.

After four years in Hawaii assigned to the Civilian Public Service in the National Parks, in 1946 he travelled to Shanghai, China, with the United Nations to train locals in how to plough the fields with tractors and improve irrigation and planting methods. In 1948, he met my mother Shirley, a Sydney girl from Coogee who had scored a job as personal assistant to the liaison officer of UNRRA. On 26 April 1949, they flew to Hawaii on the last commercial flight to leave Shanghai before it fell to the Chinese Communists. They were married two months later and honeymooned at the pink Royal Hawaiian hotel on Waikiki Beach. I still have a silver milk jug that my mother confessed to stealing from their room-service breakfast tray.

I once found a letter my mother had sent from Shanghai to her mother when she was twenty, saying she believed 'children should be brought up in their parents' faith because otherwise they won't know that they "belong".' She said her children, if she ever had any, would definitely be brought up in the Jewish faith. Well, I was brought up neither Quaker nor Jewish. We kids were welcome to explore, and choose or not choose whatever we wished to believe. We were welcome to go with our parents to the Quaker Meeting House at Devonshire Street, Surry Hills, or the Synagogue in Woollahra. For a while, I had a job at the local church teaching Sunday school to a group of little kids. A friend gave me a crash course on the nativity story, and I would spend the hour cutting out figures from pieces of felt and encouraging the children to create their own versions of the holy night on felt boards. Many eccentric characters and wondrous animals attended the manger that night if the children's tales were to be believed. I awaited parental complaints but none came. I felt reassured that, although we were taking liberties, the fundamental message was the same. A message of hope and rebirth.

For a young child, the Quaker Meeting House was never much fun. We kids were sent downstairs to hang out in a cold sparse hall being set up for after-meeting tea and cakes. Quakers just looked like old kindly people to me.

Quakers, also known as 'The Society of Friends', object to harm being caused to anyone. They believe that the essence of God is in every living being and each person has unique worth. They have no priests, gurus or mediators, and every 'friend' is free to share their experiences in a meeting. As I got older, I was invited upstairs to sit with the adults in the simple timber hall. Quaker meetings are conducted without music or ritual. When someone is moved to speak, they usually stand and convey their thoughts gently. Sometimes they share stories, sometimes observations or simply an inspiration that has come to mind. Quaker meetings were my first introduction to meditation: sitting quietly in the moment, open to whatever came along. It reminded me of the Native American 'talking stick' I had read about; a great man called Deganawidah had guided five tribes to make peace agreements using the stick. The stick was passed from person to person, allowing the holder to speak and the others to listen, absorb and reflect. As I was telling this to one of the other kids at tea-time in the cold below-ground hall, one of the older men with bushy white eyebrows, overhearing, said to me, 'Well, why don't you look closer?'

I was confused and embarrassed that I may have insulted him. The following meeting, he sought me out and asked me if I had looked closer. I questioned his meaning. He said, 'Why, the Indigenous people of this land, of course. Look to them.'

I spoke to Dad about this. Soon after, he arranged for us all to go camping to Bomaderry on the south coast of New South Wales, which was where I made my first Indigenous friend.

Red's Quaker heritage was important to him. His ancestors, as he called them, had fought for the abolition of slavery and insisted on gender equality and equal rights for women. One of them, Maria Mitchell, was born into a large Quaker family on the island of Nantucket in 1818. It was a place of horizon-gazers, seafarers and lighthouse keepers, where the men were often away. Maria declared that the laws of nature were discovered not through 'the hurry and worry of daily toil, but were diligently sought . . . And until able women have given their lives to investigation, it is idle to discuss the question of their capacity for original work. One was better to be peering into the spectrograph than on the pattern of a dress'.

At seventeen years of age, she opened her own school, saying, 'We cannot accept anything as granted.' On 1 October 1847, aged 29, she spied a new 'telescopic comet' five degrees above the pole star, which was named Miss Mitchell's Comet. She was awarded the gold medal from the king of Denmark, Frederick VI, for the first sighting of any new comet detectable only by telescope.

At age thirty-two, Maria became the first woman elected to the American Academy of Arts and Sciences, and the first to enter the American Association for the Advancement of Science. In 1865, she was appointed the first professor of astronomy at the newly founded Vassar College in Poughkeepsie—one of the earliest women-only institutes of higher learning in the USA. Her yearly salary was US$800, a figure she vigorously contested when she discovered it was a fraction of that paid to male professors. She fought this until women were given equal pay.

The Observatory at Vassar was built as a condition of Maria joining Vassar's first faculty. She insisted that it include living quarters in the north wing for herself and her father Charles to live in, and she remained there until shortly before her death in 1889. With an inner circle of six young women who she encouraged to 'think for themselves' and were self-named the 'Six Stars of the Hexagon', she held parties in the Planetary Dome, mixing poetry and astronomy with strawberries and cream. 'It was a part of science which was not all mathematics, or all logic,' she wrote, 'but is somewhat beauty and poetry.'

Red shared with me some of her quotes that he'd been told as a boy:

'Study as if you were going to live forever; live as if you were going to die tomorrow.'

'The eye that directs a needle in the delicate meshes of embroidery will equally well bisect a star with the spider web of the micrometre.'

Maria had railed against domestic drudgery, urging her female students to pursue full-time careers. For her entire life, she argued that higher education alone would give women independence of mind and drive: 'Until women throw off this reverence for [male] authority they will not develop. When they do this, when they come to truth through their investigations . . . their minds will work on and on, unfettered.'

I loved imagining Maria peering through her telescope into the night sky. I could picture her, absorbed in the vastness of space and its infinite possibilities, then wrestling with human life on earth, unable to fathom or abide male dominance and female repression. Knowing her genes were mingled with mine made me feel strong and independent.

As children, we were told stories of the Coffins, my grandmother Hattie's family. In 1602, Red's ancestors, Norsemen enroute to Greenland, were driven off-course by a storm. They came across Cape Cod, Massachusetts, which they described as resembling a 'flat pork chop' with an island now known as Nantucket to the south. The Wampanoag people lived there long before white men assumed discovery and continued to live there long after. Red's family settled on Nantucket in the late seventeenth century to become farmers and whalers. Rejecting the beliefs of Puritan settlers, they converted to Quakerism, which brought the constant threat of fines and even the penalty of death for heresy. Many Coffin men became whalers whose lives were captured in Herman Melville's *Moby-Dick.* This novel was based on the true story of the *Essex* ordeal, when a whaling ship captained by a 29-year-old man was lost at sea after being repeatedly rammed by an 85-foot whale. Twenty men drifted for ninety-two days in three small boats. Ironically as it turned out, they decided not to head for the nearest island because they believed it to be inhabited by cannibals. They chose to stay at sea, hoping to be spied by a passing whaling boat. Searing sun and the absence of food, water and sleep drove the crew mad; eventually, they drew straws to see who would be eaten. The youngest, a teenage boy called Owen Coffin, nominated himself because he was a Quaker and a Pacifist, and would not fight for his life. He apparently lowered his head, was shot and consumed.

For more than fifty years, my father planted trees all over the world, watched them grow and tended them lovingly. He sat beneath many of those trees, painting watercolours that captured the beauty of the landscape before him. He collected fallen red cedar and chunks of tallowwood, and created sculptures inspired by their grain. He not only witnessed but experienced the full cycle of life for a piece of timber, and delighted in its beauty and majesty. He spent hundreds of hours in his shed carving, chipping, sanding and polishing. He allowed a piece of driftwood to change shape and follow its own form. He believed in the beauty of change, and the natural laws that govern and struggle to govern, despite human intervention. He was concerned that speeding up change to be faster than nature could accommodate would lead to disastrous natural events. He meditated on this. He contemplated the notion of the individual and the focus on the 'I', in which each person is directly responsible for themselves and is dedicated to self-survival and the survival of the planet. He encouraged me to think in terms of 'We'. 'We' means having a responsibility to myself, others, the group and the environment. 'We' offers a uniqueness that is inherited and the insurance that there is guidance in evolution. Politics, however, involves taking sides and that rarely offers a good result. Politicians are self-serving and political parties are based on manipulation. Politics dumb things down, creating parties and divisions that insist on having followers.

It was around 1970, when I was twelve and my sister Rosemary fifteen, that Red began to disappear for twenty minutes twice a day. My sister and I were curious. He had learned Transcendental Meditation (TM) from a man called Thom Knowles in Woollahra, in Sydney's eastern suburbs. Rosemary and I showed an interest so he booked us in. In 1973 we began to drive 90 minutes into the city after school to learn the technique. We arrived early to claim the comfortable three-seater couch pushed against the living-room wall in a small white terrace house. Upright chairs sat in four rows of four, facing the front, where the teacher Thom sat next to a TV screen. The sessions began with Thom telling us the history and benefits of TM, then we would watch videos of the Maharishi Mahesh yogi, a bearded Indian gentleman who giggled a lot as he sat cross-legged surrounded by flowers. He was amusing and articulated experiences with a mixture of humanity and science. We were invited to attend the ceremony day when we would be given our mantra, and were asked to bring a flower, a piece of fruit and a new hanky. Individually, we were taken to an upstairs room where the ceremony took place in Sanskrit, we offered our gifts and were given our mantra. We had been warned never to utter our mantra aloud. Once verbally given, it became a vibration rather than a spoken or written word.

Rosemary and I began to meditate with Red twice a day in Rosemary's bedroom. I sat on a cushion on the floor, my father sat opposite me and my sister was cross-legged on her bed. The lights were switched off with only a candle burning. TM became my best friend. I felt the presence of my mantra all the time. I developed a feeling of great security knowing I could meditate anywhere and would occasionally be tugged towards it in the classroom and have to resist the temptation to be embraced by its allure. I never ever felt lonely and I rarely experienced fluctuating emotional states.

Years later, however, when I was studying acting at NIDA, it hit me that I might never be able to articulate, let alone express, feelings of an extreme nature if I kept meditating. I was concerned that my regular twice-a-day practice was infringing on me being able to feel things deeply. I wondered whether I was cheating myself of everything life had to offer. I felt inadequate as an acting student and wanted to access emotion and communicate it honestly and effectively. I also wanted to be more interesting. I listened to other people my age voice strong opinions and felt embarrassingly 'simple' and compliant. I watched them fall in and out of friendships and love affairs, and doubted that I had the depth of experience for such states of being. I wanted to feel things *more*, so I stopped meditating. And sure enough, as I welcomed new experiences, I became buffeted by stronger winds that sometimes left me flattened. Accompanying these intense feelings were associated confusions and stresses. It wasn't that I hadn't previously been feeling things; it was just that I wasn't adversely affected by them. I also thought I wasn't meeting other people's expectations of how I should behave. I thought people might assume I didn't care. I thought I had let people down by not expressing devastation over my mother's death. I felt many things about her death but none of them were bad. I felt loved, grateful, curious, in awe and definitely sad, but even the sad feelings did not threaten my sense of peace.

When I ceased meditating, I became more self-focused. I also felt smaller, less secure. Dealing with my new conflicted feelings also took up a lot of time, and the more self-focused I became, the less I could feel fully present. It became harder to access my 'centre' because there were niggling obstacles stopping me from spontaneously 'playing'. Sometimes I simply got in my own way.

Knowing something and being able to express it became two very different things for me. I gradually came to realise that all the feelings I needed were within me, because I was human and I had an imagination; I could call upon them more readily if I was calm, open and focused. I also realised that to have a long career, which I hoped to have, it would be unsustainable to let my immediate habitual reactions drive me, and just hope for the best. I would need an open heart, a calm mind and an acceptance of different perspectives.

I came to this realisation twenty-four hours after Red knocked on my apartment door in Darlinghurst one morning in 1984 when I was twenty-six years old. I had woken that morning with a painful period. My skin had erupted with pimples and I was broke.

Red stood at my door smiling. 'Well,' he said. He had travelled by train from Faulconbridge, in the Blue Mountains, where he was living, and was carrying a backpack and a wallet with cash in it. 'I have enough gear here for camping, enough food to stay in this room for two days and enough money to go to a two-day TM retreat in Manly, starting at 5 p.m. today. What'll it be?'

I hugged him, choosing the retreat. First, we pulled the sleeping bag out of its cover, wrapped it around us and ate all the food, quietly chatting, until it was time to head to the ferry and steam over to Manly. How he had known what I needed was a mystery to me.

On another occasion, I borrowed Red's car and was driving my sister to visit him in Faulconbridge. I had only just got my licence and wanted to take long drives whenever possible.

Rosemary remarked how every road sign, such as 'Springwood 5 miles' and 'Leura 16 miles', was a one-off original. This had never occurred to me; as I was thinking about that, we collided with a truck heading towards the afternoon sun.

We spun. Rosemary screamed, raising her knees to her chest. We came to a stop. Silence.

The car was badly damaged but we were unharmed. As we emerged from the twisted metal, a silhouette appeared over the rise in the road. It was Red. He'd been at home when he had a 'feeling' he should start walking, and so he did. When he saw the car ahead of him, he understood. He wasn't panicked, he said, he knew we were all right. And we were.

The car was panel-beaten and returned to Red. He put an ad in the *Trading Post* for a '4-year-old, experienced Ford Fairlane' for $99 or nearest offer. A man called him minutes after the paper hit the streets and asked if it was a prank. 'No,' Red said. The man arrived, offered him $80 and drove it away.

Red intuited rather than analysed life. While he considered things deeply, I never heard him offer an opinion. He held strong values, yet never spoke of them unless asked. He had a love for the ridiculous, and he trod the earth lightly.

'Panacookums!' he'd call out every Sunday morning. He prepared the pancake mixture each week from a soured-milk culture, which he kept in an airtight jar at the back of the fridge. The old electric frypan came out of the corner cupboard and warmed up, while he hand-mixed and beat the creamy batter. As he drizzled oil into the pan, animals, cartoon characters and plants bubbled into life. He once made me a giraffe that extended over five plates.

When we sat at the table, pure Canadian maple syrup was generously poured over the pancakes, the 'funnies' were scrambled for and the jokes page shared. We took turns reading the comic strips aloud to each other; Red loved Charlie Brown. Red listened to them as if taking in a terribly serious paper. He pretended to analyse Lucy and Schroeder's relationship like he knew them intimately. Red could be childlike, and together we would laugh at re-runs of *The Three Stooges*, *Laurel and Hardy* and the *Marx Brothers* while sharing a block of Rocky Road.

He took us on camping trips with an old tent, a billy and swags. On skiing weekends, we bunked down in dorms, ate mushrooms on toast and played in the snow. He left my sister and me building snow sculptures while he skied cross-country, which requires strong leg muscles, a skill he had acquired as a boy to get to school in the snow in Kansas. He would plant chocolate bars in the frozen ground to dig up and munch on his way home.

After he bought a canoe, we paddled the Nepean River most weekends, watching for kingfishers and fallen nests. On alternating weeks, we hiked to Wentworth Falls where, when I was younger, he had carried me up the steep steps on his shoulders without complaint.

Born with a wandering soul, Red was drawn to fellow travellers. He stopped for young hitchhikers who were searching for meaning. He brought them home and very soon the guitars came out, incense was lit and songs were sung while food was prepared. Red would promise them a bed for the night or a lift to the highway.

The year after Shirley died, Red packed up the house in Camden and went to the op shop. Here, he purchased two pairs of trousers, one wide-legged and one narrow. He chopped the legs of the slim pair at the crotch, just below the pockets, and sewed the ankles closed, creating two long tubes of fabric. He turned the wider pair inside out, cut the pockets open at the seam and attached the tubes to the opened pockets. These in turn created two ridiculously long new pockets. Proudly stepping into the wide-legged pair, he demonstrated his fabulous new super-duper trousers with pockets either side, which extended the length of both legs. In one pocket, he placed a small rolled chamois cloth, a tube of toothpaste and a toothbrush, a comb, and a small notebook and pen; in the pocket on the other side, he placed a tiny watercolour set, his passport, his wallet and a chocolate bar. Anything else, he said, he would find as he needed it.

He purchased a second-hand pair of lightweight shoes. He removed the soles, stitched elastic to each arch, toe and heel on either side, slipped them on and smiled at the comfort.

He never wanted to offend, so to remain true to himself he adopted measures to satisfy all. He wanted to travel the world barefoot and luggage-free, yet when he had to, he could appear nicely clothed and be prepared for anything.

I drove him to the airport one morning when I was eighteen. When we got there, he hugged me. Then, looking into my eyes and smiling, he said, 'Well.'

It always got me. To me it meant, *There you are . . . Aren't you wonderful?*

I waved him farewell with a lump in my chest, and he disappeared barefoot and luggage-less through the International Terminal, a free man.

When I was nineteen and had just completed my first year at Sydney College of the Arts, I accepted Red's invitation to go to Hawaii. I loved my year at art school, particularly the dark room. The thrill of watching images emerge through liquid, and pegging the wet dripping paper on suspended string lines to set and dry was mesmerising. Hours would pass in minutes. Our tutors included the extraordinary Imants Tillers, Guy Warren, John Williams and Helga Larsen.

We arrived in Honolulu late at night and bussed it to our two-bedroom hotel suite. Tired, I brushed my teeth, plonked myself on the bed and fell asleep. I awoke in a darkened room, unaware if it was morning yet because the curtains were all closed. I sat up to meditate. TM meditations are effortless; it's the gentle introduction of the mantra that initiates the experience. Every meditation is different and this particular one in Hawaii felt profound. I sat upright against the wall with my legs crossed in a room I had never been in before, in an apartment I had not yet explored. Often in meditation, my arms will feel weightless and seem to rise above my lap like they're filled with helium. On this occasion, they rose as if lifted by invisible threads, elongating to form endless graceful snake-like streamers. Each finger became an underwater anemone feeler capable of lightly caressing every surface. These feelers traced every contour and texture in the room and then continued to extend themselves into the rooms beyond. They explored the darkened living room, kitchen and bathroom. They slid over benchtops and picked at fabrics. They poked into corners and slipped behind a kettle, a toaster and a pile of towels. My arms seemed to know that, just like seaweed, if they kept floating they would live, and so they continued. They ventured towards a row of pleated grey linen curtains and ran over their curved wavelike folds until they found an edge. With the practised skill of a magician revealing an empty cupboard, they parted the curtains and allowed light to flood the room. The glass sliding doors were locked shut; the feelers felt for the small, round latch studded with a tiny glass centre. Turning it anticlockwise and releasing it with a click, they pushed the doors open and let the world in.

The twenty minutes were up and I opened my eyes. Rising, I opened the bedroom door and walked into a dimly lit central room. Everything was exactly as I had experienced it. I approached the curtains, opened them, turned the latch with the small glass stud and slid the doors wide open. The scent of frangipani (my mother's favourite flower) hit me. I experienced a weightlessness that seemed to let me soar over the balcony rail I was leaning on and travel across the beach below, out over the ocean. Just as the sun was breaking above the horizon, my body crossed paths with a plane. I knew instantly that I would be going back to Sydney where I would audition for drama school; I would be an actor and everything would be all right.

The following day, we visited the art school in Waikiki and, with Dad's encouragement, I filled out enrolment forms. That night during dinner, Dad's closest friend Sam, who Dad had met in Hawaii before the war and wrote to regularly all these years, gifted me a brand-new and expensive Pentax camera with an assortment of lenses. I felt awful accepting it. It seemed deceptive to keep it, because I knew he must have asked Dad what he might buy me and they were both hoping I'd use it in a course in Hawaii, and that Red and I would be living there.

But I knew I wouldn't be developing film at an art school, and I wouldn't be staying in Hawaii.

We returned to Sydney and I auditioned for NIDA.

Part 2
Woman

6

Miss Mumford

When I was eleven years old, I realised I was only hearing about one-third of everything my teachers were saying. It sounded something like: 'Open your books . . . all the . . . but also . . . however . . . when done.'

I sat at a desk in the back row with Alison Wootton. Alison had blonde hair with curls so tight they could hold pencils. Alison was smart. Alison wrote with a pen that seemed to have all the answers stored in its narrow ink-filled tube. She pressed the nib onto a blank sheet of lined paper and all the answers just flowed out. She cottoned on pretty early that my excellent posture was not due to deportment classes but rather was a means to cheating. If I sat up really straight and pressed my back into my chair with my eyes downcast and focused to the right, I could see at least a quarter of her answers. Alison reacted by creating a right angle on the desk with her left arm and tilting her head towards her shoulder until she obliterated her paper from my view. I felt so bad that she'd had to adopt a contorted position to compensate for my cheating that I responded with an equally self-protective pose, just to let her know that I had got the message.

At such times, I felt dreadfully alone. And ashamed. Once every couple of weeks, the teacher nominated someone who had completed all their work to clean the fish tank outside the principal's office. I interpreted this as a reward that I would never receive. One day, I placed my pen in the groove on the lip of the desk to signal I had finished, and although the teacher must have been aware I was probably lying, she let me go.

The rectangular fish tank sat on a small table against the wall between the principal's office and an adjacent staff room, opposite the sick bay. I loved scooping out the fish and gently placing them in a temporary container while I emptied the tank, washed the slime away, rinsed the pebbles and seaweed and miniature deep-sea divers, and refilled it with water and released the fish again. This gave me great satisfaction and also let me overhear conversations between the principal and parents. I could chat to anyone in the sick bay. On one occasion, I overheard a discussion involving a boy I knew. He had been accused of stealing, and he and his mother were in the principal's office. The boy was sobbing. After the mother left and the boy was sent back to class, the principal said to one of the women who worked at the front desk, 'He's definitely guilty. They always cry like that when they're guilty.'

I thought of Tommy Higgins. Tommy and I were in kindergarten together. He was my first boyfriend. One recess, Tommy gave me a ring in a small, dark-green box with a snap-shut lid. I took the ring home and put it under my pillow. The following morning, I put it on. It was a simple band of shiny gold. It slipped off all my fingers but sat quite neatly on my thumb.

My grandmother Rose, who was staying with us at the time, brushed my hair each morning for ten minutes. It stimulated my natural oils, she said. This was when she saw the ring. 'Where did you get that?' she asked with alarm.

'Tommy Higgins,' I said.

'You go to school and give that right back to him.'

I felt shocked at her reaction. I thought she would be curious about my first boyfriend and hoped we might have a girl-to-girl chat about him. Suspecting the ring was stolen, she told my mother to call Tommy's immediately.

That recess, I handed the ring back to Tommy in the playground. He took it and ran away from me. I watched him stop just before the parallel benches where we ate our lunch. He bent over, picked up a brick and hurled it at me, screaming. The brick hit me hard and cut the flesh above my left eye. Through the blur of trickling blood, I saw Tommy crying. Rivulets of tears traced clean squiggly lines from his eyes to his chin.

I wasn't sure why he was crying when I was the one who was injured. I didn't realise how hurt and possibly guilty he might have felt if he had indeed stolen the ring and already been chastised. What was clear to me, though, was that I wasn't ready to go steady.

The principal's remark about the boy confused me for many reasons. How could someone know another person's guilt or innocence after one conversation, and why was crying an indication of guilt? There must be many reasons why someone cries. I guessed that when someone had done something wrong and were found out, their feelings of shame made them cry. But what if Tommy was innocent and crying because he felt misunderstood and disbelieved?

This incident prompted me to watch people more closely. Particularly teachers. I wondered whether teachers and principals had some special knowledge. Some deeper insight. Some sixth sense for understanding people.

By high school, I had become completely obsessed by what my teachers were wearing, how they stood, what gestures they used and how they phrased their sentences. Mr Yabsley wore brown shorts, a tan shirt and knee-high beige socks, and smoked Camels in class. His right-hand fingers were tar-stained. He showed his favouritism for me by sitting on the edge of my desk, swivelling around to almost face me and blowing smoke towards me between sentences.

Miss Cameron wore red. Her black hair was piled high and her heels left tiny marks on the wooden floors as she slowly paced the aisles. She rarely smiled.

Mrs Knowles, the librarian, had an inverted U-shaped mouth. She breathed in deeply though her nose before speaking.

Mr Roby had the strangest habit of pushing his elbow into his waist like he was hitching up his pants.

Miss Dillon stared into the middle distance while we worked, as if lost in a reverie.

Mr Broadbent had the most wonderful Manchester accent and encouraged in me all my drama pursuits.

Miss Brown wore skirts so short you could see her underpants. Once, when she sat on the sideboard in the art room, I saw safety pins keeping her Modess pads attached to her knickers.

I loved all my teachers, but I would arrive home with their assignments and stare at them. My father, who was always available for me, helped me with maths and some science. He'd stay up all night reading the novels on the syllabus so he could discuss them with me. Even with his help, I felt I was drowning. I began to have those dreams about having forgotten to study for an exam or learn lines for a play, where you find yourself in front of an audience, naked and alone.

One hot afternoon at about 4 p.m., I opened my wardrobe door to find it painted black with a shelf holding a box of coloured chalk and a duster. I have no idea how my father knew this would be the greatest gift he could give me. Maybe, from his perspective, he had tried everything else and decided to go with my strengths. I removed my uniform and rummaged through a suitcase that was stored on the top shelf of my cupboard and dressed in one of my mother's knee-length woollen check pleated skirts, an olive-green twin-set, a string of pearls, low-heeled shoes and coral lipstick. Then, with white chalk in hand, I began to teach myself. I placed the imaginary me on the edge of my bed, opened the cupboard door and engaged all my skills of observing my teachers to teach myself what I had missed.

I imagined, like them, that I had a unique insight into my student. I became excited about keeping notes in class and couldn't wait to get home to share all the information with myself. I called my teacher Miss Mumford; she developed the attributes of all my favourite teachers. She always put me first, and if the imaginary principal came to the bedroom door, she said, 'I'm sorry, Mr Flood, but it will have to wait. I'm working with Heather.'

Miss Mumford listened to all my concerns, and when our work was done, she disappeared and became garments hanging in the cupboard. Every day at 4 p.m., however, she was there waiting for me. When Heather was confident again to work alone, Miss Mumford always left without fuss.

Due to the success of Miss Mumford, I began introducing other women into my secret life. My favourite book growing up was *The Family of Man*, a black-and-white photographic book by Edward Steichen, which traced the gamut of life from birth to death. Published in 1955, three years before I was born, its 503 reproductions fascinated me. I borrowed women from the book to bring to life and talk to in my room.

Although most of the subjects were American, I believed their emotional stories were universal. Each photograph offered an entry point for a story beyond the photographer's frame. One woman who, I decided, had lost her child, was being held by another woman as she sobbed into her arms. I wrapped myself in a blanket with a jumper tied around my head, knotted it under my chin, and held my dead child (a pillow) in my arms, sobbing.

At home, we had a system where no one could enter your bedroom without permission, which was given via a rectangle of cardboard hanging from a small nail on each door, coloured on one side. The coloured side meant *Do Not Disturb.* Just then my mother burst in, ignoring the coloured side, to announce that dinner was being served. I was still mourning my child and we locked eyes in silence. She carefully closed the door and walked softly away down the hallway.

We had a guest for dinner that evening. When I arrived at the table late, my mother explained to her friend that I'd had some upsetting news and offered that I could be excused if I wished to eat in my room. She said all this with compassion and did not invite discussion. I so loved her in that moment.

I never named my lost child, nor the mourning mother, but I'm sure I created them to coincide with my own mother's secret struggle, her leukaemia diagnosis. I prepared myself for her unspoken ill health by rehearsing the mourning and letting go of a loved one through death. I like to think she and I silently acknowledged that nothing needed to be said, and that she felt confident I was capable of dealing with whatever happened in my own way.

This firm belief she had in my emotional maturity had grown after I told her of an experience I had when I was six years old. We had some friends over for early dinner and one of the boys decided to play hide-and-seek outside. It was sunset. I was a bit dubious because I didn't like being in the dark, I didn't like being scared and I didn't much like the boy doing the counting. But I'd have felt pathetic if I said 'No,' so I followed him through the pungent late-afternoon smells of the back garden. He began to count and I ran off to hide. I wasn't thinking where I was going, I just wanted to hide somewhere he wouldn't find me because I was frightened that if he did, he might try to kiss me. The previous time he'd visited, he had shown me his flaccid penis and asked me to show him my 'parts'. I remember looking at the pink newborn mouse peeking out from his pants and backed out of the garage gracefully like doing a choreographed step into the wings. I have always tried to exit anything uncomfortable with grace rather than effrontery.

He began counting and was up to five before my flight response kicked in. Consumed by panic, I changed direction several times until I headed towards a white wooden fence, built of posts and crossbeams connected with wire mesh. It was only chest high and I judged it an easy climb. My heart was racing with the anticipation of being spied before I had found my hiding place. I heaved myself up. I would never attempt such a feat if I wasn't running from him. Just as I was distracted by this thought, my back foot clipped the crossbeam. I fell and hit the dirt with force. I landed with an almighty thud on my chest and, although not badly injured, I was winded and couldn't breathe.

An instant fear flooded me. I would never breathe again! In that moment, I had an epiphany: the pure knowledge that I was six years old and that, as a six-year-old, I was perfect. No one could ask or expect me to be more than a six-year-old. I could not have more cells or blood or knowledge than a six-year-old girl living in my body and living in my culture, my family, my house, surrounded by the people and experiences who made up my life. I was six. No one could take that away from me. And definitely not that boy.

This sense of singularity left as quickly as it appeared. Air streamed back into my lungs. Shaken, I stood, covered in dust. I raced off to find my chosen hiding place, a darkened wooden cupboard in the corner of the garage, resting against the wall in front of the bonnet of our Ford. I prised the door open just enough to squeeze my body in and crumpled onto a stack of papers that smelled of mould. It was pitch-dark in there. I sat for some time, so contented, so grateful, knowing I was loved and safe and always would be. I knew I would never be found. It would be up to me to make my reappearance when I was ready.

7

Are You Decent?

I was ten when our parents rented a kindergarten in Avalon, on Sydney's northern beaches, for the Christmas holidays with the Harts, our closest friends. They had been looking for accommodation to house ten people and my mother had squealed when she saw the ad for a kindergarten whose P&C committee was raising money for the school by renting it out over the Christmas holidays.

There were tiny toilets in a row with tiny washbasins, and all the play equipment was locked away in a walk-in cupboard. The small tables and chairs were replaced with beds and couches. It was a 20-minute walk to the beach and sand dunes; sadly, these are now long gone. The sand dunes rose 22 metres above sea level. We slid on our cardboard mats screaming all the way down before whingeing all the way back up. I had heard that, in the 1960s, elephants belonging to Ashton's Circus sometimes foraged in the dunes. The loose sand used to blow into the township and, although the locals protested, the dunes were eventually levelled, reshaped, fenced off and planted with vegetation to stop erosion.

One morning, I woke to find blood on my pyjamas. I hurriedly removed them and crammed them under my pillow, then showered and changed. Walking along the beach a few hours later, I told Meg, the eldest of the Hart siblings. She suggested we leave the others and walk alone. I had begun to menstruate, she explained, and it would happen every month.

'Every month? Till when?'

'Until it's over, when you're no longer fertile.'

She proceeded to describe the whole horrid truth about menstruation. The flow, pain, cramps and embarrassment. She went on to explain that I couldn't swim or ride horses or have sex. *Sex?* I thought. *I'm ten!* She said she'd take me to a pharmacy and buy me some Modess pads and a belt, which we did and she paid for. She said that while I was bleeding I wouldn't get pregnant.

Back at the kindergarten, I tore the elastic belt from its pack. The belt band, half an inch wide, was made of elastic. Front and back were pieces of identical elastic falling downwards from the belt, each about five inches long. At the tip of each elastic strip was a square metal claw. You wore the belt around your waist and slipped the ends of the pad into the claws, thus creating a thick wad to wear like a nappy. It was bulky and uncomfortable. When the blood flowed, you could feel it escaping onto the pad, squishing between your legs, until you changed it. It was awful. It made me hate the holiday, the kindergarten especially, because it reminded me I would never be a little kid again.

Period. I didn't tell my mother because I thought she would tell her best friend Jean, Meg's mother, and although they both loved me, I felt certain it would slip out during a conversation and they would betray me. Meg promised me she'd say nothing.

That period passed pretty quickly and wasn't too big a deal. The worst part was disposing of the pads. They had to be burned. Leaving them in the rubbish would smell and attract flies. Once we returned home, I could burn them in the incinerator in the block behind our house, but here in Avalon, there was nowhere. I wrapped them up in old newspapers, emptied my bag and stuffed them inside like stolen jewels, then wrapped the bag in a blanket.

Back home, I stood in front of the rusty drum in the spare lot and watched the wretched pads and bag go up in flames. I prayed to be spared from it ever happening again.

Every month, I forgot about it until the twenty-eighth day, when I began to ache in my lower back and the blood flowed again. I couldn't believe every woman alive went through this and kept it a secret, and dealt with it twelve times a year. The secrecy, the cost, the discomfort, the pain, the disposal, the dread. If it happened to men, I was sure it would be elevated to a rite of passage—money would be spent on it and big community bonfires would be created and neighbours would cheer as they drank beer, watching the fierce flames of manhood go up in smoke, their blood rising heavenward as offerings to the gods.

School was a nightmare. I carried the pads in brown paper bags inside my school bag and kept a couple in my desk. I stuffed the brown bag containing the pad under my armpit and walked stiffly to the toilets. One time, a boy I really liked was injured playing sport. The teacher called for something to put under his arm. Without hesitation, I pulled a super Modess from my bag and shoved it between his arm and his ribs. The teacher, though alarmed, congratulated me on my swift action and ingenuity.

Almost a year after I began menstruating, around my eleventh cycle, my mother came into the bathroom while I was showering.

'Are you decent?' she joked, as she pulled the curtain back a little to borrow some soap. And that's when she saw my mangled, mouldy, fungus-infested, twisted belt. I was standing naked in the bath, water trickling down the line of the embedded elastic.

She gasped. 'What is that?!'

'It's my belt.'

'What's it for?'

'My period,' I said.

'How long have you been wearing it?'

'Oh, I don't know. A little while.'

She turned off the water and helped me out. That's when I saw the red raw flesh. 'Meg said that if I wear the belt I won't get pregnant,' I said.

'I'm sure that wasn't all she said?'

'She said a lot, but that's all I can remember.'

'So, what, you've never taken the belt off?'

'Mmmm, yeah, I guess so,' I stammered, fighting back the tears.

My mother booked me in to see a skin specialist referred by her doctor. The stern angular man spoke to my mother privately then asked for me to come in. He said she was welcome to sit in the waiting room while he examined me and prescribed something. My mother complied and left.

He asked me to pop behind the curtain, then hop onto his examining table after I'd pulled off my tights and removed my skirt. I lay down and said I was ready. He slipped around the curtain, pulling it closed, and looked at the ulcerating skin around my waist.

'Do you share towels with other members of your family?' he asked.

'I guess so.'

'Ah well, that could be the problem. Sometimes, infection can be passed from one person to another on towels.'

With that, he pulled down my underpants, pushed my legs apart and opened my vagina with his fingers.

'Just checking you don't have an infection you may have spread to your waist with a towel,' he said.

This made absolutely no sense to me. What was he doing, and where was Mum?

When he was satisfied, he asked me to dress while he scrubbed his hands. I sat at his desk, my tights backwards and twisted, my laces undone, while he wrote a prescription.

He saw me out to reception. Mum stood up from an orange chair and smoothed her skirt, open-faced and eager to hear the doctor's recommendations for treatment. With matter-of-factness, he handed her the prescription and gestured to the receptionist for the bill to be paid. Again, my mother did as she was told, and we left.

On the way home, I told Mum what he had done.

She froze. Her hands gripped the wheel, her back stiffened, her mouth tightened, but she said nothing.

This was my first experience of feeling overpowered by another person. There was, of course, the time when my brother had washed my mouth out with soap when I swore at him. I'd said he was a 'bugger bum', and he held me down on the bathroom floor and shoved a cake of wet frothy soap in my mouth. I fought him hard, kicking and spitting. Once he released me, the sickly sweet soap taste made me vomit. I was shocked that he'd used the phrase 'Wash your mouth out with soap' so literally, but I also found it kind of funny.

This wasn't like that. This wasn't an annoying brother. And my mouth was different from the space between my legs. Somehow, this sharp-faced man had got me to do something I knew wasn't right. And he did it without physical force. In a moment, he had asserted his control over me, leaving all my feelings in a jumble and my senses wobbly. He also had control over my mother, it seemed, even though she wasn't in the room when it happened. She had left obediently and became completely silent after I told her. This indicated to me that her feelings were all wonky, too. It shocked me to have witnessed my mother not knowing what to do or how to react, and I felt concerned that I had worried her. We didn't mention it again. It had created a complication for us both, because we didn't want to mistrust people. We both wanted to see the good in people and we also wanted the world to see we were resilient, smart and accepting women. I have no idea whether my mother made a complaint. But I daresay, even if she had, it wouldn't have been believed or dealt with in 1969.

I lay in bed wondering whether the doctor had touched other girls or only me. I slid my hands under the elastic of my pyjama pants and touched the outside of my vagina to feel what he must have felt. I dared not go inside. I hoped he wasn't thinking about me. I withdrew my hand, shelved the experience under the title 'Sad man did a sad thing' and packed it all away.

Throughout the 1970s, my mother's generation of women began to find a voice both outside and inside their homes. I listened to them re-educate themselves and create support networks. Watched them literally burn their bras and march for equality.

About the age of twenty, when I had become and identified as a woman, I felt useless. I didn't have much to fight for. Education was free. Rentals were cheap. Friends were plentiful. Work was always just around the corner, travel was easy and accessible, and sex was available with no strings attached. I travelled, studied, worked, partied and had sex. I had sex with friends, people I was attracted to, and people I'd fallen in love with. But I also had intimacy with people I didn't like, and people I thought of as sad, so I obliged. I experienced unwanted attention and unclear messaging, as well as downright frightening, dangerous and confusing encounters.

My cousin Sue and her husband Mike invited me to use their house in Beecroft, a beautiful leafy suburb north of Sydney, to learn lines for my NIDA audition. I chose my pieces and was particularly confident about a patched-together monologue from the 1940s play *Queen of the Rebels*, by Ugo Betti. My character,

Argia, transforms herself from 'a cheap, low, dirty slut who never did a decent thing in her life' into a martyr who allows herself to be mistaken for the fugitive queen the rebels wish to execute. The play was boring and the character had virtually no psychological development, but the speech itself was gutsy. As a stand-alone piece of writing—Argia said lines such as 'His sweaty hands reached this way and that'—it would allow me to use my voice and show my 'darker side'.

I caught an early train so I could arrive at Sue and Mike's house before they left for work. Sue welcomed me on her way out: 'Help yourself to everything and see you for dinner.'

I had a wonderful day, walking from room to room, talking to imaginary people in the play. When Sue and Mike returned, we ate together, and then Mike dropped me at the station. 'The next one's straight through to Town Hall so you'll be home in no time,' he said.

Three brightly lit carriages slowed into the station and stopped. The first two were empty; in the third, a suited clean-shaven man sat on the far side, three rows from the rear. I thought it safer to sit near company and chose a two-seater across the aisle and two rows ahead of him.

The thick, slightly yellow-tinted mirrored windows prevented me from looking out at the darkened scenery. Instead, I oscillated between watching my own reflection, which featured me as a hollow-eyed hag looming large against an almost empty row of seats across the aisle, and pressing my forehead to the cold hard pane. If I maintained the latter position, although my teeth occasionally chattered due to the vibration, I could watch the evening lights flicker past as they briefly illuminated cramped backyards with tired paling fences and waiting commuters on desolate platforms. Provided I kept my forehead planted on the glass, I could also avoid any contact with the man.

He was well dressed in a dark-blue suit and tie, and had been looking straight ahead when I got on, so I thought he hadn't noticed me. When I had settled in my seat, keeping my bag straps snugly over my shoulder, resting my script and purse in my lap, he seemed unaffected by my presence.

The journey from Beecroft to Town Hall was a 47-minute trip. My numbing forehead and stiffening neck caused me to sit upright. To change posture, I shifted away from the window and towards the aisle.

That's when I saw him looking directly at me. I closed my eyes and adjusted my position to face the front. I pretended to sleep while I focused on recalling the lines I had learned that day.

'His sweaty hands went this way and that . . .' I repeated, testing and correcting my memory. Soon, I was pleasantly absorbed in another world.

I heard a shuffle and then a pressure on the top of my left shoulder. It was the man's left hand. His right hand came from behind and covered the whole right side of my face, from my jaw to the top of my head. It felt clammy and smelled of copper and nicotine. His right palm was trying to turn my head towards him. I fought the force, pushing my right jaw and temple against his strength. His hand on my cheek slipped, and my head whipped to the right. For a split-second, I stared directly into my stricken face reflected in the window, like a still from a horror movie, the stalker looming in the background.

He slapped my cheek. The sting brought my breath back. I willed myself to stand. It was impossible—my legs wouldn't engage—and I felt terrified. He jerked my face sideways, like an unhappy child ripping off a doll's head. Once he had me facing the aisle, he began pushing my resisting face towards my left shoulder and his erect penis, which was now balanced on my shoulder.

'Put it in your mouth,' he said, as the bitter-smelling flesh contacted my lips. Repulsion engulfed me. I wish I'd had the courage to bite it, but I screamed and managed to free my trapped left arm.

I seized the bottom of his jacket, propelling myself to my feet. I grabbed the back of the seat in front of me and ran, clutching my bag, bouncing between the rows of seats to my left and right. Shaking through the shuddering carriage, I got to the end. I reached for the handle for the doors between the carriages. I wrenched them open and was blasted with cold air. I navigated the unstable plates connecting one carriage to the next. I reached the guard's door, praying there was a guard in there, maybe even a couple of them. I pressed my back against the door, my hand ready to bang on it if need be. I willed the man not to follow me.

Burwood, Redfern, Central . . . I counted down the passing stations, my heart thumping in my ears. I tried to avoid breathing through my nose; the smell of copper and stale nicotine was stuck in my nostrils. I dared not let my lips touch each other. The train took an eternity to slow and then stop at Town Hall. I alighted and ran. No one followed me. I never saw that man again.

As with the doctor, and an increasing load of experiences, I dwelt on it only briefly and filed it away. I shelved this one as 'I got away, so all good'.

'Fill in the form and I'll do the rest,' Irma said.

She was an imperfectly lit version of a seventy-year-old Marlene Dietrich. I was twenty-two. Irma (not her real name) lightly rested her pale veined hand on mine and let it rest for a good five seconds. She withdrew it, her fingertips slowly leaving my skin to search her handbag for her lipstick and a circular compact. She smoothed the crimson dye over her thin lips and twisted the coloured tip down with the same hand, while she expertly snapped the mirror shut with the other. Once it was zipped away and her handbag was replaced on the floor, she ran her polished nails through her fine faded red hair, downed the last of her wine and said, 'We shall have such a time you will not forget.'

Irma was the Australian representative for an international theatre organisation that encouraged cross-pollination of theatre practitioners between countries. She was offering me a chance to be one of those pollinators. I felt lucky to have been recruited into something that was going to widen my experience and deepen my developing passion for theatre.

Days after I had been selected, I received confirmation that I would be welcome to attend an international theatre conference in East Germany, and that all expenses would be covered once I arrived. I felt chosen. I was going to a completely different culture, one in which Bertolt Brecht had created extraordinary performances challenging established naturalistic theatre. I would be attending a four-day gathering of theatre practitioners from around the world. It fitted in perfectly with my plans to travel alone to Europe and visit my bestie from art school, Robyn, who was now a practising artist in Amsterdam.

I had purchased my round-the-world plane ticket and my Europass from a travel centre in Sydney. The woman behind the counter was processing my details when I noticed a tear running down the crease next to her nose.

'Are you okay?' I asked, concerned.

She lifted her head only slightly. Still typing, without making eye contact, she said, 'It's all very well for you, I never get to go anywhere. This job is so hard.'

I had assumed that working in a travel agency meant she would be travelling constantly, getting great deals, going whenever she wanted. A real high flyer. It had never occurred to me that your job didn't match your experience of life.

Checkpoint Charlie was intimidating as I crossed from West to East Germany. I considered not going through with it. It all looked so terribly serious, why had I ever thought this was a good idea? It had looked so romantic in my head, but now, the high barbed-wire fencing stretched its long spiked fingers with a foreboding machine-like regularity. I pressed my nails into my palms to check I was actually there.

I presented my passport and a letter of introduction, and was let through. The streets were grey and desolate. I was exiting a watercolour painting and arriving in a monochrome sketch of straight lines and unadorned surfaces, colourless figures queueing for I didn't know what. Distant loudspeakers produced harsh sounds in German. My fist was clamped around the paper holding the address of where I was to stay.

I stopped, released my grip and smoothed the hand-drawn map across my thigh. I looked at the directions in blue biro. The map wasn't a great deal of help—I arrived at the address by chance because its signage was clear and simple. Its heavy doors opened into a quiet, pristine foyer.

The man behind the tall, dark wooden reception desk was stamping papers; he nodded at me to present myself. He studied my passport and letter of introduction, which I had placed on the counter, explaining the purpose of my visit. A barrage of German words challenged me; he glared at me with suspicion. Pointing to the date on my letter, he shook his head and asked for money, which was the only part I understood.

I tried to explain that Irma had said that everything would be paid for, and all I could offer were travellers' cheques.

'*Ich akzeptiere keine cheques*,' he said, tapping the date with his forefinger and raising his voice in frustration. It finally dawned on me. I had arrived a day and a half early and my allowance was not yet available. I kept citing Irma Schnapps and he checked her booking. Finally, he seemed convinced that she would arrive in the next two days.

He got up and asked me to follow him. We proceeded down a long, narrow hallway on the second floor and came to a door, which he unlocked and opened. A second door stood beyond the first. He unlocked this second door and admitted me into a small room the size of a prison cell. A single bed rested against the left-hand wall and a double-glazed window looked out at a grey sky and grey street. A small washbasin protruded from the wall by the window.

He nodded and paused, as if to explain something, then thought better of it. He closed both doors, locking each behind him, and left.

For two days, I stayed in the room. No room service was offered and none arrived. My copy of *War and Peace* was much lighter than when I had left Sydney. I was down to about a third of the book, after tearing pages off as I read them to lighten my load. I had used the discarded pages to write letters home to my father, turning each page on its side and using blue or red biro, so he could decipher my travel experiences while enjoying the cross-hatch patterns of my lettering against Tolstoy's.

I rummaged through my backpack and spent the 48 hours rationing my dried fruit and nuts, reading, and peeing in the sink, using pages 648–800 as toilet paper. I hoped Tolstoy would understand.

I wondered how long I would be left here, should Irma be delayed or not arrive at all. But after two days, she arrived with a flourish. The doors opened and she stood with the concierge, encouraging me to come out.

She insisted I share her room. 'Why waste money on two rooms when we can be together?' she turned, repeating it in German. The man nodded.

Her suite was three times the size of the one I'd been in. It had a small balcony and a couple of old armchairs opposite the double bed. She had some bread rolls and cold meats sent to the room with a bottle of Portuguese wine, and we sat chatting and picking at the food. That night, we shared her bed. She rolled towards me, her hands reaching for me, telling me I was beautiful as she stroked my face. I allowed her to kiss me.

I thought to myself, *Ah, I see, it's this or back to the room.*

The following day, we showered and dressed, ate a breakfast of bread, cheese and pickles, and walked across the barren square to an austere building where the conference was being held. It hadn't for a moment occurred to me that most speakers would be addressing their topics in German, of which I knew not a word.

A couple of hours into what promised to be a long and very academic morning, a man named Gerhard (not his real name) introduced himself to me. He offered his large, soft hand. I shook it and we snuck out to find a cafe. Gerhard, a director from West Berlin, spoke English and was gorgeous: dark, tall and gentle. That evening, he suggested we cross to the West to dine. We passed through 'Charlie', ate dinner together and found a room in a tiny hotel close to Alexander Platz. Partly intoxicated by the wine, but mainly excited by the newness of everything, I willingly undressed and lay on the bed. Gerhard pressed his body onto mine and without any foreplay attempted to penetrate me. What shocked me was not his speed, but the strangeness of what I could feel between my legs. The size of the article was incomprehensible. Was this a joke? Was I more drunk than I'd thought? The pain was excruciating as my flesh tore. I screamed. He continued to push as I thumped his back, begging him, 'No!'

He suddenly stopped.

My aunty Rosemary, my mother Shirley, and my aunty Audree in Strathfield, Sydney, in 1945, on the day Shirley, aged 21, left for China to work for the United Nations Relief and Rehabilitation Administration.

My mother Shirley arriving in Chongqing, China. Shirley was deeply affected by the children she met who had lost their parents due to the war and in 1948 she became the secretary to the Chief of the UNICEF mission in Shanghai.

Shirley and Red, my father, on a boat after meeting in Shanghai, China, 1946–47. They were very much in love and shared a passion for travel, philosophy and family.

Audree in a studio photo taken on the occasion of her engagement to Ron, 1946. I love this photo, as her gentle nature and exquisite beauty shine through.

Red on the island of Maui, Hawaii. Being a conscientious objector during World War II, he was assigned to Civilian Public Service from 1942–46. He considered Hawaii his spiritual home.

Red painting on a field trip in Korea, where he planted thousands of trees in his reforestation and erosion-control work in the late 1950s. Red carried his paints wherever he went. He did hundreds of watercolours on his travels.

Shirley and Red on their wedding day in Honolulu, Hawaii, 22 June 1949.

Shirley, holding me as a baby on her lap, my brother Steven, Red and my sister Rosemary, in Seoul, Korea, 1958.

My sister Rosemary and me singing and baking in our house in Jamaica, where we lived for two years after my father was offered work there, in 1961.

Rosemary and me playing dress-ups in the garden in Jamaica, 1962.

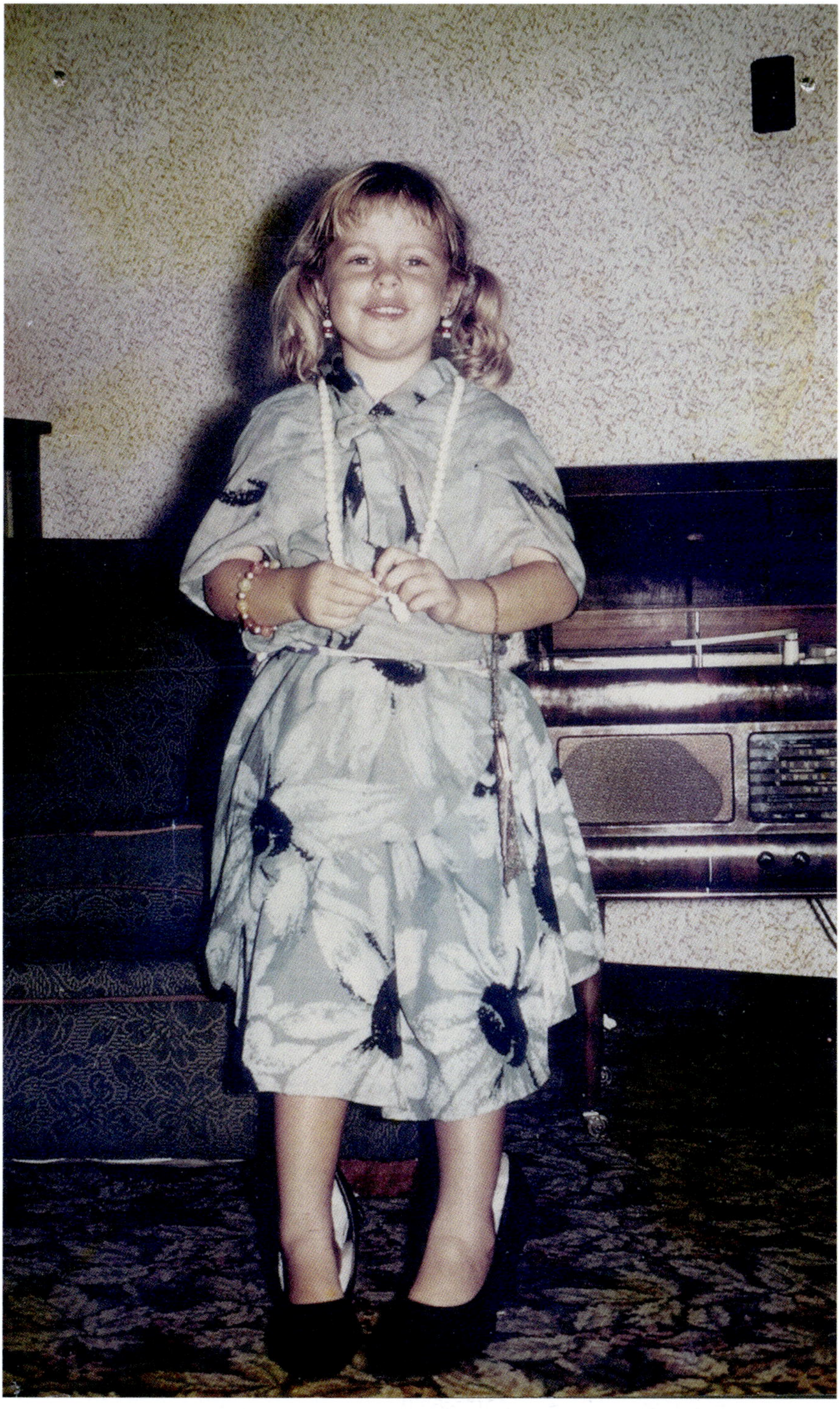

Dressing up on a visit to see my aunts in Strathfield in 1963.

Family photo taken in our garden in Camden, with cats, after we moved to Australia, 1967.

Reading in the backyard in Camden. My sister Rosemary and I loved being in the garden, which our parents created, finding special places to make cubby houses and play with the cats.

My aunty Rosemary, Ron (Audree's husband), my aunty Audree and my maternal grand-parents Harold and Rose in the front garden at number 18 Boden Avenue, Strathfield.

Shirley, Rosemary and Audree in Audree's back garden spontaneously recreating the 'Three Graces' using curtains from the spare room, while a Tchaikovsky record played, 1969.

Red and Shirley at a square-dancing party held at Audree and Ron's in Strathfield, 1968. My mother was a talented seamstress and sewed the outfits herself.

Aunty Rosemary, always smiling, holding a bunch of tulips in her Strathfield backyard, 1999.

Marty and me in Aunty Rosemary's dining room, 1990. She always lovingly prepared the table with a lace cloth, home-baked cakes, tiny sandwiches, beautiful teacups and saucers, and blooms from the garden.

Me in a photo Marty took soon after we met in 1989.

Marty's wonderful parents Kath and Brian, and family, Melbourne, 1979.

Marty and me at Rockwall Crescent, Potts Point, 1991.

Our wedding, 2 February 1992, at St Canice's Church, Kings Cross. We were married by Marty's Uncle Charlie, who was a priest. I had forgotten to organise a bouquet so grabbed a single flower from a vase as I left the hotel we were staying in.

Elizabeth and Red on their wedding day in the Blue Mountains, 1987.

Me, Red and Robyn (Ra Ra) in Blackheath, in the Blue Mountains, 1998. I met Robyn on my first day in Sydney on my way to enrol at Sydney College of the Arts in 1977. We are still best friends.

My beautiful sons Finn and Seamus sharing a book in our Bellevue Hill home, 2004.

Seamus, me and Finn at Government House after I was appointed a Member of the Order of Australia in 2021.

Me and Katrina, Lee-Anne and Edie in 2017. We have all been close friends since the 1970s. Ever since 1982, we photograph ourselves in the same pose whenever we get together.

Back row (left to right): Joanne, Marion, Lulu and Stephanie. Front row (left to right): Wayne, Fran, Sarah, Lisa and me: the 'Pilates Girls', my chosen sisters since the 1980s.

Clockwise from bottom left: Zoe, Holly, Kristina, Andrea, Annemieke, Alex and me: 'the Gang'. Our sons went to Woollahra Public School together and continued on to high school. The mothers partied hard while the boys studied.

Me and Hugo Weaving in State Theatre Company South Australia's *Private Lives*, directed by Rodney Fisher, 1984. PHOTO: DAVID WILSON.

Me, centre, in Sydney Theatre Company's *The Harp in the South, Part One and Part Two*, directed by Kip Williams and adapted by Kate Mulvaney, 2018. PHOTO: DANIEL BOUD.

Me with Richard Roxburgh in Sydney Theatre Company's *Burn This*, directed by Wayne Harrison, 1990. PHOTO: BRANCO GAICA.

Me as Ruth Bader Ginsburg in Sydney Theatre Company's *RBG: Of Many, One*, directed by Priscilla Jackman and written by Suzie Miller, 2022. PHOTO: PRUDENCE UPTON.

We rolled away from each other. And we both cried. I cried in pain and he, I considered later, cried for his misfortune.

He rose to walk to the small bathroom and that's when I saw it. It was the size of a family-sized Coke bottle, the ones on the TV that flash large on the screen, dominating the takeaway burgers because it's a bonus with every meal.

We lay awake all night as he wept and told me no woman had ever been able to accommodate him. I felt sorry for him, but not for long. My compassion began turning to anger as I witnessed myself comforting him when I was the one in physical pain.

Hours later, we passed back through Checkpoint Charlie. I returned to the hotel, hobbled through the foyer, eased myself upstairs, packed my bag and slipped away.

I hurried back towards the checkpoint guards, who by now were familiar to me. I had no more passes to re-enter East Germany, so this was it. I was leaving after two days in a locked room, kisses from an old woman and an unnatural injury I hoped not to die from.

I limped my way to the taxi stand. I flew to Amsterdam and cuddled up to Robyn in her white loft room, sipping vodka as we chatted about love and loss and art and dreams. I'd been travelling for a couple of months now, and I had seen enough. Robyn took me to the airport and handed me a sleeping tablet she'd been saving for a sleepless night. I flew to London, where I changed flights. I was in so much pain, I thought I was going to pass out. The queue for the flight to Sydney stretched for miles and people hoping to get aboard were offering money to booked passengers in exchange for their ticket. I refused a decent price, so determined was I to get home.

I saw, ahead in the line, a very large man holding his boarding pass. Feeling my own discomfort, I wondered how he would fit into a seat without being in agony.

We boarded. I adjusted the crotch of my jeans, which I wanted to tear off. I longed for pain relief and would have settled for some rescue remedy when the large man, checking seat numbers, caught my eye. He smiled and deposited himself next to me.

His bulk extended to the closed tray table on the back of the seat in front of him. His shoulder and forearm enveloped mine, and I tucked myself as far into the window cavity as possible. We chatted about Amsterdam and, as soon as we became airborne, I swallowed the pill.

I slept for five hours and woke to the smell of curry and the sight of a man's hairy arms reaching across my chest, tearing a bread roll in half.

'Oh hi,' he said. 'You slept well. Are you hungry?'

'No.'

'Great. Hope you don't mind me using your table. Mine's stuck.'

I closed my eyes and breathed all the way down into my vagina.

I shelved this one away as, 'I healed, so I guess no harm done'.

Lee-Anne Donnolley, or LAD, and I met at a holiday drama camp in 1973 when I was fifteen. I thought she was the smartest, most fun friend anyone could have. She included me in everything.

She lived in Canberra and, during her second-last year of school, organised bus trips with other drama-interested students to theatre productions and musicals in Sydney. The most memorable was when *The Rocky Horror Show* opened in Glebe. She had the bus driver stop in Camden to pick me up. She seemed to know everyone and could talk to them about anything; she could laugh more wholeheartedly than anyone else my age.

When I finished school, LAD invited me to live in her shared rental terrace house on Glenmore Road, Paddington. There were five of us. All the others were in their final year at NIDA: Edie as a designer, and Brian, Ray and LAD in stage management. For $15 per week, I slept in the back upstairs room, a disused kitchen. The parties were plentiful and the people thrilling. I remember a young Richard Wherrett leaning against the wall surrounded by eager faces, listening to his plans for a new theatre. The following morning, Edie and I scrubbed from the living room walls a blue band of hip-high markings made by sweaty blue jeans.

One morning, I walked from the house to the corner of Oxford Street and Glenmore Road past two closed antique shops opposite the Victoria Barracks. In the window of the first was my mother's pale-blue handmade Chinese shot-silk dressing gown, which she'd had made for her honeymoon. On a small round side table sat her brass 'wild horse' screw-on earrings from Shanghai, which was where she had met my father. I wondered whether I was seeing things—if this was unexpressed grief playing tricks on me. I paced about until 11 a.m. waiting for the shop to open, wondering how my mother's things could possibly be in that window. The only thing that made sense—which I later found was indeed the case—was that my father had sorted my mother's clothes and given a large bundle to St Vincent de Paul. By accident, he had included the dressing gown and earrings. The antique store must have bought them at a bargain and was trying to make a nice profit.

When the store opened, I went inside, not knowing whether to tell my story or not. I asked the price of both pieces: the dressing gown was the equivalent of a couple of months' rent for the tiny room I was sleeping in. The earrings were a little cheaper; I put them on lay-by to collect a few weeks later.

I walked back down Glenmore Road, wondering whether more of Mum's things were floating around out there like lost ghosts. It was warm on the steps back at the terrace house, so I sat to watch the shadows fall across the signage of the charcuterie opposite.

'Hi, Heather.'

I looked up at a pleasant-looking man of about 40. He extended his hand and announced himself: 'Tim Spare. Beautiful day! I knew your mother—wonderful woman, always had time for everyone. May I?'

He side-stepped through the open wrought-iron gate, hitched his trouser pants with his hands and squished next to me on the red-painted concrete step, pushing me hard up against the railing. I was surprised to be sitting so close to this stranger, who had made himself so immediately intimate with me. He told me he had seen my mother at a Save the Children rally and the Vietnam moratorium marches, and that he practised Transcendental Meditation. He spoke so knowledgeably and without pause that I didn't feel it appropriate to ask questions.

He assumed I knew him, or had heard of him, so I remained silent, embarrassed that I may have forgotten him. He asked me what my plans were. I told him I was at art school but had just been accepted into NIDA.

'I imagine you'll need money, then?' he said. 'Would you like a job?'

I looked directly into his blue eyes.

'What job?'

'Come on down to Melbourne, and I'll set you up over the holidays. Got your licence?'

'Yes,' I said.

He looked pleased. 'I drive ice-cream trucks in summer holidays. It's a blast. You'll love it and the pay is great. You holiday and work at the same time.'

He gave me his card and said to get in touch.

I spoke to my dad, saying what a lovely man Tim (not his real name) was and how he knew us. Dad agreed to drive to Melbourne with me and deliver me to Tim's address in Ferntree Gully. We had a wonderful leisurely drive to Melbourne, arriving at about 3 p.m. at a suburban house in a quiet street surrounded by gum trees.

Tim greeted us in loose calico drawstring pants, a fine Indian cotton shirt, beads, bare feet and a cloud of patchouli. I wasn't sure if it was him at first, and neither was I sure if I liked this Tim as much as the other one. Dad seemed pleased to meet him. We were welcomed into his almost-unfurnished home. He explained that he was mid-moving; this had been his deceased mother's place and he was literally squatting there till the last of her things were removed. It would then be sold and he would move back to his city pad.

He poured herbal teas into mismatched cups and motioned us to cushions on the floor. We sat and drank as he asked us questions about our trip down. Dad liked the casual atmosphere and approved of the 'squatting' style Tim was living in. I had told Dad that Tim knew Mum, but he asked Tim no questions about their connection. I was sure that, like me, Dad was embarrassed he didn't remember Tim. He also might not have wanted to discuss Mum. He didn't broach the subject and neither did our host.

Red rose, hugged me, pressed an envelope of cash into my hand and said he would now 'take off', because he wanted to see friends in Melbourne before heading back to Sydney in the morning. He thanked Tim, walked down the leaf-strewn path to the car, turned, waved and drove away.

I felt suddenly alone and a little frightened, but accepted the feeling as excitement. I returned indoors. Tim showed me my quarters for the night: a pleasant room with a double mattress on the floor, a small desk and pretty curtains around a rectangular cottage-style window.

Tim prepared steamed vegetables with rice, refusing my help, and served it in bowls as we sat on the cushions. After dinner, I fell asleep, listening to branches scraping the roof. I woke in the dark with warmth on the back of my neck and a pressure on my back. Tim's hands were reaching for my breasts through my T-shirt and his stiffening penis was pushing through my pants between the cheeks of my bottom.

I began to cry. It seemed like the best thing to do at the time. I was alone in an empty house surrounded by bush with a man I didn't know. I cried quite genuinely, and was surprised by how readily and forcefully the tears came.

Tim appeared shocked by my response. He withdrew from the room, apologising I think. Somehow, I must have dozed off again, as I woke to my alarm clock. I dressed without showering and sat for a long time on the mattress, listening for movement in the house. I heard none. I walked into the living room and through to the kitchen. A note sat on a small table against the wall. The note sat under a glass with a sprig of flowers and a bunch of keys.

Tim had written that he was sorry if he'd frightened me and that it was probably best if I did the driving job alone, because he had other work to do in the city. He also left instructions for me. A station wagon was parked in the driveway. I was to drive to Rosebud or Dromana, I can't remember which, where I was to leave the car at a caravan park. I would then walk to a garage where the 'Mr Bunny' van was stored. I would collect the ice-cream and chocolate mix from a cupboard at the rear of the garage. I would then drive the route to Portsea daily, visiting caravan parks and carnivals. Each evening, I would roll the money in brown paper from a box in the garage, lick the sticky sides closed, pop it in a cotton bag and deposit it in a bank deposit box.

I would be paid at the end of the holiday period, and Tim would pay me extra for doing the job alone. The figure he quoted would pay for my whole first year's fees at NIDA and almost cover the purchase of my mother's dressing gown as well.

I felt so relieved I was doing it alone and that he had apologised, and was excited to be going on an adventure. I thought Mum and Dad would feel proud of me if they saw me now.

At the bottom of the note, Tim added that I could sleep in the station wagon, because there was a sleeping bag there, and I could use the caravan park toilets. It all sounded kind of perfect.

I have no memory of how long I followed Tim's instructions. It may have been as little as a week or as long as a month, but I will never forget the 'Greensleeves' melody that accompanied me.

Alas, my love, you do me wrong
To cast me off discourteously . . .

It still turns my stomach. The batteries in the compartment below the roof's loudspeaker would tire, transforming 'Greensleeves' from a bright, tinny, almost jaunty tune to a distorted, agonising drawl, which eventually slowed to an excruciating death. I bumped down into the caravan parks, Mr Bunny's song causing dogs to bark and frenzied children to beg their parents for money. Sleeping babies woke up and started crying. Parents hated me and let me know. Angry mothers dragged their pleading children back to the lunch table, and excited dogs leaped at the sliding serving window and peed on the tyres.

Despite the resistance, parents and children did buy the whippy ice-creams and I made good money every day. I felt guilty about what I was serving because it didn't appear to belong to any real food group, and my being Jewish made it worse. I was pouring massive tins of liquid pig fat into the van's 'inner kitchen', deceptively seducing children with its transmutation from brown sludge into a bright, white, creamy, twisted and pointy dessert. It wasn't even cold; it had a bizarre temperature that made you assume it was cold when it was actually a non-temperature. You could dress it up with hot dipping chocolate sauce, which sat in a crockpot clamped onto a little shelf, and you could sprinkle it with tiny dots of sugar and pierce it with Flake bars, but it was still crap and I knew it.

The night-time carnivals were worse. I wasn't allowed to park near the rides, so I had to park near the road. Groups of mainly young men drank beer and flagons of Ben Ean, smoked dope and whistled at young women, and sometimes jumped on the bumper bar of the van to terrorise me. One night, I hadn't secured the melted hot chocolate and the crockpot rocked off its perch. Soon, liquid chocolate coated the floor. It was pretty much the last straw.

The day came when I'd either decided 'Enough' or had reached my end date, I can't remember which. I left the station wagon locked, put the keys on a back tyre and drove Mr Bunny to a house in Frankston, where I was supposed to drop it off with the keys and pick up my pay.

As I drove there, I promised myself a flight back to Sydney. I was so tired. I had lost weight and wanted to go home. I was relieved when I turned a corner and saw a couple of 'Mr Whippy' vans covered in similar colourful children's comic characters as my 'Mr Bunny'. I parked, slammed the driver's door for what I hoped was the last time ever, and found the house.

A neat path led to a front door. I pressed the doorbell and heard the *dingdong* repeat several times before footsteps. A woman in an apron and slippers answered.

'Hello, I'm Heather.'

'Yes?' she questioned.

'Tim Spare sent me, to be paid. Here are the keys.'

She stared at me. She called for what turned out to be her husband. A man in shorts appeared behind her, and she repeated what I had said. They invited me in, which I was reluctant to do because I just wanted to keep going. But the way they were looking at me made me feel like I didn't have much choice if I wanted the money.

We sat in their kitchen and ate soup from a bowl. They talked to me but the words weren't penetrating. They had to say it all again before it landed. 'Tim', whose real name was something else, they told me, had once worked for them. He had taken one of their vans and, although they told the police, he had never been charged and the van had never been returned. They had felt frustrated but had to let it go. It seemed he was at last returning the van through me, but had gone to a lot of trouble to make money out of it first. The only change on the van's exterior was the name 'Mr Bunny' which, the husband said when he looked closely at it, had been painted by 'an amateur'. He sounded personally insulted.

They seemed like honest and kind people, and I slept in one of their beds for hours. They paid for my train fare, sitting up rather than in a sleeper car, back to Sydney.

I didn't tell my father about the experience, but I did tell him about my mother's dressing gown. When he had given bags of her clothes to St Vincent de Paul, he had mistakenly added the gown and earrings. Red bought my mother's honeymoon dressing gown for me and I paid off the earrings.

Years later, while shooting a film in Batemans Bay, I had dinner in the restaurant of the motel where I was staying. It had small four-seater tables. My dear friend Robyn (Ra Ra) had driven from Canberra where her parents lived to stay the night with me. (It turned out that Robyn's and Leeanne's mothers were each other's bridesmaids; it was a complete coincidence that Ra Ra and LAD became two of my dearest friends.)

Ra Ra and I were finishing our meal when I looked across the room. I saw Tim. I'm sure it was him. He was dining with a young woman. I did nothing. I shelved it under 'Some experiences just make great stories'.

Theatre dressing rooms are some of the most fun places to be. They can also be the most intense. Some theatres have communal dressing rooms with benches along the walls and chairs spaced in front of a lighted mirror. Others accommodate two to three people, and there is sometimes at least one room for an actor who requires or prefers some privacy.

Each room has the classic mirror surrounded by lights and, if you're lucky, a small drawer or cupboard to store valuables and make-up. The costume rack is usually wheeled in daily and crammed into a corner if there is space. Larger theatres are more likely to have multiple dressing rooms, allowing actors to have individual spaces.

The dressing room is where I create the life before the show. The process begins the moment I arrive backstage. Having a positive, harmonious, respectful and fun atmosphere backstage makes a thrilling transition from life outside the theatre to life onstage. If a dressing room door is open, it generally means others are welcome to at least stand at the door and have a chat. If the door is closed, it's closed for a reason: predominantly privacy.

The caravan or trailer on a film set is similar, and its unspoken rules are the same. Who you share your room with, and who spends time in your room or van, can make all the difference between having an enriching experience and a depleting or even terrifying one. Ninety-nine percent of my dressing room experiences have been joyous.

I was in my early thirties and performing a role opposite a male lead. The plays chosen usually offered the lead roles to men, giving them opportunities to travel huge emotional distances. Women were usually given short strolls. In this case, the male actor had been given a beauty. My character was there to support his journey.

I didn't object to the need for the female character or I wouldn't have done it, but nor could I throw myself wholeheartedly into the role. I did, however, object to the techniques the male actor used to access his emotional energy each night. He either ignored or shouted at me, both onstage and off. He pushed past me in the communal passages and, one night in front of a full house, he put his hand over my entire face and pushed me to the floor. I couldn't believe the audience accepted it as part of the show, but he did it with such conviction it was a wonder they didn't applaud.

On another show, an actor knocked on my door minutes before the start, demanding I tell him why I wouldn't return his obvious affections. He refused to let me pass until I agreed to meet him between shows. He threatened to hurt himself if I didn't reciprocate.

Another time, while I was resting between shows in my dressing room, a male actor came in uninvited and lay down with me on the floor. I joked with him, telling him not to be silly, to go out and get some rest. Eventually, I got up and left him on the floor.

While sleeping in a van on a film set, I opened my eyes to find a male actor kissing me, his tongue in my mouth. Another male actor was standing behind him, God knows why or what their plans were.

The only time I found the courage to fight back was quite by accident. I was having a tricky time with an actor, who I felt simply loathed me. Maybe he loathed my performance, maybe just me, but more likely he loathed himself. Every performance was an exercise in positive thinking, reminding myself that he was probably nervous, struggling with personal issues or perhaps even health problems. All I could be thankful for was that, as each show finished, it was one less to go until the season was over.

At interval, I put a tampon in my pocket. I made a cup of tea, drank it and went to the bathroom as the bells rang for the audience to take their seats for the second act. I washed my hands and waited in the wings. When the lights dimmed, I took up my position on stage. Not long into the scene, I felt a trickle. I was horrified to realise I had removed a tampon and not replaced it. I felt in my pocket and there it was. My mind raced ahead but I couldn't think of an opportunity to leave the stage, nor could I fabricate a reason to. The more I considered it, the more panicked I became, and the less I could follow the scene I was in.

I was so distracted, I skipped a line, and had to make up a couple to get back on track. I sat on the small settee on stage, spread the skirt of my dress, pushed the cotton tampon through the cellophane, released the string and, easing my hand furthest from the audience's view, slipped it under my skirt. Lifting the buttock of my crossed leg, I slid it under my undies and pushed it in. I rose from the seat and, walking gingerly because I hadn't inserted it far enough, stepped towards him and wiped my finger lightly on his chest as I said my line.

I looked him straight in the eye with a confidence I'd never dared before. I felt triumphant.

I put the experience on the shelf towards the back of my mind, titled, 'A small victory'.

It was hot and sticky. We had both shed our clothes and were lying naked on top of the sheet, under the ceiling fan rocking in its shoddy fixture. The party had been a huge success. Everyone had come and we'd eaten, drunk and danced from 8 p.m. till 3 a.m. Even so, Marty and I tidied up afterwards, adding our bottles to all the restaurants' piles in the laneway for the early-morning garbage truck, which smashed its way into our dreams before dawn, six days a week.

Our bedroom was upstairs with a balcony and stairs leading down one flight to the footpath of Rockwall Crescent, Potts Point. Marty had purchased the lower-ground and ground floors of the five-storey terrace in 1986, three years before we met. In 1990, I moved in. Downstairs, there were black slate floors. A black metal spiral staircase led to a landing with tall glass panels overlooking a small courtyard, a garage door and the back laneway. You opened the panels by pushing the base of the window at an angle; because they could not extend more than a few inches, we often left them open overnight to encourage air flow. A small bedroom led off the landing, and also overlooked the courtyard below. A narrow hallway stretched away from the panelled windows towards the front of the house and was flanked by floor-to-ceiling cupboards. At the end of the hallway was our bedroom and ensuite with two sets of French doors opening onto a small balcony with stairs leading down to street level.

We had passed out, assured of a leisurely day ahead. Then I heard the creak of the old floorboards under the beige carpet. I felt my skull press into the pillow beneath my head. I heard it again. My neck stiffened and my jaw clamped. I began to count. I was one. I was one person lying in bed, here and now. I counted two, which was Marty, his body warm beside me. Who the hell was three? I counted again . . . one, two . . . three. If there were two of us in bed, then who was making the boards creak?

I froze. There were three of us. My blood turned cold and my eyes dried open. I tried to close them. I so wanted to be asleep, or look asleep, or not be there. I hoped I couldn't be seen; that I had somehow evaporated and this third person would vanish, too.

But there he stood looking down at me. He was huge. His hair was black and his eyes wide. I may have been mistaken but he looked alarmed to see me, too. I immediately sensed that he hadn't imagined he was walking into a bedroom, but had hoped for a living room with handbags and jewels strewn around, waiting to be collected.

My arms were stiffly by my sides. I forced the fingers of my right hand to curl. I dug my nails into Marty's left thigh. It was like he had been on the blocks in start position, awaiting the gun. He sprang into action. In one fell swoop, he was standing on his side of the bed, brandishing an American Civil War sword across my body and pointing its blade menacingly towards the intruder. I saw the silvery length of steel and Marty's naked form, his own less lengthy member swinging. The sight of the two swinging rods made me laugh. Not a big laugh, but just enough to let warm air fill my frozen lungs, my blood to flow and my senses to return.

The large man began to back down the hallway. Marty was clearly intent on pursuing him. My frozen terror had transformed itself into a manic fever. I threw my naked body to the floor, grabbed Marty's left ankle and begged him not to follow the intruder. I was projecting vivid images of carnage and bloodshed. I knew that one of them would be injured; in no time, there would be a dismembered body and Marty would be either murdered or a murderer. I searched my vocabulary to find the strongest, most compelling and convincing word I knew, but all that came out was the word 'beg'.

'I beg you, I beg you. Please, don't go after him. Please, let's just get out of here. I *beg* you!'

I laughed at the absurdity. A naked knight with a sword and a woman getting carpet burns, begging him not to slay the dragon. Marty kicked shut the bedroom door and, with his spare hand, riffled through the cylindrical wicker laundry basket. He threw me some fabric, grabbed something for himself and ordered me to open the French doors. We escaped down the stone steps, opened the gate and ran to the corner of Rockwall and Macleay streets. We caught our breath, checking that we were indeed alive, and that's when I sobered up.

I turned to Marty. He was standing under the lamplight in a pair of tracksuit pants holding a sword. For me, he had found a crumpled and grease-stained tea towel. No matter how I fashioned it, it covered very little. Just then, the intruder passed us. He was labouring beneath a heavy load of cameras. He ran across the road, staggered over a brick fence and disappeared beyond the Nikko Hotel carpark.

'Where the hell did that sword come from?' I asked through chattering teeth.

'Carla gave it to me. It's always under the bed.'

Because Marty was with me, because there was his ex-girlfriend's sword, because we escaped and no one was hurt, our adventure was given airings at dinner parties. Had I been alone and frozen, I daresay it may have been a different story.

Then there was the flasher in Balmain, who used to hang around in a back laneway.

The father of a girlfriend, who tried to kiss me in the kitchen when I stayed over one night.

The seventy-five-year-old father of another friend, who invited me into his marital bedroom while his wife was in the kitchen, and showed me framed family photos on their dressing table before smothering me in awkward wet slobberings.

And there was the fair-haired young man who, on a beautiful Sunday morning as I was walking down High Street, Kensington, to NIDA, asked me, 'Are you wearing pants?' I ignored him, but he increased his speed to match mine and asked again, 'Are you wearing pants?'

'Yes,' I said dismissively.

'Doesn't look like it,' he replied.

I took a sharp left turn into one of the university entrances, about three gates up the hill from the NIDA gate.

He followed.

My only options were to turn back towards him or pass through a narrow passage between two buildings. Less than halfway along, he shouldered me to the brick wall and began to undo his fly. I pushed him and ran and ran. He scared the hell out of me.

All these incidents caused huge physical reactions in me. They sharpened my survival senses but, eventually, left me feeling more sad than scared.

The shelf where I stored these experiences was getting crowded. I knew that too many more may cause the shelf to crack under their weight. I could either protect myself by avoiding the world, or develop an attitude to suit the environment. I chose the latter. It was in my control; it made me responsible, not for the actions against me, but for the state of mind I could adopt; and it cost me no money.

Armed with nothing but a set of survival skills, I acknowledge now how fortunate I've been that I avoided greater harm.

As a young woman, I had no understanding that many of these uncomfortable and threatening experiences would be, in years to come (and were even at the time), criminal abuse. With each of these encounters, I sensed a violation of trust and a betrayal of my social expectations, but what was more at stake, for me, and more threatening than any potential physical harm, was the loss of trust. This I feared more than the violence itself. I feared losing my enjoyment of life and my excitement about the future. This outweighed any desire to complain, report or avenge.

And so I muzzled myself. I began gathering, collecting the individual experiences and storing all their unique fragments. The sensations, the images, the sounds. I catalogued them for future reference. I felt enthused about having new insights to draw upon in my acting life. I replayed the incidents in my mind, taking mental notes, then I filed them away again.

This process made me feel energised; it put me in control. I could recall the moment on the train when the man pushed my face towards his penis. I could re-experience several intense reactions that seemed to happen simultaneously. My nostrils stung with a sharp, stale scent of nicotine and copper. My right cheek felt hot and clammy. My stomach churned with bile while a trapped voiceless scream was suffocating deep inside me. Then a shock of electricity raced through me. I assumed a dreadful feeling of inevitability, connected to my action of having chosen to sit near him. These thoughts were accompanied by feelings of falling, sinking and drowning, which were followed by a gut-wrenching queasiness. The thought that I might die was overridden by a white-hot 'No, I fucking won't!' that directed me to grab his jacket and pull myself up.

Because I had got away, my heart rate then calmed, and I began to breathe regularly again. My tingling skin settled and my body heat cooled. My frantic mind quietened, and I reminded myself of my good fortune.

All this I could re-create and convert into feelings of power and control. I hoped to use it creatively in the future. Years later, it shocked me to realise that I had ignored any thoughts about these men potentially continuing their behaviour elsewhere and causing serious or irreparable harm to someone else. I began to imagine the devastation you'd experience when the perpetrator was someone you love. Someone you trust and have invested your time, energy and heart in. I began to acknowledge how this could not only lead to an irretrievable mistrust in the perpetrator, but a loss of trust in yourself and even in the whole damn world.

What concerned me now was the thought that, maybe, I had been encouraged to not ask questions. Maybe, I had accepted that it was up to me to find a way to deal with things and stay silent, because I was a woman.

For a woman of my generation growing up in the seventies, one of the expectations was to push back against the prudish mores of our mothers' generation. I felt women were encouraged to explore new sexual freedoms. In doing so, I gave myself permission to have fun, and discover and expect sexual satisfaction. Somewhere mixed up in this, however, I silently accepted bad behaviour as simply that: bad behaviour, not damaging behaviour. I forgave others and I forbade myself. I forgave (or tried to forgive) those who may have harmed me, believing I may have given confusing signals. Then I forbade myself from speaking out in fear of being shamed, blamed or implicated in the 'She asked for it' narrative. I associated loose behaviour with words such as slut, whore and slag, accompanied by the terror of not being believed, the distress of upsetting people, the unavoidable self-doubt and the fear of fear itself.

I reflect now on the daily morning ritual at my primary school, when we all dutifully recited the motto: 'It all depends on me'. As a grown woman, this could mean that it depends on me to speak up and take action, but as a little child, it felt like a heavy burden and meant: 'It all depends on me to be a good girl. To deal with things and accept responsibility'.

As I got older, and fell in love and had children, a niggling question formed. Was this 'getting over things' and 'filing them away' possibly my own positive spin on what I was really doing, which was self-silencing? Only in the past ten years, since more women have felt empowered enough to speak out, have I acknowledged to myself that my habit of 'moving on' had cost me and others. Back when I was young, after a particularly upsetting incident on a film set, I had decided never to work on screen again. I assumed I wasn't cut out for it. I believed I wasn't hip enough for the male-dominated, cocaine-sniffing, beer-drinking cast and crew I was working with. I assumed I was a bit of a prude and a bore. So I turned to my theatre family again, and they welcomed me back. When I encountered similar disturbing behaviour there, I felt momentarily disillusioned but, too afraid to lose my place and even more my love of theatre, I forgave. A power imbalance had needed addressing and I had felt ill equipped to take it on.

Every generation demands change and there is always resistance, especially when those being challenged are in a privileged position. The younger generation are now challenging my generation, wanting accountability. They feel increasingly powerful and are refusing to be silenced. They are teaching my generation of women, and indeed of all genders, to speak out. Ironically, it's often men, especially men in privileged and powerful positions, who are yelling the loudest, desperate to protect their reputations.

Occasionally, I wish we could go back, revert to factory settings and begin again.

8

Standing in My Light

When my agent Bill Shanahan called me in one morning in 1982 suggesting I meet with one of the only casting agents in Sydney, I leaped at the opportunity.

In his kind voice, he relayed that he'd been putting me forward for roles in films but this particular casting agent had turned him down each time, refusing to see me.

'Heather, you need to sort this out. She seems to have a problem with you. Call her and meet with her.'

I went into Bill's office, a narrow terrace house in Woollahra with a sign saying 'Shanahans' by the front door. Bill sat in a snug, light-filled room with Brenda, his co-agent, and Brenda's daughter Sharon. The three of them sat at a large desk, which from memory was at least two tables pushed together. In the centre was a lazy Susan, with all the actors' files kept alphabetically on its dial. The cardboard manila folders fanned out from the axis, and within their creased covers were handwritten notes and typed contracts. All files were labelled and replaced to their correct slot after use. Covering the walls were black-and-white head shots of all the Shanahans clients. The phones were constantly ringing.

Bill seemed unusually disturbed about my unexplained rift with the casting agent, as though there was a ticking clock and a now-or-never opportunity to right a wrong. I called from the phone on his desk and made an appointment to see her in three days' time.

I was twenty-four years old and, although not brimming with confidence, knew that my future was going to be as an actor. I arrived early to the casting agent's waiting room, introduced myself to the person in reception and waited, scanning a collage of small black-and-white photos from film shoots that plastered one of the walls. I was careful not to appear too interested in them so as to avoid looking like a novice.

'Well, hello there,' she said. I turned to see that she had descended the stairs herself rather than have me sent up. This seemed promising. I followed her up the narrow carpeted staircase and entered a rather ordinary room partitioned by a couple of dividers, with desks, chairs, lamps and the odd plant. Framed posters of Australian films, which I assumed she had cast, hung on the walls and bound scripts sat in piles on shelves along with VHS tape boxes.

She offered me a seat in a corner alongside a desk and sat opposite me. She crossed her legs. Her slacks had the neatest crease down the front, and revealed her slender ankles below the hem. It occurred to me that she liked her ankles.

She offered me tea, which I declined. After a couple of pleasantries, she said, 'Well, Heather, you're terrific on stage but you'll never get a film role because you don't have "IT". Some people have IT and some don't. And you don't, I'm afraid.'

I felt relieved that I hadn't accepted the tea. I wondered whether I had misheard her and should ask her to repeat it, but I felt foolish enough for not having the 'IT' she had just mentioned. She said it like it was common knowledge, as if everyone knew it but me. I felt embarrassed to be wasting her time on something so petty, and wondered why she hadn't simply told Bill and saved me the humiliation.

I remember smiling at her, not wanting her to feel uncomfortable for saying such an unexpectedly horrid thing. My first instinct was to protect her from discomfort, and bow to her superior position and wisdom in such matters. I wanted to ask her what *IT* even was, and whether it was something I could acquire but, instead, I thanked her (not knowing what for), picked up my bag from the floor, hooked it over my shoulder, thanked her once more, gave a little wave and descended the stairs. The person on the desk was on a phone call. As I reached the door to the street, she called after me, 'Pull it hard, please, it's real draughty in here!'

I stepped into the cold air and wished I could travel back in time. Back before the agent had said the words: 'You don't have IT'. If I had doubted hearing her correctly in her office, I certainly didn't doubt it now. It sat deep in my chest like a purple plum swallowed whole. I felt the hard seed through the soft ripened flesh; it hurt.

What was I thinking? Who was I kidding? Only myself? I recalled the visiting director who, two years earlier at NIDA, invited us to perform scenes for mock auditions to prepare us for the industry. He apparently possessed some extraordinary insight into who would make it and who wouldn't. If he permitted you to complete your monologue, then you were on a short list. If he interrupted you, then you were out. I performed a piece that had previously received positive feedback and launched into it confidently. Moments into the audition, he said, 'Stop . . . Thank you . . . Next!' He dismissed me, leaving me with my mouth open mid-sentence and my hands neither up nor down, but on their way to becoming a gesture.

With the few others who had also failed to be considered, we wrote him off as a silly old fool. But was he right? I thought of my close friends who had been backstage after my recent show at the Drama Theatre in the Sydney Opera House, who sat in my dressing room, drinking my wine, avoiding speaking about the play they had just seen and especially, it appeared, my performance. *Did they know?* I thought of all the actresses my age, who had already worked on film sets, flipping through their faces like cards being dealt out on a table and wondering what they had that I didn't. What the hell was *IT?* Why had no one ever mentioned this before? Why had I spent three years at NIDA, and why had it never been part of the course? Discovering IT. Acting IT. Being IT. It was outrageous! It was unfair! It was not my fault!

And why had she said, 'You're terrific in the theatre, but . . .' as if the theatre employed a lesser type of actor who has nothing unique to offer, an actor without IT. Or did she mean theatre actors were actors who shouted, wildly gesticulated and were 'theatrical'? People who had no subtlety, no subtext, no X factor. That's what she meant, I decided. She was talking about the X factor! The elusive quality, the unnamed, the thing no one can put their finger on because it's simply . . . IT. And only those skilled enough to recognise IT—and who are the gatekeepers and caretakers of IT—can identify IT.

I'd had enough. I was now angry and upset. The plum had become mushy, its seed had split open and its jagged edges tore at my throat. A stinging sensation pierced my eyes and I started crying. I was so embarrassed. I lowered my head, walked down the footpath and turned left.

I was living in Crown Street, Darlinghurst, half a block from the Italian cafés in Stanley Street and directly around the corner from Liverpool Street. I could see the casting agent's sign from our own bathroom window! Although I was sharing with wonderful friends who would have been supportive, I needed to walk outside. Our terrace house had been a brothel, and the bathroom was one of its largest rooms. Directly off the kitchen through glass French doors was a fully tiled room with a large square spa/bathtub in the centre. There was nothing else in the room. I don't recall ever having a bath in there, but it was a great entertaining room and definitely a talking point.

I walked the five or so blocks to Centennial Park and set off around its curved track, a gentle breeze pushing me forward. I oscillated between feelings of failure and blazing anger.

How could she, who's never even acted, know what IT feels like? How does she even know what IT is? Why didn't I force her to tell me? Why did I flee? Why didn't I ask her, 'Are you born with IT, or can you develop IT? Are you chosen to have IT? Are you the only one who can see IT? Does everyone know I don't have IT?'

My belief that I would act in films was hit head-on by her certainty that I would not. I pictured her sitting opposite me in that mean little office. It dawned on me that she didn't look happy. Her mouth was tight and thin; her short hair, although thick, was dull; and the room had no warmth. Even the girl who was going to make the tea for me looked disproportionally dejected when I declined. I began to see the casting agent as someone who was vulnerable, and possibly lonely and overworked. Her creased slacks were a bit desperate and the cold, cramped chair pushed against the wall was unwelcoming. A thought popped into my head: *She takes the shape of the last chair she sat on.* Someone had said this to me once, describing a person they had little respect for. What did it mean, and why did I think of it now?

Had she judged me based on her current success? She had recently taken complete credit for 'discovering' an actress a year earlier. The actress was brilliant and was always going to be recognised (in my opinion), regardless of this agent's involvement. Has she decided that other actresses had to take the shape of her latest triumph and, if they didn't fit the mould, then they were of little consequence? Was she the sole dictator of the audience's taste and box-office success?

And was I not doing something similar? I was allowing the discomfort of the chair on which I received the bad news to stay with me and wrap around me, like the very upholstery was stuck to me, and its weight was dragging me down with every step. Was I willing to live with the heaviness of her negativity for one moment longer? Did I not have the right, like anyone else, to choose what chair I wished to mould me, and to sit in as many as I desired? I had to shake these feelings off and not accept her narrow, prejudiced, possibly self-serving opinion, which could potentially affect me adversely in the long term. I would *not* take the shape she wanted me to take. I would *not* let her views restrict my belief that everyone has the right of expression and to find their own way. I would *not* let her words shape my body, my mind and my feelings. I began to walk faster, stretching my legs out and dramatically swinging my arms. With every stride, I pushed myself further away from that chair. I shook it free and began walking as if I did indeed have IT.

I began to think, *Maybe I have IT and she just can't see IT? What does IT feel like? Maybe this!*

I began to lighten up and even find the whole experience amusing. I walked myself out and, by the time I arrived home, I felt ready to prove her wrong.

As far as I could see, she was simply standing in my light. All I needed to do was shift my position and find it again. On stage or on a set, when someone stands in your light, it means you are cast in shadow. Usually, this happens unconsciously when the other actor is simply focused on what they are doing. When it's brought to their attention, they apologise and adjust their position. But sometimes, it's intentional. I have performed on stage with a stunning and highly experienced actress, who throughout the performance would take small steps backwards as she delivered her lines until she was dead centre, facing front, and you had your back to the audience. Another would repeatedly angle her body or introduce an unrehearsed physical move during a take, to obscure or cast a shadow across her fellow actors. The great thing is that, once you are aware of it, you simply make adjustments.

I called Bill Shanahan and told him about the conversation. He wasn't happy. He said, 'Good actors are good actors regardless of the medium. You are a good actor.' Beautiful Bill, who encouraged and nurtured you, yet made you do the legwork. He gave praise when he felt it was earned and stayed silent when he didn't. Bill believed acting was an honourable profession; he didn't agree with actors doing fashion shoots and self-promotion. He believed in the actor's craft and its development. He valued the connection with an actor's work, the pride in that work, the longevity of their career and their unique journey. He also had the most wicked, mischievous sense of humour to balance every serious discussion. He reassured me that I would be fine, and that things change every day in this business. No one person had a monopoly on everything and, in the end, success is about generosity, compassion, and a willingness to try things and take risks.

Some months later, on my way to the Drama Theatre to perform in a matinee at the Sydney Opera House, I turned the corner from Oxford Street into Crown Street and ran into Bill. He was standing in a queue with other potential buyers to look at newly renovated one- and two-bed apartments in an old Art Deco building called Royal Court. He said he was looking for a friend of his and that I should come on in with him.

The foyer doors opened and people raced up the large central staircase as if vying for the best dodgem cars at a fair. Each apartment had a price tag attached to its door and an agent standing ready. Bill headed straight to the first-floor two-bedder, which had a curved stone balcony overlooking Oxford Street. Buyers were given ten minutes to appraise the apartments and talk to the agents before the next group was allowed in. If you were interested, you wrote a cheque for ten per cent of the purchase price and you had right of refusal for the next 48 hours.

Bill wrote a cheque for five or ten per cent of the $68,000 asking price, turned to me and said, 'There you go, it's yours. You'll pay me back in no time.'

Bill bought me that apartment, and I repaid the deposit swiftly because he believed in me and encouraged others to do so, also. John Gaden cast me in a school's production of *Macbeth* for the STC without auditioning me. George Ogilvie cast me in the film *The Place at the Coast* without a screen test; Rodney Fisher cast me in *As You Desire Me* sight unseen and George Miller and the directors of the *Bodyline* series responded enthusiastically and cast me based on Bill's recommendation.

Now, at the age of sixty-three, I've participated in more than forty feature films, appeared in almost one hundred TV productions and played hugely satisfying roles in more than sixty theatre productions.

Bill passed away in 1991 aged forty-eight from AIDS complications. Bill had IT.

9

Raining Silver

A girlfriend had gifted me a session with a clairvoyant in Paddington for my twenty-ninth birthday and I'd made an appointment. We had spoken a few days before on the landline when the clairvoyant had requested I arrive on time at 3 p.m. and to bring some flowers maybe, plus a cake or some small cakes, maybe even a lamington as she loved those—but not the ones with jam. And then she added, 'Would you kindly call me "Granny" when you arrive at the gate? I live in a religious retirement village and some of them here, well, some of them wouldn't appreciate me doing my thing, you know, my gift . . . my readings.'

I agreed, of course, and asked if I needed to bring anything else.

'No, just you, the cakes and a small tape recorder,' she said.

I arrived at 3 p.m. promptly. She was waiting under an awning in front of the reception area.

'Hi, Gran?'

'Oh great . . . You're here.'

With wide and welcoming arms, she embraced me, ooooooed and ahhhed at the flowers and the lamingtons and ushered me along a curved path into her tiny, neat, dimly lit, one-room bedsit.

The kettle was boiled and tea poured. We sliced the lamingtons into quarters. I pressed the button of the tape recorder and sat upright, awaiting my future.

Between bites and wiping her mouth with the back of her fine, purple-veined hands, she began. For at least an hour, she mentioned an odd assortment of seemingly unrelated events that I had supposedly experienced, but my recollection suggested otherwise. There were names of siblings I didn't recognise, and hobbies and pastimes I had no interest in. I sat back and decided she was probably lonely, and this was an imaginative way to lure visitors and earn a little money on the side. I was happy to think of it as a lovely interlude with a charming old lady.

Then, emphatically, she pushed the teacup aside, sighed, checked her teeth for coconut and said, 'That thing,' pointing to the tape recorder. 'That thing still going?'

'Yes,' I said.

'Okay, then, let's get into it.'

She shuffled her cards and began to lay them out like she was playing single-handed solitaire. She turned and swapped them and tutted and muttered, 'Pick one and place it on that pile, now this pile.'

And so it went. Eventually, she sat up straight with fingers splayed slightly on the green faux-leather card table and said conspiratorially, 'Well, you are going on a trip, a big trip, but it's not easy, not easy at all. But you must go. Oh yes, you simply must.' Then she said, 'You will meet a man, and he will be broad at the shoulders and tapering at the waist.'

I may have made a phew sound.

She looked at me with a mischievous glint. 'You are going to meet your guardian angel. I can't tell whether it's a person, an animal or what it is, but it's there waiting for you and don't you worry, IT WILL MAKE ITSELF KNOWN TO YOU.'

These words seemed so odd to me and her certainty even odder. She pressed on as if there was a fast-approaching expiry on her memory. 'You will be surrounded by silver, silver everywhere you look, as far as the eye can see, silver.'

'Gold?' I gently questioned.

'No, definitely silver,' she snapped, possibly a little insulted by my playfulness. 'And you're getting a job, so be ready.'

With that she whacked the table with both of her small fists and said, 'That's it.'

I pressed 'Stop' on the tape deck and glanced at my watch. I'd been with her for more than two hours. We chatted about her bad back, the other people who lived in the complex, the garden and the weather. She said she was a little tired, so I should probably think about making a move. We walked leisurely to the front gate, admiring the small bright flowers that lined the path until we reached our farewell. We hugged as I thanked her and said how lovely it had been. In a projected voice, she asked me to pass on her love to the rest of our family.

I let myself into my apartment in the Royal Court in Darlinghurst. The answering machine was flashing. I pressed 'Missed calls' and recognised the voice of Bill Shanahan.

'Call me. You need to be in Broken Hill by tomorrow. A role has come up and they're already filming. Someone must have pulled out and you need to fly first thing tomorrow. There is a slight complication as there's a pilots' strike, so you'll go by Hercules. Call me!'

I called Bill and got the details. The pilots' strike was severely disrupting domestic air travel in Australia. Then prime minister Bob Hawke declared a national emergency, and allowed Royal Australian Air Force planes and pilots to provide limited services. Amazingly, this little film *The Water Trolley*, which went on to be nominated for an Emmy Award, was deemed important enough to fly me to Broken Hill. The passenger list looked like an emergency military deployment. *If they ask me to attach a parachute,* I thought, *I'm not boarding!*

I landed in Broken Hill in the dark and was met by three figures: Noel Price, the director; Bob Donaldson, the first assistant director; and Martin (Marty) McGrath, the director of photography. The air was close and still. I felt like a grungy Ingrid Bergman arriving in Casablanca. The cast and crew were all staying at a 1960s horseshoe-shaped, single-storey, blond-brick motel with front-facing cars parked at each door. A large neon sign announcing the 'Hilltop Motel' adorned the reception office. The rooms were basic; each had a bed against a wall opposite a large aluminium-framed window with sheer pale curtains. A small bench ran adjacent to the bed and tucked up close to the bathroom. The ceilings were rough-blown concrete with a half-moon frosted light-fitting planted dead centre. A plastic kettle, two cups, some biscuits and a small bar fridge completed the sparse decor.

The first day's filming required me to operate a Morse Code machine. I love how actors playing supporting roles often arrive on a set with little briefing of what they're to do. I was once cast as a nurse without a name, and was sent a call time and an address but nothing else. I was handed a white uniform and taken to the set. The director was briefing the main cast, followed by a rehearsal. When they got to the part where the lead actor sat in a chair, I was pushed forward. I was expected to perform an eye examination using an optometrist's machine. I had no idea where to begin, so I fiddled with dials and pushed buttons until the director shouted: 'Cut! What the fuck is she doing? Are you a nurse?'

'No, I'm an actress.'

'Fuck. Will someone get me a real nurse?'

I was ushered off set and left on a cold chair in a draughty passageway. As I waited in the lunch queue, wishing I was dead, the make-up artist leaned towards me and whispered, 'Don't ask, just follow me to the toilets.'

She removed my dress and presented me with it; the white fabric was now soaked in menstrual blood. She washed it, dried it with a hairdryer, helped me back into it and kindly led me outside. Lunch had finished so there I sat for another four hours until, humiliated, I was finally released.

The Morse Code machine experience was much more forgiving. The camera was angled to suggest I was an expert rather than expose my ineptitude. The character was also in a panic, which allowed me to appear flustered and therefore not in control of my actions. I wore a simple shapeless cotton housedress, no make-up and had my hair tied back; yet later,

Marty would say that I was one of the most beautiful women he'd ever met. The following day's filming was followed by rushes, which is when the director, producers, cast and crew watch the chosen takes from the day before. Although it's not a lot of fun watching yourself, I always loved being part of that process. It rarely happens these days.

After rushes, we walked en masse to the centre of Broken Hill to dine at the Pink Pussycat. I remember excusing myself to use the bathroom. It was when I returned that I noticed his absence. Marty had seemed very pleasant, kind and calm, but I hadn't really noticed him until now, when all I saw was a room without him. And then a lightness when he returned a few moments later from the direction of the bathrooms, where he later admitted he was hoping to bump into me privately.

After dinner, we landed loudly at the bar of the Barrier Social Democratic Club and drank Argadalas, a dangerous and disgusting mixture of Cointreau, Baileys and vodka. Marty and I sat on two high stools at a sticky round table, talking about family and passions, only ceasing when the bartender shoved us out. We discovered we were the only two people left.

Out on the street, the rain was pelting down in massive droplets. We paused under an awning on the corner of Oxide and Beryl streets and kissed. Back at the Hilltop, drenched to the skin, Marty invited me to Room 17 (he still has the key) and we made love. My back was pressed against the cool wall. We were facing each other. I was trying to look into his eyes to gather insights into how he was feeling. The neon light from reception was creating a silhouette of him. I noticed his broad shoulders and tapered waist.

That very second, Marty said, 'I feel like I'm your guardian angel,' a phrase to which he later confessed, 'I have no idea where that came from.'

I froze. My vision expanded to the space beyond his darkened cut-out form to the massive rectangle of silver rain in the window, falling like streamers all around him. From where I lay, he was a landscape of hills and valleys surrounded by silver. Moments later, he reached to get something from his jeans pocket. He placed a silver ingot in my hand. It had an imprint of the Broken Hill mine and the words 'City of Silver'.

I shivered and tried to breathe normally. An alarm went off and Marty rose, showered, dressed, kissed me and closed the door. He and the crew were expected on set at dawn.

I thought I had the day off, but soon Marty opened the motel room door again. 'There's a change of schedule due to the rain and you're on,' he said. 'They're looking for you. They've woken the hotel manager because you aren't answering your door. They're really worried. I'm leaving now. Probably best you get to your room and let them know you're okay.' He kissed me and left.

He closed the door as I threw on the crumpled black dress I'd worn to dinner the night before, picked up my shoes and slipped out, panicking. The neon sign, which moments earlier had created magic, now exposed me. I walked barefoot, tousled, mascara smeared, from Room 17 towards the figures calling my name and banging at Room 25. The concrete path seemed endless as the eyes of the crew, awaiting instruction, watched from their vehicles. I dug deep for my dignity as I stepped out the slow walk of shame.

Noel, Bob and the motel manager swung around as I blurted, 'Hi! Sorry, I just went for an early walk.'

They looked at my dry clothes amid the torrential downpour and smiled. I like to remember it as a smile; it was probably more a smirk. Marty and I ignored each other for the remainder of the shoot. Someone told me he was married (he wasn't), and another told me to avoid on-set romances because they never last. But after we landed in Sydney, standing at the airport, we agreed to share a taxi to the eastern suburbs together. We engaged in small talk as we travelled. As I alighted, I offered him my number. Our friendship developed and we would meet up in different states wherever work took us. We both acknowledged that, somehow, we would be together. Nothing felt more certain to me. Nor to him. After all, a week earlier, an elderly woman had seen it in the cards.

About a year later, I played Marty 'Gran's' recording.

I moved in with Marty with one suitcase, a teapot and a large framed photo from a production of *Macbeth* I'd been in, directed by Richard Wherrett. A year earlier, I had invited him to the opening night of *All My Sons* by Arthur Miller, directed by Gale Edwards at Wharf 1 for the STC, but he gently declined. He thought that committing to an opening night and watching me on stage was too intimate an experience, while there were still things to sort out in his previous relationship. I loved that he felt this. He actually asked me if I felt comfortable about him going to stay with her 'to sort things out'. And so he did. When he returned a couple of weeks later, our relationship developed.

I was deep into rehearsals with Richard Roxburgh for *Burn This* by Lanford Wilson, directed by Wayne Harrison, when Marty, who was shooting a television series in Melbourne, flew to Sydney for my birthday. We had just had our first dress rehearsal at Wharf 1. I was completely consumed and sharply focused on fulfilling all the notes Wayne had given me, and making the role and the production the best it could be. Marty collected me at about 11 p.m. in a taxi on Hickson Road and we drove towards Potts Point, where he lived. He had booked a room at the Nikko Hotel, previously the Chevron and now the Rockwall Garden apartments. I thought this strange because his place was diagonally across the road. We had a light supper and drank cocktails in the bar. By 3 a.m., we arrived in the hotel room a little drunk and tired. I felt concerned about whether I would be firing the following day for the second preview and wanted to sleep.

Marty got down on one knee and proposed. He held a small box with a gold ring with four emeralds embedded around the band.

Not now, was all I could think. *Oh please, not now.*

My head was full of Lanford Wilson's New York love story, which was fraught and complicated and that's where I wanted it to stay. Somehow, accessing my feelings for Marty was going to get in the way of my performance and I wanted to remain in that world, at least until after opening night.

'I need to think about this,' I told Marty. 'But as it's my birthday, can I keep the ring?'

I thought keeping the ring was also a way of saying I want to do this but not right now.

We didn't sleep. We walked around Rushcutters Bay Park at dawn and then flagged two taxis. Marty disappeared towards the airport and I travelled to my apartment in Darlinghurst, where I showered and readied for work. The answering machine was flashing and I rewound the tape while drinking tea.

Marty's mother's voice carried the first message. 'I am so thrilled you're going to be my daughter-in-law!'

His sister Madelin followed. 'Congratulations. Welcome to the family.'

Feeling ill, I threw the tea down the sink. What had I done? I adored his family and, clearly, they could see no reason why I would not have said 'yes'.

Marty remained loving and attentive, but never mentioned marriage again. The play finished and another one began. I realised how unsure I was about what marriage meant for me. The idea of a wedding made me feel uncomfortable. I was concerned that our relationship, which was working so well without marriage, could change unless we were engaging in it for the same reasons. I eventually brought the subject up; in doing so, I realised I believed that marriage for me meant children, illness and soon after, my death. How simplistic my thinking had become, how obvious to me now that I had not yet sorted through the implications of my own mother's death! How crazy it now seemed that her story should be mine. How clearly I now realised the importance of breaking family cycles and creating new ones for yourself.

I released myself from my mother and began a conversation with Marty about marriage, and what we both wanted and how we should do it. We were married in 1992 at St Canice's Church in Kings Cross. Marty's uncle Charlie, a priest, performed the service. Surrounded by our families and friends, we read our favourite e.e. cummings poems 'i carry your heart with me' and 'somewhere i have never travelled, gladly beyond', followed by a big party at the Wharf where we danced till our feet hurt. At about midnight, it poured, and after farewelling my sister in the street, Marty and I stood in the sudden downpour, relishing the silver sheets of water as they fell around us.

10

This Is Going to Hurt (Warning: Feelings May Arise)

It was the size and firmness of a frozen baby pea. For three years, my left hand travelled to it at least ten times a day. As it grew, my touch became more specific and my forefinger traced its circumference as if moulding it into a small, perfectly round ball of Blu-Tac. Touching it became as habitual as a child sucking their thumb while twisting their hair, or an adult reaching for a sip of wine while talking.

It's not that I wasn't concerned, it's just that I had been told repeatedly it was nothing to worry about. My doctor had sent me for annual mammograms, which all came back clear. Understandably, she tried to assure me that it was a benign lump or cyst. I tried so hard to believe her but a niggling voice, which was loudest on waking and just before sleep, kept drawing my attention back to the site. The lump was situated high in the breast, and it occurred to me that the mammogram machine may not have captured it. I became worried about the efficacy of the machines as well as the lump, and then became concerned about my doctor's diagnosis. Worry is a strange thing. It appears unexpectedly and presents in many guises, sometimes as a bad temper, sometimes as being unable to concentrate, but almost always my worry was louder than other noises. This was why I tried so hard to push it down and get on with more important, more worthwhile, more satisfying things. I was good at smothering worry and even better at listening to people who I believed had more knowledge about myself than I did.

I met with a friend who had been diagnosed with breast cancer and showed her my lump.

'Nah, that doesn't look like breast cancer. Mine was much bigger and more spongey. You're fine.'

I canvassed other mothers with young children, who tried to comfort me with their stories of blocked milk ducts, lumpy breasts and multiple cysts. I mentioned it to friends, who thought I was too young and not someone who'd get it, but said if I *was* worried I should continue to do regular checks. Nothing anyone said reassured me, and although I appreciated their personal and practical insights, none of them had helped to assuage my fears.

We flew to Los Angeles with our two small sons, so that Marty could take some meetings. I saw the trip as a wonderful opportunity to see our friends Joss and P.J., and their children Lily and Spike. Marty had introduced me to Joss and P.J. when we were all in our late twenties while Marty and I were working temporarily in Melbourne, in the early days of our relationship, and the four of us had formed a close bond through our love of film and laughter. At the time, Joss had written and was directing the film *Proof*, on which Marty was the director of photography and I played Hugo Weaving's mum in the flashbacks. We spent weekends pushing Spike in his pram around the Melbourne Botanical Gardens, stopping for breakfasts and sharing funny stories. We all went on to do *Muriel's Wedding*, which P.J. wrote and directed, and our lives became intermingled.

We had been in LA for only a couple of weeks when Marty was offered a film in Thailand directed by Prince Chatri Chalerm Yukol. The prince insisted we enjoy a week at the Six Senses, a Thai resort, before filming began. I felt it was a shame to leave Los Angeles so soon; I had envisaged Marty getting offers that kept us in the States, and was looking forward to getting in touch with my father's family and giving our boys an opportunity to establish a connection with their grandfather's past.

Marty was intrigued by the Thai project, however; in the prince's twenty-third film, *The Legend of Suriyothai*, a historical saga about four Thai dynasties, 3,000 Thai army soldiers played extras and 160 elephants were at the Prince's disposal. It sounded like a fabulous adventure, so we exchanged our woollen coats for cotton shorts and flew to Bangkok.

I was lying on a simple padded massage table on a Thai beach at sunset. It was postcard perfect. There was a soft warm breeze; the sound of water lapping; the scent of jasmine, coconut and lemongrass; and gentle Thai murmurings among the girls who welcomed tourists onto the sand to disrobe and relax. Marty had taken the boys for a dip in the pool, giving me a moment alone to be pampered. Massage is one of my most cherished pleasures. I hope that death will be one long massage and that, as I'm dying, someone will literally rub my life away. From the time we met, Marty has massaged the small of my back every night as I fall asleep. Even if he falls asleep before me, which is always, he will wake to move his hand gently on my back. Seamus, our younger son, is a brilliant masseur who has given me shoulder rubs since he was young. Most evenings, he will arrive at my bedroom door as I'm settling into bed, lean against the doorframe and say, 'Well, well, well, it must be hard being perfect. I imagine you'll be needing a shoulder rub,' and massage my shoulders deeply.

'Roll over now, please,' the masseuse whispered near my ear, drawing my attention away from the lapping water. *Roll over,* I thought. *Oh wonderful, that means we're only halfway done.* She placed a light cotton sarong across my bare torso, stood at the head of the table and began gently touching my upper chest. I remember inhaling deeply and sighing. The next moment, as her hand pressed lightly over my right breast, I sat up and projectile-vomited onto the sand. I was to spend the following couple of months in determined denial.

After six days of luxury, we were driven hundreds of kilometres from the glamour of the Six Senses to two simple dark-brown rooms on the edge of Bangkok. Marty was working long days in pre-production, so we only spoke late at night in hushed tones before he fell into a deep sleep. I woke each day and gathered the boys into a taxi. To escape the intense heat, we spent hours in air-conditioned shopping malls; on the top levels were games and rides for small children that seemed to meander for miles. The Thai people welcomed Finn and Seamus wherever we went. On alternating days, we travelled to a water park straight out of a 1950s brochure for family escapes. It had large, lagoon-shaped pools surrounded by pale-blue concrete walkways and benches. Small merry-go-rounds and dodgem cars were scattered around the place, and because the park was vast and the weekday visitors few, we had the pick of every ride. On weekends, the place teemed with families. The massive water slide was opened and queues of excited kids climbed the tall ladders and screamed their way down. Our sons loved it and splashed around, licking ice-creams, while I fought an overwhelming tiredness.

I was offered a part in a play back in Sydney called *Through the Wire*, written and directed by Ros Horin. It involved harrowing, compassionate true stories of four refugees in Australian detention. The writing was compelling and one of the actors, Shahin Shafaei, was to play himself after fleeing Iran and spending ten months isolated in Curtin Detention Centre, wondering if he would stay alive and, if he did, stay sane. My long, hot days in Bangkok were bliss compared to the unbearable cruelty explored in the script.

The boys and I returned to Sydney, unsure when we would see Marty next, because every day the Prince created more elaborate scenarios for his epic film. It's not often a producer/director has an entire air force and military at his disposal, and as many elephants as there are in his country.

I felt relieved to be home. Rehearsals for the play began. Rehearsal processes for plays are fairly similar. The director and stage manager will usually create a daily or weekly schedule, and actors are called when required. Commonly, you are called every day, and I'm called all the time for most shows I'm involved in, either due to the role, or because the director's vision involves actors playing multiple roles, moving sets, or simply because it builds better relationships for everyone to be present and aware of the creative process. Each play has its own life and tone, with each person essential to its success.

It was a Tuesday morning and I wasn't due in till midday. Marty had returned from Thailand for a visit; he had taken the boys to Canberra for a few days, so I thought I should grab the opportunity to see my doctor. She had an early slot free. We chatted about travel and I mentioned my lump. She examined it and referred to my past two annual mammograms, which were both clear. She suggested it was nothing to be concerned about, but that I was soon due for another mammogram so why not do it now to alleviate any undue concerns? I felt immediately irritated hearing the word 'mammogram'. I was certain the machine wasn't capturing the site and asked if it was all that could be offered. She said they could do an ultrasound, but why not wait until the show was over and do them both then? *Why did she mention an ultrasound only now?* I wondered. *Why not three years ago?*

I folded the referrals and phoned the scanning facility.

'Well, we have a cancellation in 15 minutes if you can get here, but you have to tell me now because there are others I can give it to.'

'I'll take it. Thank you. Please don't give it away.'

I left the car where it was parked in Paddington, walked to St Vincent's Hospital in Darlinghurst and entered a packed reception area. People sat on plastic moulded seats, flipping through roughly treated copies of women's magazines and daily papers, or chatting quietly. A TV screen suspended from the ceiling was playing an interview with an opinionated witness to some event, standing on the front lawn of a suburban house, pointing to the neighbours and saying, 'I've never seen anything like it.' A young child stood in front of a rectangular fish tank, chasing a blue-and-orange striped fish with his finger across the thick glass casing, leaving smeary snail-trails. He swiped the glass from right to left with his palm as if trying to change the screen to a different channel. He appeared confused and increasingly frustrated that the fish scape remained. He looked to his mother for help, but she was uninterested, staring blankly and crushing a small white paper cup in her right fist.

I turned my attention back to the unmoving queue of two people in front of me, when a woman with a tight low bun sitting behind the counter peered around them, raised her eyebrows and looked over her glasses directly at me, with a look that said, *Calm down, please, wait your turn, I'll get to you.* I flushed and wondered whether I'd inadvertently made a noise. I must have clearly projected my impatience. My skin prickled. I felt like I was about to miss the last train because the ticket seller was chatting to a friend in the tearoom. I was about to explain indignantly that my appointment was scheduled for 45 minutes earlier when a young woman with multiple tubes attached to tape-concealed veins and pulling a beeping machine on wheels came into view. I sat, contrite and apologetic, and waited.

Eventually, I was given a number and told I'd be seen to 'in good time'. It occurred to me what a strange phrase 'in good time' is. I'd assumed it to mean ahead of schedule and here I was, in good time for my appointment, being told to wait to be seen in 'good time' when there was clearly going to be a long wait. I guess she meant that, if I was patient and waited a 'good *length* of time', I would eventually be seen and that would be the 'good time' for the appointment. My thoughts were travelling down little laneways of words and their meanings when my name was called.

'Heather Mitchell? This way, please.'

When I was in my early thirties, Marty and I had gone to Poland and Shanghai to shoot a children's series called *Spellbinder.* Shanghai still had only a few tall buildings, and bicycles were the primary means of local transportation. I could fantasise being there in the 1940s, when my parents had met in Shanghai as twenty-three year olds. It was an amazing experience, especially because the entire crew and many of the lead actors were native Mandarin speakers. We had learned only enough Mandarin to say pleasantries and to show that we enjoyed a sense of humour. I stood before a row of smiling crew members, extended my hand and said, 'Ni Hao. Wo Jiao Heather Mitchell.' ('Hello. My name is Heather Mitchell.') To which the first smiling person repeated my name back to me. 'Happy Meechu.'

So Heather Mitchell became 'Happy Meet-you'.

Hearing my name now, it sounded so separate from me. I tried grasping at it from the thickening air as I walked to the door, which a man in a blue cotton knee-length coat held open for me. I evaporated from the room full of strangers and entered the rest of my life.

The clear gel was cold and the apparatus hard. The ultrasound technician angled the rectangular screen away from me, while maintaining the most noncommittal facial expression possible. He slid and circled and dipped and gouged with the prod until he was satisfied. He repeated the movements on my left breast, offered me a handful of tissues to wipe off the sticky gel, and excused himself with 'I'll be right back.' I tried to interpret what those words meant. Urgency? Or were they routine?

Within minutes, he returned with a woman. Together, they repeated the process. She glanced at me, smiled sweetly and left. I felt a rush to my head. My heart actually hurt. New words were cramming into tight spaces. *Fuck. Please no. I knew it. I thought I'd be older.* Then phrases began forming, as I imagined what they were about to tell me:

'I regret to inform you . . .'

'As you're probably aware . . .'

'Is there someone we can call?'

'Did you drive here yourself?'

I wasn't ready for any of them, yet I knew that they were coming. They had always been waiting to be heard in their own 'good time'.

They booked me in for a biopsy that same afternoon. I felt conflicted. I was conditioned not to disappoint others in the theatre rehearsal room, and was due there in half an hour. This conditioning had started in my first professional show, when the director had yelled at me for being late. I had one word to say in the entire play, as well as a long scene in which an elderly bearded actor shouted his lines over my deceased body. Each performance, I had to run on stage from the wings in the dark, climb into a double bed, close my eyes, quieten my breathing so my chest wouldn't rise and fall, and, without blinking or twitching or moving, endure being spat on for at least four minutes. With the actor spraying his consonants across my face, being dead would have been a relief.

One day, I misread the schedule and arrived late. They were already rehearsing one of fifteen scenes I wasn't in. The director turned to me, pointed and shouted, in front of a roomful of Australia's most esteemed actors: 'YOU FUCKING AMATEUR!'

On another occasion, a director insisted I attend rehearsal when I had just rushed my one-year-old son with pneumonia to hospital in an ambulance. Via the stage manager, she said that regardless of 'the situation', they could not move forward without me. I felt so angered by her lack of compassion, yet equally determined to prove my professionalism, that I asked a girlfriend to sit with Seamus once he had been admitted, while I taxied through heavy rain from the hospital to the rehearsal room. I waited there the entire afternoon and was never called on. I returned to my son's bedside five hours later, soaked from rain and tears.

I decided then to weigh up my options, remembering that there is always a choice to be made. I must remember to choose the option I can live with.

The look on the hospital worker's face said, *Take the appointment.* I accepted the suggested time, ordered a cup of tea and a piece of toast at the kiosk, and flicked through a stack of *Home Beautiful* magazines.

I was led down narrow corridors and given instructions. I was offered a cubicle to undress in. It was like a toilet without the toilet. A change room without the mirror. A broom cupboard without the broom. The bottom of the door ended just below my knees and it amused me momentarily to think I must have looked like a flip book, where you can put a chef's head on a ballerina's body with giraffe legs.

I removed my clothes, turned them right side out and folded them. They reminded me of a missing person's clothes, piled and neatly abandoned on a deserted beach. Clothes that a detective would bag and hand to some nameless faceless subordinate to label and take to the station as evidence. I slipped on the white cotton front-opening hospital gown. Although it was freshly laundered, I could sense within its weave the thousands who had slipped their arms through the slits, and struggled with the twisted ties that offered flimsy modesty. I recalled visiting someone in hospital and averting my eyes as a patient walked the halls with their buttocks exposed. I perched on the edge of the small, cold, hard metal bench of the changing cubicle, feeling like a game-show contestant who has been isolated in a soundproof booth to test whether their answers match their potential partner's, resulting in them either winning the money and the mate, or going home alone.

I tried to project ahead an hour and see myself, relieved and heading back to work, apologetic but happy. But I couldn't make the image stick. My stomach turned.

The core biopsy was more invasive than I'd imagined and made me feel vulnerable. I wanted my mum and reverted to being eight years old again; I'd just woken from having my tonsils out, the raw burning pain in my throat cancelling out the promise of the post-surgery ice-cream. I had looked for a familiar face but saw none. My favourite pale-violet flannelette nightie was sticky with sick, and my hair was scented with antiseptic and loneliness. I was surrounded by two rows of elderly women, not the 'Kids just like you' I'd been assured of. A woman in the bed next to me was doing a crossword puzzle from a folded newspaper, chewing the end of her pencil. Tiny flecks of chipped paint gathered near the corner of her mouth and, although I watched her for some minutes, she failed to notice me. A woman who looked at least a hundred was knitting and listening to a program on her transistor radio, the small tinny box with its straight metal antenna nestling in a little valley in her pillow, the tiny holes of the speaker pressed to her ear.

I felt trapped by the pressure around my legs from the overly tucked-in sheets; I would have done anything to be home again. When my mother finally arrived with my doll Fatima and the thickest ever jumbo dot-to-dot book, I cried with relief and begged her not to leave me. My mother was trying hard not to look distressed. I overheard the ward sister, who wore a white winged hat just like Sister Bertrille in *The Flying Nun*, say to Mum: 'There are simply no beds available in the kids' ward, so she'll just have to brave it and be a big girl and make do with where she is.'

To cheer me up and give me something to look forward to, my sister helped my parents paint my bedroom. When I finally got home, I sat in my bed with crisp clean sheets, wearing a new peach-coloured nightie, sipping bubbly lemonade from a tall glass, surrounded by freshly painted walls and thinking I was the luckiest person on Earth.

The core biopsy was taken with a thickish needle or probe, extracting tissue that would then be tested in a laboratory. It was like a narrow gun that made a loud clicking sound as its spring sucked up tissue from the foreign body in my breast. Although it was mainly fat tissue, and therefore not hugely sensitive, I found having my breast jabbed an emotional experience. Only a year before, I had breastfed Seamus, and having it butchered after it had so recently been a vessel of nourishment and comfort felt like a sort of betrayal.

I hopped off the table, walked down a hallway towards a dead end, felt mildly dizzy, turned, retraced my steps, found the change room, dressed, retrieved my car from Paddington and arrived at rehearsal for the final hour of the day.

The call came at about 5 p.m. on Friday 1 October, 2004 which happened to be the first day of Breast Cancer Awareness Month and just before a long weekend. A scene was being rehearsed, which I wasn't involved in, so I crept to my bag in a far corner of the rehearsal space and checked my new first-ever mobile phone for messages. The phone rang instantly, I answered it to kill the sound. Any external disturbance in a rehearsal space is frowned upon. I looked at the stage manager and mouthed 'Sorry' as I lifted the phone to my ear.

Dr Misaki Ikegame, my new doctor, was quiet and clear. 'I'm afraid it's breast cancer. I think you'd better come in. I'll wait at the surgery till you get here.'

As I hung up, a loud, long, guttural sound filled the room. It resembled an animal in pain. A primal wail disconnected from me. It stopped suddenly. The room fell silent.

The director Ros rushed to my side. My friend Lucy, who was acting in the play with me and had discovered only that morning that she was pregnant with Nina, her third daughter, offered to drive me to the surgery. My friend Deidre, who was also in the show, said she would come to the appointment with me. Rehearsals ended abruptly.

The rain was bucketing down. We jumped puddles, shook ourselves off and entered Misaki's rooms. Gently and calmly, she said she was sorry but it was breast cancer, a high grade, and should be removed immediately. She recommended Dr Andrew Spillane and suggested I call him in the morning. I thanked her and left. But what I wanted to say was: 'You don't understand, I have two small children. I have absolutely no time for this.' I wanted things to rewind, for her to say that she was wrong, it was all a horrid mistake.

I phoned Martin in Canberra. Poor Martin received most news by phone. He had been away when I found out I was pregnant with Finn, when Seamus contracted meningitis and when my father died. Whenever I was stressed or in need of the comfort only Martin could give, his work seemed to take him away. But I have never felt he wasn't with me. Nor have I ever resented him not being there when such things happened. I've felt frustrated and overwhelmed, but never resentful. He has always listened, and done everything he can to understand and offer support. I have undoubtedly cursed him under my breath a few times, but over menial things like wet towels on the bed or a stove being left on, never because he hasn't been there for me. In our vows, I think we had silently agreed never to bring one another down.

I spent the night gathering information from people, websites and articles. I spoke to Bev, a friend who had been through breast cancer, and a breast cancer support group. By morning, I had filled nearly a whole exercise book with names, treatments and side effects. I decided to approach it like researching a script, which helped me feel almost excited about the information I was collecting and the overall story my research was compiling, and enthusiastic about the prospect of meeting some of these new challenges. When I was in this state of mind, I could even imagine a version of me who might enjoy the adventure and look forward to seeing where the story would take me.

At other moments, I remembered my mother's death. She was only five years older than I was now. I felt that my death was inevitable and imminent—it was written in the stars—and that I was always going to get cancer once I married and had kids, because that's what had happened to her. I almost felt relief that it was happening. Some part of me had always been waiting for it.

These feelings were followed by terror that I would be leaving Marty and our beautiful young sons.

I bobbed around on a sea of calm, only to be dragged to a murky bottom and thrust up again through layers of tangled kelp.

I acknowledged to myself that the coming months and years would pass more tolerably if I pretended it was all an adventure: not pretend it wasn't happening to me, but rather that whatever was going to happen had the potential for opportunities. One of the best things about living as an actor is that you have to surrender yourself to the unexpected. Any freelance artist must embrace uncertainty. If you choose this life, you permit yourself to be a limpet tossed in the sea, looking for a rock to attach yourself to. Some rocks are in your path, others you have to fight hard to even get close to, and then there are months of just bobbing around, avoiding snags and trusting the tides. At every moment, an actor is choosing consciously and unconsciously. Choosing a perspective in which to frame a character's thoughts. Deciding what's already fact and what's yet to be known. Listening for truths and lies and what to believe in. When an actor begins a rehearsal process, they don't have the answers; all they have is curiosity, imagination and time. Even a brilliant script with a beginning, middle and end is open to interpretation. Rehearsals are about exploration, excavation and examination, and it's the quality of the questions that make it most rewarding. A good director, like a good doctor, will have a vision and offer you suggestions and hope, and the opportunity to find solutions that will make the story sing.

I had good doctors. I put a great deal of energy into preparing myself for treatment but was unprepared for the gratitude I would feel for the doctors and carers I encountered. The enormous admiration and genuine affection. I discovered from Day 1 that I needed all of them, not only the finest oncologist and surgeon, but also the harried-looking woman on the admissions desk.

Dr Andrew Spillane showed Marty and me into his rooms at the Royal Prince Alfred Hospital. Before he even offered us a seat, he looked at me, shook my hand and said, 'I'm sorry.'

This was not what I'd expected from a surgeon, a profession with a reputation for being clinical and uncaring. Andrew was compassionate and a great listener. Marty sat on one of the two chairs, while I slipped behind a curtained-off section where the examination table was. I removed my top half and he proceeded to examine me, speaking into his dictaphone: 'Heather Mitchell presents today with a Grade 3 infiltrating ductal carcinoma.' Then I'm pretty sure I heard him say, 'She is geriatric with low-slung breasts.' *What the fuck?* I nearly guffawed out loud. It was bad enough to be shivering topless with a cancer inside me, but to be called geriatric at forty-five, and as for the 'low slung'! I gave a short laugh and noted to myself, *Tell Andrew later, should we get beyond formalities, that he might consider reassessing his choice of words.* We discussed options such as mastectomy versus lumpectomy and decided, based on good information, that a lumpectomy followed by chemotherapy and radiation was the best solution.

Anyone who has travelled through a diagnosis then treatment knows it is a rollercoaster, and the rises and falls can make you ill. At any time, you can choose to get off, but you'd be left with a niggling feeling that you hadn't been brave enough to see it through.

Anyone who has travelled through any crisis also knows that everyone else has something to say about it. One friend grabbed my hand, insisting I meet her tear-filled gaze as she told me, 'Oh yes, my sis-in-law died of breast cancer. It was just awful.'

Another person said, 'I didn't think of you as someone who lets stress get the better of them.'

Or: 'I hear the treatments are great now, you don't feel a thing.'

Not to mention: 'I know you don't have breast cancer, it's the medical system trying to control you.'

Or: 'I never liked your hair anyway.'

The best was a prominent director, who said to Marty in a busy theatre foyer: 'Heather's here? My goodness, I thought she was dead.'

And everyone wants to tell you about their health problems, or never wants to talk about health problems so avoids seeing you in case the topic of health might come up.

The first surgery was straightforward. It involved not only removing the lump and a margin around it, but also the lymph nodes underneath my armpit. Called the axillary lymph nodes, they are typically the first place a surgeon will check to see if breast cancer has spread. Fabulous little bean-shaped lymph nodes are found throughout our bodies, fighting infection and carrying fluid. If any cancer cells break away from the primary cancer and travel to the closest group of lymph nodes and beyond into other nodes, the chances of cancer cells travelling into other areas of the body increases. My first surgery resulted in the discovery that I'd need to have all the nodes under my arm removed, as well as the nodes around my breastbone.

I left hospital a day later and went straight to the theatre for a matinee performance. It was wonderful to be working and the cast were sensational.

Performing while another part of your brain is struggling to comprehend life-changing information is a wild ride. One moment, I felt completely present in the life of the show; the next, I was prey being swooped on by an eagle and lifted high into the limitless sky. I witnessed myself as an insignificant speck before being shot back down to earth, landing with a thud on the feverish ground. My mind begged me to focus and stay connected to my task, but the need to escape and make sense of the shock my body was dealing with was sometimes too tantalising.

And so, I 'dried'. In the theatre, when someone 'dries' on stage, the stage manager who calls the show may prompt from the wings. This is the actor's lifeline when all else fails. If the actor is in the grip of terror, they might not hear the prompt. The anxiety of being so completely exposed intensifies until they hear nothing but the sound of failure in their head. I imagine this is the feeling some people articulate when they say they would rather die than be on stage or speak in public.

In every live performance, an actor dares this to happen. It eventuates only rarely, but when it does, the actor's training, imagination or survival mechanisms kick in, and usually save them before the prompt. If the actor cannot continue, does not hear the prompt and has no one to help them, then admitting to the audience that they have dried, and allowing themselves to be completely vulnerable and transparent is often the best idea. I remember a production of *Ring Around the Moon*, in which Hugo Weaving, who was playing twin brothers Hugo and Frederic, had to appear as one brother, then exit stage right, tear off his clothes, re-dress, race down a flight of stairs, run through the vomitorium, up another flight of stairs, breathe in and casually walk on stage left as the other brother. On one particular night, early in the season, Hugo had just entered as the brother Hugo and was about to launch into a lengthy speech when he paused, looked at the audience and said, 'Ladies and gentlemen, I'm terribly sorry but I've completely forgotten my lines.'

The audience broke into spontaneous applause. They loved him for his honesty and self-deprecating humour. Later, he told me that he had been standing on stage about to begin the speech. He was having such a good time, and the thought popped into his head, *Oh, I'm doing so well tonight, I'm really flying.* With that, he completely dried. He had been floating above himself, in 'the flow', feeling that absolute rightness when everyone is in harmony, nothing can go wrong and you feel invincible. Your consciousness gets seduced by your own magnificence.

There are hundreds of similar stories. During a production of Ray Lawler's *The Doll Trilogy*, after an inspiring yet gruelling nine hours of performing all three plays back to back, Harold Hopkins, who had been sensational playing Barney, dried. He sat on the couch centre stage at 10.30 p.m., having begun the first show at 10 a.m., and could not think what to say. He sat with his elbows on his knees and his head bowed, and called for a line. I was watching with Rodney, the director, in the glassed-in bio box at the back of the theatre. Our hands gripped each other's. An actress who was on stage with Harold exited, I assumed to ask for his line. She returned with a glass of water and no line. Harold called for a line, slightly louder this time. The stage manager could be heard throwing him the line with increasing volume. But Harold's fear must have prevented him from hearing it. This went on for minutes. 'Line . . . line please . . . line . . . LINE!' By the time he heard the line, the audience were nearly on their feet shouting it at him. It was one of the most agonising experiences I've witnessed in the theatre.

Many years ago, I was doing a play at Wharf 1 at the STC and, at the fifteen-minute call, an actress had still not appeared backstage for a Saturday matinee. The stage manager called her home and eventually roused her. In what must have been a shocking rush of adrenaline, she threw herself in a taxi and arrived shaken and confused after the performance had already begun. She'd clearly had a big night the previous evening, had overslept and was still somewhat under the influence. She was helped dress and was gently pushed on stage. The scene involved the two of us. My character was to sit centre stage on a garden chair being encircled by her character, who was feeding me information about neighbourhood gossip that included vital plot points. On this occasion, we swapped. I walked over to her, met her bewildered gaze that was screaming for help and led her to the chair. She plonked down onto it, wiping her sweating upper lip and brow as I began circling her. I could see she was still agonisingly adjusting to her new surroundings. She had no idea what to say, let alone who I was. So I began to grill her, eking the vital information out of her. I began:

'I know you're thinking . . .'

'I can see what you want to say . . .'

'I know you want to talk about so and so . . .'

'You think that so and so . . .'

Until I had covered as much of the essential information as I could recall and, in a dark scene change, dragged her stumbling offstage.

On the opening night of *The History Boys* at the Opera House, I dried. I was sitting between John Wood and James Mackay facing the audience as a panel of teachers, addressing the boys after they had sung their valedictory song. My character, Mrs Lintott, was to finally let loose and say what she really thought. The song finished and there was silence. After thinking someone else had forgotten to speak, I realised in a blinding flash of rising panic that it was me. I calmly crossed my legs, looked briefly to John, who I knew would be no help because he had enough lines to deal with, then turned to James and said, 'Irwin, do you have any idea what it is I'm wanting to say?'

'Yes,' he said. 'Something about . . .' And he fed me my line.

'Wonderful, thank you. Now boys, as you know . . .'

There is nothing like panic to focus all your senses and remind you that you're truly alive.

The beauty of a dry is that it's one of the most understood and recognised human flaws, and as long as you can ask for help, you will be fine.

But on this particular matinee, the day after my surgery, it felt all too hard. I breathed in and out, placed my hands on both slightly bent knees like I was experiencing a dizzy spell, whispered, 'Please save me' to myself, stood up, smiled to the audience and continued.

My second surgery only weeks later was performed the day before my forty-sixth birthday. This surgery involved completely removing the lymph nodes and attaching a bag that collects the fluid from the nodal area. Friends brought me fancy little knitted bags to cover the plastic goo.

My friends Joanne, Lulu, Wayne and Stephanie visited me in hospital and brought me flowers, hand creams and cakes, and we were hushed for laughing too much. Vicki, who I had known since school, her husband Marc and their beautiful son William popped in with flowers. Vicki has always known when to appear and her timing is always perfect. They came not only with gifts but, more importantly, with distractions. They looked at me, not with pity but with a sensitive understanding that the key to being happy was getting away from too much 'self-focus'. I had received beautiful messages, which they read out to me and I felt truly blessed to have such friends.

Marty had called in the morning to say he was busy with the kids. I assumed he would come when a babysitter arrived.

My friends Stephanie and Peter arrived at about five o'clock with a selection of beautiful moisturisers. Later, during the months of chemotherapy, I became friends with a woman behind the David Jones beauty counter, who slipped me samples of expensive elixirs and oils. (She'd had a sister with breast cancer and wanted to spoil me.) Going into shops with a bald head, especially whitegoods stores, with two small children often afforded me what I termed the 'cancer discount'. Everyone still had cordless phones and ours had just died. We couldn't afford to replace it. I stood in Harvey Norman, thin and bald, with a child on each hand, looking longingly at the phones and tutting at their price tags. The friendly assistant asked what I was looking for.

'Well, I need a cordless phone and a new answering machine, so I don't miss any important medical messages. Do you have any cheaper models, please?'

Finn and Seamus looked up at him with forlorn eyes, as if some terrible fate would befall them without a phone from this very shop.

'Mmmm, well, these are our top-of-the-range and most popular models, but I tell you what. I'll sell you an inexpensive answering machine and you can have this demonstration phone, which has never been used. And it's top of the range.'

We all smiled.

Steph and Pete had given me an incredible gift of ten appointments with Dr Zhou, a Qi Gong master before my second surgery. Each session would involve a transference of energy from him to me. I would experience a sensation of light energy ripple through my body. He asked me the date and time of my surgery; I told him and thought no more of it. As I lay on the gurney prior to being wheeled into surgery, I glanced at the wall clock, which read 11 a.m. A bolt of light shot through me. I immediately felt serene and certain everything would be fine. I arrogantly thought I'd somehow made this happen. When I next visited him a few weeks later, Dr Zhou asked me whether I had received his qi.

'You?' I said. 'You sent that? From here?'

'Yes,' he said. 'Where else? I'm happy you got it.'

Marty arrived at about 5.30 p.m. He looked awful, suddenly thinner and grey. He held a small paper bag in one hand and, as he leaned to kiss me, stroked my forehead with the other. Steph and Pete left, saying, 'We'll see you soon,' more to Marty than to me. I asked what was in his hand. He passed me the creased brown bag. Inside was a small hardcover book called *Tamburlaine Must Die*, by Louise Welch. I had this painful image of Marty wandering the streets of Kings Cross, looking for something to buy me. Obviously, nothing would have seemed enough to him, so he would have strayed into Macleay Bookshop. Spying a spine with the one word in its title he most feared—*Die*—he purchased it. Poor Marty. He was suffering so much more than I was. He kissed me, said he was having dinner at Steph's and would see me tomorrow.

My birthday came and went. Thank God for morphine.

Meeting Michael Friedlander, who is affectionately known as Prof, was one of the unexpected gifts of having breast cancer. He sped up the agonising pace of medical time with his wealth of experience. He could tell me the truth, yet not make it shocking. And for someone who never turned away a patient, he made me feel like I was the only one.

My introduction to him was through a friend who had recently completed treatment, and she made me promise I would call him.

The day before my second round of chemo, Marty and I went into Gowings in the city. Gowings was in a large multi-storied building with menswear and had a small traditional barber shop down one end. I'd always had a thing for the big red leather barbershop chairs with metal footstools and wanted to enjoy having a complete shave. Days earlier, my friend Shahen had cut my hair short for me and my dear friend Robyn (Ra Ra), who can turn even the most menial task into an artwork, was collecting handfuls of hair and reminding me of the special nature of the moment.

We walked through Gowings' glass doors onto George Street and drove home excited, Marty occasionally looking at me and smiling, admiring my perfectly smooth skull.

Chemo was conducted in a compact room with six comfortable reclining armchairs. The drips were on a rotation, constantly being checked; once they were all flushed through, I was reminded to take my anti-nausea drugs and could leave. The first round had been pretty uneventful and, although I felt squeamish, I had no really bad days. Michael Friedlander had warned me that the treatment is accumulative; therefore, the later sessions could be the hardest. I heard the words but thought I'd be the one person to sail through with my positive mindset overcoming any negative or unexpected reactions. I always found that the first few hours after chemo made me manic due to the steroids. I would clean the house and bake. The nausea rarely kicked in until the following day and, although the drugs took the edge off, it was still much worse than morning sickness.

On 22 December, I helped the boys pack their little wheelie bags for a Christmas in Melbourne with Marty's family. We'd spend Christmas Day in Mt Evelyn at Marty's mum's magical house. Kath, Marty's mother, lived with her husband Stan (not Marty's father Brian, who passed away at age fifty-seven) in the family home that Kath and Brian had built in 1968. It was a low brick dwelling with sliding glass doors along the whole north-facing side, giving immediate access to the glorious sloping grassland and bush block. We loved going there. Marty's six siblings and their partners and kids would all converge on Christmas Day with yummy dishes and presents; the whole place was infused with the smell of gumtrees and wood fires and birdsong.

The plan was that I'd have my fourth round of chemo on the 22nd, then we'd all fly out the following morning. Marty drove me to the hospital and planned to stay with me for the treatment. I had the routine blood test, which gives an indication of the patient's white cell count. A normal white blood cell count is between 4,000 and 10,000. Someone who is receiving chemo or radiation may experience a count of about 3,000 to 4,000. Mine was low, and Michael said definitively that I would not be having chemo that day. We went home and I insisted that Marty and the boys still fly to Melbourne. I'd sleep well and redo the blood test the next day, followed by the chemo, then I would fly down on Christmas Eve. Reluctantly, he and the boys left, while I returned to the hospital. The new test produced a very minor improvement and Michael advised me to wait another day. I begged him, 'Please, please, give it to me now. I'll be really good and fly down and rest. I promise.'

He acknowledged that it was my decision, but advised against it. But unable to bear the thought of missing Christmas with the boys, I went ahead.

Each time, how painful the process was shocked me: not the actual chemo but getting the bloody needle in. The nurse could only use my left arm, due to the absence of nodes under my right arm, and my veins were petrified. They loathed the needle. Either it sank deep into the sinews of my forearm, or my veins bulged and knotted, screaming 'Closed for entry!'

Each attempt began with a nurse apologising: 'This is going to hurt.' It was sickeningly painful. On this particular day, it took over an hour and required four different people attempting it before the magic flowed.

Some people are scared of chemo and I understand their fear. But chemo to me was magic. Whenever the metallic multicoloured liquids flowed slowly into me, it was a chance to renew myself. I imagined the microscopic cell in which the cancer had originated before it multiplied and spread, being drowned and flushed away. At night in bed, I would visualise it being blasted, rubbed out or smothered. If I went to the origin and destroyed it, all the other cells followed. It was the queen bee cell; the other cells would not survive without it. And yes, I know a lot of good cells were also pummelled and thumped, but I felt confident that they would return healthier and more robust than ever. I also imagined there were other stealthy things going on inside me, which I was completely unaware of, and they too would be cleansed. I felt certain that science would do its job brilliantly, then it would be up to me to complement it with healthy and positive lifestyle choices.

I treated my cancer as a character. I learned what cancer liked and didn't like, where it lived and where it hid. When to talk to it and when to ignore it. Hardest of all, I learned to let go of any expectation about what it might do next.

I left the hospital and jumped in a cab to the domestic airport. I was wearing jeans, a long-sleeved T-shirt, scarf, mask, hat, sunglasses and gloves. Although I felt woozy, I was sure I would be protected. A woman of about sixty, sitting across the aisle, leaned towards me, smiling.

'Excuse me, I know you, don't I?'

I blushed, confounded that anyone, even a family member, would recognise me in this gear, which covered everything but my neck and fingers.

'Sorry,' I said, 'I'm not sure . . .'

'Yes,' she said, 'it's you. You took the car space I was trying to get yesterday. I was really pissed off, but then I saw you get out of your car and you looked, well, you looked pretty sick. I thought, well Margaret, there's a lesson for you right there. Don't go getting all het-up over things when you don't know the full story 'cause there's always someone else worse off. That's how I see it, anyway. Nice to see you're going on a trip. Somewhere nice, I hope, for Christmas. Family? In Melbourne? Anyway, you just have a nice time. You deserved that car space, so don't you worry about it.'

I apologised and said I hadn't even seen her car, so I guessed that was my lesson, to be more aware. That was nice of me, she said, and reached over and squeezed my forearm. When we landed, she insisted on getting my carry bag from the overhead compartment and we walked separately through the concourse to the baggage carousel like we were best friends pretending not to know each other.

Edie, my dear friend now living in Melbourne, met me at the airport. She drove me to a hotel where I would spend the night before joining the boys. The nausea hit me suddenly and I searched for the pills I'd been warned to take prior to nausea kicking in. The nausea from chemo was similar to motion sickness but much worse. It made morning sickness during the early months of pregnancy a mere tummy upset by comparison, and alleviating it wasn't easy. I spent the night reassuring myself it would pass, and by morning, it had settled.

Marty and the boys collected me, and we drove to Malvern to stay the night with Richard and Liz, Marty's closest friends from school, who generously shared their home with us whenever we stayed in Melbourne.

Christmas Day at Mt Evelyn was joyous. Marty's sister Carmen, who was living in the Netherlands, had arrived, making it even more special. Kath was the loving matriarch, soft and gentle with a razor-sharp intelligence. She never imposed her views about the state of the world or the family. No family member, whatever their difficulties, was of lesser importance. Without ever offering advice, she managed to guide and influence us all with her succinct and delicate observations. She was also a businesswoman; as with so many women of her generation, I wondered what parallel life she might have lived had she not had seven children.

We returned to Malvern on 26 December. Although I was feeling very weak, I was determined to take the boys to the National Gallery of Victoria and then the cinema. We caught the tram to the gallery. My friend Carolyn, who had been a godsend to me when Finn was a baby and I was out of my depth, met us in front of the wall of water that cascades constantly on the façade. I had underestimated how busy the gallery would be on a holiday; the noise of excitable and complaining children, including my own, made me feel unstable. The sometimes too-close proximity of a passing person made me hold my breath; the sweeping strokes of a Turner painting caused bile to rise into my throat. My hands and the back of my neck became clammy; throwing up was my only option. I managed to hold it down while Caro drove me home, leaving Marty and the boys to wander the city and find fun things to do.

For the following two days, I heaved continually day and night. On the evening of the second day, Marty called Caro, who stayed with the boys while her husband Simon drove us to Epworth Hospital. Richard had rung ahead and contacted a brilliant doctor so we were admitted instantly. Tests were run as my shaking expulsions increased.

The doctors at Epworth could find no reason for my violent symptoms, except for chemo. They suggested I return urgently to Sydney to Michael Friedlander's care.

I was lying on my bed, preparing to go to hospital, when our neighbour Antoinette, who had generously taken the boys to her home to play, knocked at the door. Sheepishly, she told Marty that Finn and Seamus both had nits. She had given them a treatment, but maybe they should come home now.

I was horrified. *Nits! My kids? What?* I was more appalled that my boys had nits than that I may soon disappear altogether. If nits moved in, they wouldn't leave for years.

I was losing weight fast now. Seeing myself naked in the mirror horrified me. I had lost all hair from my body, including my eyebrows and eyelashes, and every bone jutted through my flesh. Nothing bore any resemblance to me whatsoever. I was admitted to hospital and tests were performed, but no results could confirm the reason for the violence of my symptoms. Marty looked so concerned, the boys were visibly scared, and a few friends who visited couldn't hide their thoughts that they were looking at me for the last time. I was down to 41 kilograms.

Prof came into the room. He told Marty and me we had to make a decision. His instinct was telling him I had picked up giardia in Melbourne, but none of the tests had confirmed this. He was reluctant to treat me for it, because the drugs for giardia are severe. He asked my permission to make the call and do it, and I agreed. Within hours of swallowing the huge tablets, I stopped vomiting and the symptoms ceased. Once again, Prof saved my life.

This meant that the chemo had to be delayed until I had gained weight and my immune system had recovered. Treatment was suspended for a few months. The final four rounds of chemo were tough and I can't believe now, when I knew it was saving my life, that I honestly didn't think I could go through with the final one.

After finishing chemotherapy, I was halfway through radiotherapy when I began to question the treatment I was receiving. My skin was burning in an area that made no sense to me. I was being treated for a Grade 3 carcinoma and complete removal of the axillary nodes under my right arm and internal mammary chain. Why was I burning in an area unrelated to each of these? I asked the nurse again and again. Each time, she said that the doctor would let me know if there was a problem. On the morning of my final radiation, the day when the bell would be rung for me (a bell is rung every time someone finishes their course of radiation) after I'd had 60 sessions, I was now suffering from third-degree burns. The nurse asked if I would like to come in now rather than my scheduled time, because my doctor was in the ward. I was shown into a small room with my radiologist, Dr Blah (not his real name), who I hadn't seen since he planned the treatment three months earlier. He looked at me over his glasses and asked who I was.

'I'm Heather Mitchell, your patient,' I said, as he checked a photo on the corner of what looked like my file. He opened it, turned the pages, each of them blank, and closed it again.

'Well, you've finished. Well done.'

'Have I?' I said.

'Well, who's been your doctor while I was on leave?'

'On leave? No one.'

'I left Dr Fetch [not his real name] in charge of my patients.'

'Well, I don't know him,' I said.

'Well, you've had a successful completed treatment.'

With that, he excused himself and left the room. I looked at the nurse, who looked back at me. We both held our breath.

'You're my witness, right?' I said. 'You saw that file.'

'Yes,' she said.

I ran out of the place and caught a cab to the Sydney Dance Company to see my friend Leigh, who was the general manager and a brilliant letter writer.

'Okay, we're writing to the hospital to get answers,' she said, perked up by a challenge and the desire to help.

The following day, I received a request from the hospital's head sister to attend a meeting. Marty and I sat opposite her in her office. Two other people were present, a woman taking notes and someone we assumed was a lawyer.

'I received your letter. What are your intentions?' a commanding woman in white asked.

'My only intention is to live,' I said.

'So, what do you want?' she prodded, gently but directly.

'I want to know whether I have had the correct treatment and, if not, what I am to do about it.'

'Then I suggest you make an appointment with your specialist, Dr Blah.'

She looked at me dubiously. Marty and I chose to leave rather than become embroiled in discussions about suing, which we had no interest in doing. The swiftness of her response to Leigh's letter made me concerned about how often such letters landed on her desk.

That afternoon, I was called by a man identifying himself as Dr Bangle (not his real name) from another hospital. He said he had been made aware of my situation and wanted to help. He invited me to meet him at his office in a tower on the hospital grounds at 9 p.m. that evening. I thanked him and, without even considering what his motives might be, called Robyn, who picked me up and drove us through bucketing rain. We arrived in a lonely car park and found our way via a lift into a series of dimly lit corridors. As it dawned on us how desperate we must look, how gullible, how eager to trust a complete stranger because he called himself a doctor, we held hands. It seemed feasible that we were going to be murdered and our bodies disposed of to cover my radiologist's potential error.

Doctor Bangle opened his door. He was far too pleased to see us. He was jovial, even. He told us proudly that he had a spot on TV as a medical adviser on some morning or afternoon show. I was so unimpressed, I think I stared at him with my mouth open. He finally asked what was concerning me, listened and took notes. Then he put down his pen and gave a long rant about the other doctor, how fortunate I was to have him, and how impeccable his reputation was. The chair beneath me hardened. It was a set-up. I realised how silent the building was—I could hear the faint hum of a vacuum cleaner. It was just us and the cleaners. Of course, this is how desperate people are manipulated. People who feel they are sinking, and are frantically reaching for the upturned boat, rope or plank of wood . . . they will even settle for a lump of drifting cork.

He began typing without explaining what he was writing. We sat and waited. He produced a letter, which he wanted me to sign. The letter articulated that I had presented at his rooms at 9 p.m. in a state of distress, and he had managed to assuage my fears and that Dr Blah was an eminent specialist and that I would not be taking the matter any further. It stated that I had been alerted to the dangers of accepting further radiation, that my treatment was complete and that I had no desire to take any legal action. I read the letter and fought with my conflicting feelings. I felt betrayed, abused, foolish and scared. I folded the letter.

Robyn and I stood, opened the door and walked swiftly to the car.

I demanded an appointment with Dr Blah to ask him what should be done. Supported by my friend Peter, a film and TV director who had once practised law, we sat in his rooms. He leaned back in his chair, put his feet on the table, and reiterated that I'd finished all my treatment. He continued, 'How foolish would I look if I admitted you'd had insufficient treatment?'

'Are you saying I've had the wrong treatment?' I asked.

'I'm saying you shouldn't have any more, and if I admitted you'd had the wrong treatment, I would look foolish, wouldn't I?'

As far as he was concerned, that was that.

Friends spoke to friends and journalists began to call.

'Would you like to do a story on this?'

'We really think this would be an important story to tell.'

I had absolutely no interest. No interest to tell, no interest to sue. I wanted to hear 'Sorry' and be guided as to what to do next. I spent the next three months collecting all my reports, and creating timelines and communications between myself and my specialists. I had chosen to have treatments in three separate hospitals. I had initially chosen my surgeon and oncologist because they were highly recommended and both were exemplary people and experts in their fields. However, they operated from different hospitals. I then chose Dr Blah because he was at a hospital that was easier for me to get to; radiation is a daily treatment, so I thought it unwise to travel too far. I was already having to regularly attend five different hospitals for different treatments and surgeries. It had not occurred to me how unwise this was. I didn't understand each hospital's brilliant systems of multidisciplinary meetings, in which all patients are discussed individually by a collective of specialists. That information is all kept in-house. I, on the other hand, had scans, pathology results and progression notes all over the place. Vital pieces of information were not necessarily being communicated as effectively as they could have been in the one place.

It took three months to collect all my medical reports and canvass expert opinions. I sent my files to six major hospitals. Caro and Simon, my constant support, introduced me to a specialist at the Memorial Sloan Kettering Hospital in New York, gave me the address of someone at the Marsden in London, and told me about another four Australian hospitals specialising in cancer. All responded quickly. Three gave sound and sobering reasons to abstain from further radiation: 'Your chest wall could cave in, your skin may not heal, you may get radiation poisoning, it may affect your heart and lungs.' The other three were undecided and, although not recommending it, acknowledged that the target area was probably untreated. One of these people said to me, 'I really can't advise you on this matter, but if you were my wife, I'd want you to do everything you could.'

That did it. It came down to what I was prepared to live with and I knew I needed to do it.

I did the rounds of every recommended radiation oncologist at every major Sydney hospital. I had many refusals before I met Denise Lonergan. Denise considered the situation very seriously then said, 'I'll do it.' She spent weeks meticulously plotting and planning so as to avoid organs and any overlapping of the previous rays. She was dedicated and kind. She was a mother and wife and a brilliant radiation oncologist, and I was aware that I was in good hands.

Each day, I arrived and sat in a hallway that led to the Radiation Room. Each day, two orange chairs were waiting and each time when I arrived, a man in green overalls was sitting there staring ahead. He was handcuffed and had ankle bracelets, and was accompanied by two police officers. The officers leaned against the windows chatting, as he and I sat and waited. A small pot plant on a low table separated us, but he was close enough for me to catch his scent of Pears soap and laundered clothes, and to hear his breathing. I always had a book with me to read as we waited, but I never absorbed a single word. This stranger and I spent every day sitting side by side at the same time for three months, never permitted to make eye contact or speak.

Neither Marty nor I had worked for over a year. As freelancers, there is no sick leave, no long service leave, no buffer when there is no work. Marty had tried everything, but there seemed to be a cloud of 'failure' around us. Initially, there was the feeling that people were showing respect, that people were genuinely concerned, and either offered help or kept away. This gradually developed into a generalised impression that we were struggling, that 'Heather was not doing well', that 'Marty was having to look after the kids', and before you knew it, work dried up. We began to think people were saying we were no longer capable of work or would be unreliable, and we tried hard to reassure ourselves that this was not the case. The stress of having no work, and therefore no income, plus many unexpected expenses made the situation so much worse. Marty kept from me that he was repeatedly extending our line of credit with the bank.

It became clear that selling the house was the best option and, quite frankly, we felt grateful to have a house to sell. We polished it up and put it on the market. The day of the auction, we sat in the living room while the auctioneer tried to enthuse a small crowd. We had asked a friend to begin the bidding, and for some bizarre reason he began $300,000 lower than we had asked him. We were struggling to get up to our initial first bid, let alone near our reserve. We feared not selling, or selling for a price that would leave us with nothing. Through the reflection of the fridge, I was watching a bidder offering small advances in price, and I decided he wanted it. I instructed the agent to tell the auctioneer to tell the man what we wanted. He refused, saying he would never do that. I insisted. His junior went over to the man, whispered to him and, sure enough, he bid against himself, jumping $400,000, and the house sold. Without that offer, we would have been left with nothing once all our debts were repaid.

While I was undergoing my second round of radiation, I heard that Dr Blah had died. Apparently, he had been on leave during my treatment due to an illness. I received the news with disbelief. The realisation that he may have been suffering with his own illness while supposedly treating me put a new spin on things. He was human after all; he had made mistakes. I felt for his family and his loss of life, but it didn't remove the taste of his arrogance and lack of concern for me.

The treatment was nearing its end. I felt like crap, not ill as much as empty. I was putting so much energy into not succumbing to the feelings of victimhood, which invade, especially late at night or standing naked, hairless, before a mirror. I so wanted to be working, to feel involved in something other than my health. Months earlier, I had begged my agent to send me for work. I don't think anyone had the courage to tell me how frightening I looked. And so, I was booked in with a casting agent to put down a screen test for a role in a TV series, playing a woman with breast cancer. *At last*, I thought, *a role I am more than qualified to play.* A role that I was sure was mine. A role that no one could argue I wasn't well prepped to play. The research was all done and there was no need for make-up and hair. A huge saving for the production. This was it. My comeback. I even considered that I had breast cancer so as to be ready for this role. Suddenly, something made sense. Art was imitating life.

I woke early, took my anti-nausea tablets and moisturised my pale skin. Nothing more to be done. I wondered whether I looked sick enough, and then I thought about older actors who 'act old' in shows, not realising they actually *are* old. I was forty-five, weighed 41 kilos and was bald. Yes, I looked perfect. No shading needed. No hollowing of the cheeks or under the eyes necessary. Just me with cancer. How could I not be believed?

I'm not sure whether the casting agent thought I was the most committed actor he'd seen, or if he thought I was mad, but we filmed the scenes a few times and then I left. I waited as all actors do to hear the news: 'Yes' or 'No'.

'I'm sorry, Heather, they've gone another way,' my agent reported.

Another way? What other way was there?

Almost a year later, I was shopping in Woolworths. While waiting my turn in the cashier's queue, I picked up a women's magazine. The cover thumped me in the guts. 'Brave Actress Shaves Head to Play Cancer Patient.'

Brave actress. What was brave about shaving your head for a role, which you're paid money for and which has no illness attached? No vomiting, no cannulas, no slicing of breast tissue, no real tears.

By the time I reached my car, I realised I wasn't really upset that I hadn't got the role, and quite frankly I would have been an insurer's nightmare, but I was more impacted by the fact that I was standing on the reverse side of the argument that an actor is able to play roles beyond their personal experience. I had always believed that the imagination is an actor's greatest friend; once truly imagined, the good actor can translate and transmute an experience so they and their audience believe it's 'real'. It was a valuable lesson to be feeling the hurt associated with watching someone *assume* to understand something that I, now effectively an audience member, actually knew about. I sat in the car folding and refolding my parking ticket into smaller and smaller squares, questioning my right as an actor to portray people's experiences that were beyond my own. I had always been sure that humans are capable of every emotional state and that these states were universal and that actors train themselves to delve into 'feelings' beyond their own narrative to express these truths. What I believed in was empathically identifying and understanding a character's motivation for action and locating the associated feelings, and as sincerely as possible finding ways to express them.

I had never been a fan of the branch of 'method' acting, which encourages the actor to remain fully immersed in the character's life, maintaining the link between the character's emotions and the actor's own unique personal memory of an emotional state. I thought this extreme approach could be detrimental not only to the actor themselves but to the other actors they work with, and certainly the people they live with. It was seductive to go down this route, especially because film cameras can pick up every detail of a sweat gland on a nostril. In a world where being *authentic* is both the challenge and the goal, it is understandable for the actor to employ the 'method' as a protection, and live it and be it. No craft is required, no technique, only pure emotional connection, which no one can argue with.

This train of thought led me to a question about the *right* of storytelling, not the *ability* for storytelling. Actors were capable of expressing truths but did they have the right? Can the actor's 'talent' combined with their craft actually cause hurt to others by usurping or stealing their experience? This sense of stealing is what causes pain and anger; ownership is being fought for. It was too vast a subject to simply reflect on in the now-stuffy car, but a door had been opened for me and it needed real examination.

Sitting in my bedroom at the age of thirteen, holding a pillow and crying over the death of my pretend baby had felt wildly liberating. I had felt deeply connected to grief and was able to truthfully express it. Even at my young age, living in a happy white loving family, I believed I could convey grief convincingly. If I was before an audience right now, then they would have believed it. The argument might be: 'You're thirteen and have not experienced the death of a child, so how can you possibly know the overwhelming, earth-shattering pain?' What I would answer now, but couldn't then, was that I was transferring my fear of my mother dying into the baby. I was using my terror of loss to practise for the moment that would inevitably come. Although I had not experienced grief yet, I was wholeheartedly experiencing it in preparation.

I started the ignition and drove towards the parking station exit. I had been there for over an hour and the boom gate didn't rise, so I pressed the intercom. After about five minutes, the wait accompanied by a dreadful beeping tone, a tinny voice asked what my problem was.

'I've lost my ticket, I'm sorry,' I said, looking at my ticket, which was a torn and mangled piece of thin paper in my lap. 'I came only just over an hour ago.'

'Do you have any other proof of that?'

Because I had no proof, other than the scraps of the ticket that I'd said I'd lost, they said I needed to pay $36.

I felt mistrusted, misunderstood and unfairly treated. I wanted to prove my sincerity to this 'voice box'. If they could actually see me, they would believe me. Then I felt angered by these stupid human-free contraptions, which didn't allow the victim a fair trial.

The car behind was tooting, not aggressively, but persistently enough to tell me that my actions were causing annoyance. So I dished out my credit card, paid the money, grabbed the receipt and was released into the fresh air.

As I drove home, I reminded myself that it was immensely important to me that no one gets hurt. That people are respected and that, if we are told that telling someone else's story creates pain and anger, we listen to why. It was important to me that stories were told because they matter, not only to the teller but to the listener. Well-told stories can create change in the individual, in the family, in society, in the fabric of how we choose to live. Young people, especially young people who have not yet been able to look back too far, are the people whose stories I had become most interested in, now that two young boys had become the centre of my life.

I made myself a cup of tea and sat in the kitchen, thinking about the depth of human suffering. I thought about the isolation that so many people suffer in wanting to protect their reputations and privacy. I thought about all the people I'd met though my two-year treatment period who were intelligent, patient, stoic and compassionate. Most had survived their treatments and were desperate to be seen whole again. For some, post-treatment side-effects were long lasting, and others seemed to bounce back. Either way, they no longer wanted to inspire fear; they wanted to get back into life and experience fulfilment and pleasure. Some needed to hold on to their treatment almost as a badge of honour, while others never wanted to be reminded of it. Someday, I hoped I would be given the opportunity to use my memories, imagination and knowledge wholly and authentically to represent the experience I had been through. And it would be informed and enriched by other people's stories because, having met them, they became part of mine.

I cannot thank Michael Friedlander, Andrew Spillane and Denise Lonergan enough. Denise, who devoted herself to helping me, tragically passed away only months after my treatment finished. My feelings of gratitude for her are with me every day.

Part 3

Mother

11

Even the Kindest People

While leaning into the cramped space between the baby in the capsule and the backseat door frame, I dropped the car keys.

'Oh, shit.'

I closed my eyes and exhaled, dropping my head and reversing my bent torso into another parked car, which barely gave me room to squat and twist to pick up the keys. I had quickly redirected my thoughts from *Please stop crying,* to *Get the keys now or you'll regret it. It'll be too hard when you're holding the baby.*

He was still 'the baby' during moments like this. Moments when I felt I didn't really know him, wasn't yet sure of his needs and wants. This morning, he had woken up crying, and no amount of milk or cuddles or rocking would calm him. And now, just as we arrived at the crowded rooftop carpark, the high-pitched crying was piercing not only my ears but also my heart. I wanted to go home, to get him out of here, to be somewhere quiet and calm, but the lists in my head chastened and hastened me. I reminded myself of the long flight tomorrow. I needed to buy tiny individually wrapped toys for his brother Finn, who was now two years old, so he could open them on the plane at well-spaced intervals to keep him happy and distracted.

Another deep breath. I shoved the keys in my bag, strapped on the Baby Bjorn (the pouch in which I carried him against my chest), untangled my hair, untwisted my T-shirt and gently placed his warm red face next to mine, kissing him before securing him. I adjusted my bag on my shoulder, slammed the door, locked the driver's door, and dropped the keys in the bag. Let's get this done.

I walked through the aisles of Kmart in a daze, my eyes scanning for small things. But every small thing looked too small, too dangerous, too easily swallowed or lost between seats. My mind created vivid images of Finn choking on a plastic cow and miniature marbles disappearing up his nostrils and into his ears. I saw angry passengers objecting to being asked to reach under their seats to fetch pieces of Lego that had repeatedly fallen from Finn's tray table. I regretted coming and reprimanded myself for thinking this was important when there was so much to be done.

'Give him Phenergan, it's brilliant,' a friend of a friend had said. 'Mandy slept for hours when we went to Fiji. And it's safe. On the way back, she slept right through and woke up and said, "When are we leaving?" We laughed so hard but she was cranky because she'd missed out on the plane's complimentary colouring book. Kids!'

I can't give him Phenergan, I thought, as outwardly I thanked her for the tip and struggled to hide my annoyance at having to listen to her success story. Only months before, Finn had visited the hospital outpatients section to have a CT scan of his heart. It was a quick procedure. They wanted to give him a sedative because they said he needed to be very still. I requested to read to him instead, because he was such a placid child. Even throughout his gestation period, he had adopted a position like Rodin's *The Thinker* and barely moved from it the whole time. I was confident he wouldn't fidget but they insisted, and gave him Phenergan. Within minutes, he went ballistic. He tore around the ward, hitting his head, pushing small chairs over and scattering coloured crayons and pencils. It took three nurses to hold him down as they injected him with something to counteract it and admitted him for observation. The following day, they did the scan while I read to him.

Standing here now between the My Favourite Pony and a boxed tea set, I reassured myself that activities were the way to go, and dumped into my trolley Little Golden Books and toys he could shake but not swallow.

Seamus was born by caesarean section on 15 February, a week before his due date, which also happened to be Finn's birthday. I was forty-one when we had Finn and forty-three when we had Seamus. My male obstetrician strongly recommended that, being a geriatric, I should have my tubes tied to avoid the risk of future pregnancies. I was appalled by his attitude and smarmy tone, but agreed to have it done, not due to my age but because we were over the moon to have beautiful babies and felt deeply content.

Marty had been present for both the boys' births but he had had to leave for Canada in a matter of days after Seamus's. He had landed a job to shoot a film in Vancouver and I encouraged him to accept it, saying the three of us would join him there in four weeks. 'It'll be a wonderful adventure,' I'd said.

I hired a lovely English au pair to help until we left, found a wonderful couple to sublet our rental apartment, bought a double-decker pram, and asked Ra Ra if she would like to come with us to help me on the flight. Then she could go off on her own travelling. She agreed and everything felt so right.

I grabbed wrapping paper and sticky tape at the cashier's counter and felt lighter, remembering how much as a kid I loved wrapping the gifts for the lucky dip at school fêtes, decorating the big cardboard boxes, and labelling them for 50c and $1 prizes. This was going to be fun. I would get us home, feed and settle Seamus, play with Finn, have a cup of tea, check all the suitcases were by the front door, leave the boys with the nanny while I parked the car somewhere long term, fed us, slept and set off early for the airport. It was all under control.

I woke at 3 a.m. with my engorged breasts leaking milk. Why hadn't Seamus woken for his feed? I fumbled for the night light and rolled over to his bassinet, which extended beyond the edge of my bed. As I reached out for him, panic roared through me. A heater had somehow fallen into his bassinet. My thoughts became stuck on a loop: *Why is a heater in his bassinet? What the fuck's going on? A heater in his bassinet?*

My mind was trying to latch onto a clear thought as my hands searched for him. Finding the edge of the muslin wrap, I thought I was unswaddling him. Although I could feel the weight of him in my hands, I could not see him. The white muslin revealed a nothingness. It was like a nightmare magic trick. The hanky had made the rabbit in the top hat disappear and that rabbit was my life.

I fumbled for the lamp switch. As it flicked, I felt my skin peel back and thousands of ants crawl up my spine. Seamus's legs were purple and his face so mottled I thought he had turned to marble. I focused on the heat, praying that heat meant life. I had obviously made a sound, or I had run and woken her, but either way Julie, our au pair, was beside me.

'Stay with Finn,' I said.

The next conscious moment I recall was racing along an almost deserted street, clutching a baby in a car capsule, searching for a car. *Am I doing the right thing? Fuck! Where's the fucking car?*

I tried to picture the car. Where had I parked it? I ran, adjusting the capsule in my grip, conscious of my footfall, aware that any moment I could trip. I was out of my body, propelled by some external force into Kings Cross and past the El Alamein fountain. A couple of sex workers I knew by sight rushed over to me and helped me find the car. Once I turned the ignition and increased speed, I returned to my body. I began to shake uncontrollably. *Why haven't I called an ambulance? Why did I run?*

This was before mobile phones. The kitchen landline had seemed so far away when I was careering for the door.

At the hospital, they took Seamus from me without any questions. They just took him. I watched the plastic-flapped doors slap shut and began to blubber. The triage nurse took my details. I was walked through the doors and put onto a bed to wait.

'We think it's meningitis,' they said. 'Do you have any other children?'

'Yes, a two-year-old.'

'Can someone bring him in immediately?'

They called Julie and she woke Finn. When the ambulance backed into the emergency department at about 4 a.m. and the doors were opened, Finn was sitting on a trolley beaming. They checked him out and sent him back home. He seemed thrilled by the experience and it lit my heart to see his beautiful, open, happy face.

By 4.30 a.m., I had cancelled the flights, called the women who were to be moving in, told Ra Ra the trip was off, and waited. They performed several lumbar punctures on Seamus and resuscitated him. They gave a firmer prediction of viral meningitis.

I called Marty. I called Carmen, Marty's sister in the Netherlands, my dear friend Joanne who was out of town, and I prayed with all my being that Seamus would be all right. That he would live. That he would live.

We spent the following weeks in the hospital. While I was there, I met shattered parents, heroic children and dedicated, caring nursing staff. When the paediatric specialist said we could go home, he told us that only time would reveal whether Seamus had any lasting problems resulting from the fluid on his brain. He thought Seamus was very fortunate; the outcome might have been much worse.

'And you can fly to Canada in two months, should you still wish to,' he said.

The boys and I flew to Canada with Ra Ra, who generously agreed to help me on the flight. By the time the plane reached cruising altitude, Finn had opened all his little surprises. He slept across Ra Ra's lap for many hours. Then began the diarrhoea. He went through every nappy I had, so I created nappies out of all the changes of clothes I had packed for him. By the time we landed in Los Angeles and transferred to the Canada terminal, we'd missed the last flight and had to wait another six hours in a deserted lounge. I had exhausted all my pieces of fabric and, like a strip poker game, was down to my jeans and T-shirt. I checked for hidden cameras and contemplated removing the fabric upholstery from the airport chairs.

We arrived tired, cold and smelly in freezing Vancouver, where Marty welcomed us warmly. Seamus, four months old at this point, hadn't slept more than half an hour at a stretch for the whole trip. Swinging him in his car capsule seemed to soothe him, so Marty and I took turns throughout the night, me with carpal tunnel splints straitjacketing my arms, and Marty with a wide elastic brace to ease the strain on his lower back.

One night at about 4 a.m., Marty received a call while swinging Seamus. It was 7 a.m. in New York and Harvey Weinstein was on the line.

'Who ever thought an owl would be funny anyway?' he shouted.

Previously, Marty had been told that the film's director had randomly called a woman on his staff into his office and asked her if she thought owls were funny. She had apparently laughed, which confirmed to him that they were, so he'd convinced the studio that 'An owl is definitely funnier than an eagle'.

The director, clearly avoiding Harvey's calls, had flicked the problem over to Marty, the director of photography. Marty was leaning against the bedroom wall, wearing his back brace and swinging the car capsule to keep Seamus asleep, placating Harvey Weinstein with his limited knowledge of birds, saying that he'd heard owls could be funny.

Over the next few months, each day became more and more ridiculous; each night, our pain intensified and our sleeplessness made us feel progressively more insane.

A 'normal' baby is ideally supposed to begin crawling anytime between six and thirteen months, or so the poster in the baby health centre said. Seamus, while keen, was not achieving more than a bumpy sideways drag. Although we cheered him on and showed him by example, he didn't catch on. Getting on all fours was difficult, and if I helped him into the position, he would fall to one side and roll over. Propped up on the couch, he crumpled to the left and face-planted in the soft cushions. Finn had taken his first steps at about 3 p.m. on his first birthday, moments after his cake had been cut. He grasped the handle of his new plastic melody-playing lawn mower and pushed it the length of the living room. I assumed Seamus's delay was due to the meningitis, and that we should continue with his exercises and encourage any movements he made to travel from A to B.

When he did eventually walk, at about 17 months, he curved in an arc to the left because his left shoulder was somewhat lower than his right. X-rays revealed scoliosis and various people gave him specific exercises to do in conjunction with the speech exercises, and fine and gross motor skill exercises, and focus and reading exercises. Everyone we saw had something to offer; however, a weekly 30-minute appointment often only created more feelings of guilt in me. I always felt that maybe I wasn't doing enough and that if he didn't show signs of improvement each week, it was my fault.

A neurologist gave me the best advice I was ever given. We were back in Sydney. After cancelling numerous appointments with him due to head lice and colds, we finally saw him at the outpatients department of Prince of Wales Children's Hospital. He was tall and kind and gentle. He spoke to Seamus and then told him he'd now like to speak to me if that was okay. Seamus said 'Yes'. The neurologist told me to spend 20 minutes every day, preferably at the same time, doing something with Seamus. This something should not be exercises unless he initiated them himself. Seamus was to choose the activity; therefore, my job was to make sure we were in an age-appropriate safe space. For example, not on a cliff walk or in a park with big dogs or near a fire. Seamus would choose the activity, and whatever he said or wanted to do, I had to follow. I was not to allow myself to be distracted or say 'no' to anything. I must be completely there for him and with him. And then I should do the same thing with Finn.

I created a wall chart with photos of possible activities we could do together. While I was with Seamus, Finn would watch *Play School* or *Baby Mozart*, and vice versa. It didn't always run smoothly but the results were profound. Seamus began to sleep more. He looked forward to doing his exercises. He enjoyed interacting with other children more, and he gave me time to do whatever I needed to do without demanding attention.

'Your son has autism spectrum disorder,' I was told. The title wasn't a complete surprise, but the words and what they potentially meant opened a chasm in me and had me teetering on the edge. I reminded myself to breathe. I focused on a disposable coffee cup in front of me. Then the vast expanse began to close and the earth felt solid once more.

'Nothing has changed,' I told myself. 'Autism spectrum' could have infinite meanings. Our job now would be to interpret and explore what those words meant for Seamus and no one else.

Seamus was three and a half years old at the time, and had been assessed by Tumbatin, a children's developmental service, which was a branch of the Prince of Wales Hospital. We were given lists of therapists, and were told that the label was necessary if we were to get any assistance when he eventually went to school.

School was generally a happy place for Seamus. He was popular, made friends and wasn't teased. Teachers liked him, and many went way beyond their jobs to ensure he remained involved and accepted. Our dear friend Suzie Miller helped us get him into Woollahra Public School, where Seamus thrived. Surrounded by women in particular who cared for him and challenged him, he felt happy and supported. Lori made Seamus feel special. Ms Reynolds made him feel smart. Ms Hallahan gave him recognition. Sharon 'shadowed' him in class a few days a week and made it fun.

Whenever we went to LA, we stayed at the Oakwood apartments in Marina del Rey, an apartment complex with short- and long-term occupants. The more permanent tenants or owners would invite the transients to movie nights and eat-outs. Although we didn't accept the invitations, we enjoyed watching them from our balcony. The first time we'd stayed, I was six months pregnant with Finn. We had a small room overlooking the common area and swimming pool. It was a happy time divided between spending days with our dear friends Joss and P.J. and their gorgeous children, strolling along the canals of Venice Beach, or waiting for phone calls from Marty's agent.

The second time we stayed, Finn had been born in Sydney and was now about 15 months old. It was Marty's birthday. We were returning to the Oakwood from a walk when we saw a couple lounging on day beds by the pool, while a boy of about four years old in an ice hockey outfit wandered around, kicking pot plants and throwing pebbles into the water. We said 'hi' to him. He replied quietly, 'I've got no one to play with.'

I looked over at the couple, who appeared to be his grandparents. They were reading and dozing. The boy asked who was in our pram and I lifted the shade cloth so he could see the sleeping Finn. The boy smiled and pulled some leaves off a nearby plant.

We wandered away from the boy, but my heart ached for him. He looked so lonely. We entered our beige apartment, wheeled the silent pram into the bedroom, closed the door and conceived a brother for Finn on the living room floor. Seamus was born the following year.

The panic began one evening at a poolside party at the Oakwood. We had returned to LA, this time with two little boys. As the sun was setting, inflatable waterlilies bobbed on the water, and canapés, pierced with decorative plastic sea creatures, were being handed around. Hours before, we had been playing with the boys in this pool, but now Seamus began flapping his hands in distress and crying. He was pointing to the floating lilies and wrestled with me to release him from my arms. He wanted either to flee or gather them up. He seemed worried about the lilies and wanted them out . . . Now!

'He doesn't like the flowers,' Finn offered.

'Yeah, I think you're right, Finn.'

I returned to the apartment with Seamus but he wouldn't be consoled. Later that evening, with the party over and the pool returned to a still body of water, I carried Seamus around it. Although his bottom lip quivered, he seemed satisfied that the whole horrid flower invasion had passed. This began an obsession he developed for things that moved in the breeze. A stretch of sand with sunbaking bodies and belongings was potentially the worst scenario. Gathering as many towels and bags as he could, he would drag them into a pile and make me sit on them while he went to save more. Confused, angry or sometimes amused beachgoers would chase him, trying to gently prise their possessions back from him.

In kindergarten, he scored the role of Mary in an outdoor Christmas nativity scene with his best friend Tom playing Joseph. He seemed delighted, but when the white pillowcases and sheets came out of a box to serve as costumes, and the parents gathered with their prams and baby wraps, he tore off Mary's garments, stripped Joseph naked and desperately tried to undress the wise men and all their sheep. What terrified him most was washing on a clothesline. He would check multiple times before bed that our clothesline was bare, and the pegs were counted up and in their ice-cream container with the lid on tight. He feared for the clothing's safety throughout the night and would not sleep until every garment was accounted for.

One evening at dusk, he was inconsolable. He begged to be taken out the front door, down to the street. He dragged me by the hand, pointing agitatedly down the side of every house and block of flats. In the backyards, we could both glimpse washing on Hills Hoists, and if we crept a little along the paths and passageways, we could see towels on side rails or racks in open garages. I tried using language and reason. I tried all the tools we'd been given by experts to help him with anxiety. I tried detective thinking, reasoning, worry beads, reminder stones, stress balls, positive mantras, deep breathing and, in exhaustion, distraction. Nothing worked.

'What are the chances of clothes flying away?' I would say. 'Have you ever seen clothes fly away? Between one and ten, how bad would it be for that sock to fly away?'

And on and on. None of it resonated. None of it helped. It was as if he had given every piece of clothing, every sock and every towel, a beating heart and their flimsy lives were in jeopardy. The potential for them to flap free of their pegs and be caught in an updraft and be lost in the never-never seemed more real and threatening to him than any other fear.

I knocked on strangers' doors and introduced myself, asking if they might remove their washing from the line, now that the sun was going down, but even the kindest people did not understand this urgency.

Just before dark, I would bob down and almost crawl below windows where families were eating dinner or watching TV, and go and remove the pegs. If the clothes were dry, I would fold them and leave them in a basket by the back door. If the clothes were still damp, I would hurry them home, throw them in the dryer, fold them, and lay them on porches and in foyers or back common areas. I was amazed the local paper had never published a column about the washing fairy, who worked through the night pressing the neighbours' knickers.

I knew this was what therapists would call 'enabling'. They would tell me I wasn't helping my child. But neither Seamus nor I could go without sleep any longer. I was the mother and he was my child, I had clothes-folding skills and he did not, and clearly the neighbours were lazy or didn't care, so it became the best solution.

And it worked. Seamus began to worry less and trust me more, and we both began to get some sleep. And sleep was always the best solution of all.

Finn played basketball and had always been good with chasing, throwing, bouncing and chucking balls, big and small. So Seamus tried. He was six years old when he got the basketball bug. At first, Seamus loved running the length of the court, looking down and watching his long legs move below him. He seemed to enjoy seeing his feet follow through with every step as he travelled. He was like a young foal delighting in his limbs as he discovered his muscles and developing strength. His first team was the Stingrays, next the Red Devils and then the Bondi Lions Blues. His jersey was Number 11, and to his embarrassment, I'd call from the sidelines: 'Go, legs eleven!'

He joined teams and played afternoons and weekends. He began to take it seriously, maybe too seriously, because he would chide himself horribly if he felt he'd missed shots, been excluded by teammates or injured himself. And then he met Peter.

Peter was a young man who became Seamus's coach and mentored him physically, mentally and emotionally. All the other therapies ceased; basketball became his teacher. He learned how to be in a team, to lead, to develop plays and to think constructively, strategically and empathically. His fine and gross motor skills became more refined and dependable. And he began to put all his energy and time into his love for the game.

One day, at an appointment for yet another opinion on his back, new scans were done that revealed that Seamus's 'scoliosis' was more likely the result of a break when he was very young, probably as a baby. The probability was that, while being resuscitated at five weeks old, his upper spine may have cracked, which explained his months of screaming, his inability to crawl and his permanent lean to the left.

Seamus bought free weights and a pull-up bar, and studied the skeletal and muscular structures. He did a fitness training course. He improved his diet. He began to read, something he had always struggled with. He read a book a week, then a book a day.

'There are always going to be pros and cons, whatever path you take,' Seamus said to me. 'Trying to find good solutions is what gives hope.'

Seamus is now twenty-one and a basketball coach at the prestigious Cranbrook School, which is soon to become co-educational. He is passionate about encouraging all genders to play basketball. He says he wants other people to gain the benefits he's had from the game he loves. Basketball 'is not about wins or losses,' he reminds me, 'it's about confidence, teamwork and leadership. It's about acceptance and acknowledgement.'

He has already coached eleven individual teams as well as private clients. In 2021, his Year 8 girls' team had 19 wins and 3 losses, ending with a triumphant Grand Final win. The pride he feels for all these teams makes my heart beat faster.

12

The Spaces Between Things

'Apparently, the nuns used to own it. Isn't it gorgeous?'

It certainly had huge proportions. Its polished timber–floored, soaring-ceilinged living room opened onto a stone-balustraded balcony overlooking Challis Avenue and its renowned cafes and restaurants. Challis Avenue slopes from Macleay Street down towards Victoria Street, Kings Cross, and you have three choices for walking: to the right into a cul-de-sac; to the left, along a street lined with massive plane trees that would take you past St Vincent's College Catholic girls' school, up into the heart of the Cross; or down the 113 sandstone Challis Steps, also known as the 'stairs of doom', built in 1904 and offering access to the lower levels of Woolloomooloo, where Sydney Harbour hugs massive naval ships. Further along, past Harry's Café de Wheels van with its famous pie floaters, is a pier with a hotel and restaurants. Meandering towards the city, you find the Art

Gallery of NSW and the Botanical Gardens, the Andrew 'Boy' Charlton outdoor pool, and eventually the iconic Opera House, the ferry terminals at Circular Quay, the Rocks and the STC and arts precinct.

From this massive, entire-floor, second-storey vantage point, I could see a black-clad figure with a rectangular tummy of white, resembling a baby penguin, pushing small chairs under tables and leaning to and fro, assessing their alignment. The Fratelli Paradiso sign had gone up only days before, and I assumed the lunch crowd was being prepared for; the smell of fresh coffee, linguine and frangipani seduced me into signing the lease immediately.

The balcony would have to be made childproof if we were to move in. Finn was already testing whether he could squeeze himself between the huge stone blocks. I was booked in for a caesarean in a month and wanted to get settled somewhere soon.

'You may have seen me on the morning show?' the agent said. 'I do the infotainment.' She must have noted my confusion because she added, 'You know, the infomercials. I'll be moving on to demonstrations soon. That'll be amazing.'

'Oh wow,' I said, far too loudly. Maybe I looked like I watched the morning show infomercials, but the truth was that while breastfeeding Finn in the wee hours (this was before streaming and iPhones), I sometimes switched on the telly without sound and watched the all-night ads to keep me awake. I even placed an order for a white plastic mask that sent vibrations into your cheek muscles to lift them, which the promotor promised would prevent me from getting jowls. I cancelled it the following morning, which is maybe why I now have jowls. Guess I'll never know.

'I'm just doing real estate letting for a friend,' she continued. 'Isn't this divine? I don't think anyone's ever lived here. Aren't the renovations to die for?'

Now she was beginning to irritate me, which I knew was unfair, but to my ear, her voice was a grating, broad, cultivated melody of ups and downs. Her smiley self-assurance rose in inflection for no reason, and everything she uttered was either a question or a statement.

Anyway. What was she talking about? Didn't she just tell me the nuns owned this place? Wouldn't they have lived here, being so close to the school? It was one of the oldest three-storey buildings in the area, so of course it had been lived in. In fact, I'd seen people coming in and out of it over the years. The Le Trianon restaurant, which opened in the 1980s and later became Cicada, was smack bang next door. I remember hearing that, although it was a top-end fine-dining establishment focused on the evening clientele, you would often spot mothers and daughters taking lunch in its glassed-in verandah, sipping bowls of light broth from silver spoons. I recall seeing a woman and what may have been her daughter coming out of the apartment building years before. After shutting the gate, they walked five steps along the path and entered Le Trianon. It seemed so quaint to think they would dress up, leave home and pop in next door for a quiet lunch.

I watched Ms Infomercial open a door leading off the living room and wondered whether she had ever really looked at her own reflection. Her insanely high heels created the illusion she was teetering with every step. Not only were they pock-marking the floor, but her back was arched in an uncomfortable bow, which threw her short-buttoned jacket tail out. It seemed impossible that her toes alone could bear her weight. As she passed through the doorframe and began to navigate the three-deep wooden steps leading down into the bathroom, which was strange in itself, I jumped in with a possibly aggressive: 'Yes, I can see it from here, thanks,' if only to save myself from watching her sidestep any more uneven surfaces.

The bathroom was weird. The three unexpected timber stairs descended into a small, rectangular, floor-to-ceiling white-tiled space. Directly opposite these stairs were another set of three stairs and an inward-opening door. This meant you had to walk up two stairs, turn the handle, step back one stair while you opened the door, then step up the further two. Beyond this second door was what she described as the 'master bedroom'. Once you were in the bedroom, to close the door you had to step down two stairs, grab the handle and pull it shut behind you as you ascended again. It reminded me of a trap room into which you were led and the lights were turned off, and you had to find your way out by touch alone because you didn't recognise anything. Or a cool room for hanging meat. Or an easy-clean room for the perfect murder.

There was nothing masterly about the master bedroom. It had no windows, but I noted it would be quiet. The 'other' door in this room (there were two doors to each room) led to a spacious but useless room that resembled a reception area for more rooms. To the left and right were two identical rectangular rooms with built-ins and windows looking out to a back laneway. Between the master bedroom and the left-hand bedroom was a laundry and second toilet, and opposite the right-hand room was a long louvre-windowed walkway leading back to the living area. This had clearly once been an exterior verandah, which the renovators had closed in, but they had overlooked including any insulation, as we would soon discover, for it became freezing in the winter.

The tiny kitchen was off the living room and, although functional, was undersized for the proportions of the living area.

Even with all these quirks, the rent was more per week than we wanted to pay, but it was light and quiet, and I was so very tired with another baby on the way. Finn was now leaning against my sweaty leg, twisting and sucking on the hem of my dress. He was pulling at it, trying to drag me to the front door. I should have seen this as a sign but, instead, I heard myself ask, 'How much is the bond?' And under my breath, 'Does it come with a set of steak knives?'

'I'll take it,' I heard myself say.

The first time I heard him call out 'Dead babies!', I was lying drenched in sweat. This terrifying cry and the image it conjured, I assumed, were part of the same nightmare I'd been swooning towards and away from for hours.

A blinking red light on the ceiling, which I struggled to register as a smoke alarm, jolted me awake. That's when the actual nightmare began. Marty was in Canada, or I would have elbowed him to deal with it.

Finn was two and standing up in his cot, gripping the wooden frame with his right hand and pointing with his left towards the closed built-in cupboards across the semi-dark room. He looked less like Finn and more like a crying baby from a Loony Tunes cartoon, who had lost his tweety bird. He was red faced and on a cliff edge, screaming. I lifted his stiffened body and carried him across the threshold, his outstretched arm still reaching away from the direction we were headed in, as if trying to save something from falling. We plonked ourselves heavily onto the couch. His flailing subsided, followed by deep sobs and, finally, sleep.

We lay there for some time in the cavernous room. The curtainless glass doors invited a dirty yellow light from an old street lamp to cast a pallor of gloom over us. I sank deeper into the cushions as my muscles recognised each unwelcome knot and gave in. I longed for sleep but couldn't. My body resigned itself to numbness and a quiet passing of time. Finn's weight across me was a comfort, and his gentle breathing and occasional grunts calmed me. I felt so connected to him. His limbs jaundiced in the yellow light, his beautiful full lips gently parted, he was feeling safe again in a peaceful sleep.

The days passed joyfully with playtime and visits from Leigh, who lived next door. Leigh and I had met when she worked at the STC in its early days at the wharf. The only real benefit of this apartment was its proximity to her. Her practical, uplifting, no-nonsense approach was a balm to my tiredness and procrastination. Sleep deprivation may be the greatest challenge for any parent, and I felt truly challenged. Seamus, our second child, was only just out of hospital, and my body was still reeling and recovering from the sleepless nights spent keeping a vigilant eye on his tiny body.

My brain would tell me to put the kettle on and my legs would respond by walking into the kitchen, but sometimes that was as far as it went. I'd lean against the doorframe and stare at the bench, trying to remember why I had come here and what it was I wanted, and waiting for a new thought to rise and settle.

'Ah yes, a cup of tea, yes tea, yes, that involves boiling water, yes okay, I'll use the kettle . . . that's a good idea . . . there. I'll fill it with water and boil it. Great. Now don't lose it, keep going, you can do this . . . get a cup and a tea bag and . . . ah great, there's the tea bags, now pour water into the cup. That's great. Fuck, we're out of milk. Never mind . . .'

Sleep. I had no idea it had to be taught. No one told me that the first couple of years of my children's lives would be about needing sleep. Nothing made me feel less adequate than hearing parents tell me how their babies slept through the night. Carolyn Burns, a mother of four who was visiting us from Melbourne, taught me to soothe and swaddle and not project my inadequacies onto the baby. The women in my life who have helped me, and whose practicality comforted me, have taught me some of my greatest life lessons.

'Come on, time for bed,' I'd say, with a story about Finn the cat and Seamus the mouse, and a song and then sleep. Each night, Finn would get into his cot without fuss and, resting his beautiful soft chin on the palm of his bent wrist, fall towards sleep. Then at about 2 a.m. each morning, when the streets were at their stillest, when the restaurants had smashed all their bottles into a skip, and late-night lovers had given up their arguments or reconciliations in the laneways, the pleading and screaming would begin.

'Dead babies, dead babies, dead babies!'

Apart from those distressing words themselves, Finn had a limited vocabulary. I couldn't fathom where he had heard such a coupling of images, let alone believed he could see them. Every night, I picked him up, and lay on the couch or my bed with Seamus on my other side, also awake, waiting for the sun to rise.

For weeks, we accepted and fought against this mad ritual of sleeplessness. For weeks, we wiped imaginary cobwebs from our faces or took turns crying.

'Buzz and I'll let you up. First floor.'

I hadn't seen Angela for a while. I was reluctant to see her because I looked and felt like rubbish, but the thought of her company gave me a rush of adrenaline. We hugged at the door, but she seemed less than excited to see me.

'You live here?' she asked.

'Yes, come on in.'

Tentatively, she walked to the centre of the room and turned 360 degrees.

'The balcony is the same but everything else looks different,' she said.

We passed to the left of the dining table and stepped down onto the slightly sloping worn wooden planked floor of the louvre-windowed passageway.

'This used to be open,' she said.

'Have you been here?' I asked.

'Yeah, before it was renovated. I realised it was the place when I was downstairs, but this is the actual apartment.'

We had arrived at the small foyer-like space with too many doors. Angela stopped.

'I had an abortion in that room when I was still at school. My brother drove me here from Newcastle. And that's the room.'

She gestured towards Finn's room and then pointed to the closed door next to it. 'That was the recovery room and this was the waiting room.'

We looked at each other. We hugged. I think we cried, although maybe only she did or I did. Either way, I recall we wanted to.

After she left, I felt relief. There was an explanation, however uncanny, for Finn's behaviour. I didn't spend any time wondering whether or not it made sense, whether it was fanciful or even madness; I just knew with certainty that I wanted to leave.

Marty flew back from working abroad. His first day home, he picked up Finn, walked out onto the carpeted landing and fell twelve steps to the bottom. We broke the lease, packed our bags and shut the door.

Eight years later, on a wintry night while telling ghost stories around an outdoor fire in the Snowy Mountains with friends, Finn paled and walked inside. I followed and watched him as he stood, facing the kitchen bench of a house we barely knew.

'I remember,' he said, impossibly quietly.

I leaned forward, making sure I had grasped his words. They hung in a tiny bubble between us. I grabbed for them, terrified of frightening them away.

'What do you remember?' I asked, afraid my voice would break the spell he was in.

'The babies. There was blood everywhere. There were babies falling out of the cupboard and there was blood.'

I looked at him. His gentle features lowered towards his chest. His apologetic and disbelieving eyes finally looked towards me.

'What was that?' he asked.

'I don't know,' I said. 'But I believe you.'

Finn sees the spaces between things. Where others see lines, he sees form. I was walking home from a matinee during a season of *Strictly Ballroom: the Musical* in Brisbane in 2015, when I passed an art shop selling sheets of black paper, which were laid out in thick wads on a sale table. I collected various sizes, located some soft white charcoal pencils and a rubber, paid and left.

'While I'm out tonight, do me a drawing,' I said, kissing the tops of the boys' heads as they watched a movie on the TV.

I arrived home at around 11 p.m. On the coffee table was a sketch of an owl. What struck me was it had been drawn with a single light source in mind. Finn had captured the light in his sketch. I remembered my school days and the blackboard that clarified things for me. The white chalk on black that helped me to understand meaning, not just information. When things were reversed, hidden knowledge became present and alive; my brain would relax and my vision would clear. It reminded me of kaleidoscopes in which, as you turned them, filaments would rearrange and mirror themselves to create new patterns. The transparent pieces would overlap and separate, turning yellow into amber and pale green flakes into a dense forest.

Walking past the table still covered in black paper a week later, I wondered if Finn would have discovered his talent by some other means. Would he have made adaptations in his brain to find a way to express himself, no matter what? Chance encounters and unexpected outcomes are so often the experiences I cherish.

Watching your children's relationships grow is one of the most fun and fraught pastimes. It is constantly fascinating to me how each family member is so unique, and everyone's memory of a single experience can differ so vastly, and each relationship with the parents and other siblings is so unparalleled. I have tried to treat my children with respect and have always been in awe of them. A friend once said that awe probably wasn't a healthy emotion to have for your child, but I can't help it. Even from birth, I found their personalities so strong, and their presence so mysterious, I treated them with a dose of reverence. I suppose this feeling has unconsciously stayed with me because I always loathe telling them what they should and shouldn't do, even when situations may have had better outcomes if I had. I am aware, however, that I've been far too involved in alleviating their struggles, and have possibly delayed them from discovering their full independence by supporting them, or interfering, depending how you look at it, in their daily tasks.

'Don't worry, I'll empty the kitty litter,' I would say, even though Finn had promised to.

'You go to bed, darling, I'll finish your homework,' I would say, when Seamus felt overwhelmed.

The constant internal tussle between intervening or not intervening. Correcting or believing their skills for self-correction will manifest with maturity. Encouraging without too much praise, or questioning them without losing their trust.

Finn was reluctant to go into lifts after an experience at his school when he was about seven years old. The lift had shuddered to a stop between floors and the rocking sensation was unnerving. He also felt uneasy about underground car parks. Not a huge problem really; as a parent, however, I wanted to help him overcome his fear should it limit his enjoyment of future experiences. And so we booked him in to see a psychologist. This woman came highly recommended; she was brilliant with children, I was told. I asked other parents how many sessions we should expect and how much it might cost. The consensus was that the therapy might vary from a couple of sessions to ongoing, depending on what was unearthed. On the day of the appointment, we drove to Macquarie Street in the city where beautiful old early to mid-nineteenth century sandstone buildings lined the street.

We passed the Treasury building, and Marty pulled over for Finn and me to alight. Marty explained to Finn that he would go and park the car in the Opera House underground car park then walk back up the hill and join us. Finn and I entered a massive mirrored and timber-panelled foyer. There was a lift that had a concertina metal grille across its sliding wooden door. Finn looked up at me for confirmation that the stairs would be our means of transport; I smiled in agreement. We held hands as we ascended the wide white marble steps. Six floors later, we arrived at her door. Her name was written in gold lettering on a nameplate. Finn looked up to me again for reassurance. I gave him my look of *Oh, what fun*, which I knew he was too smart to buy. We waited on comfy chairs and played the hand game where you pile your hands on top of the other person's, slipping the bottom one out each time and putting it on top until you're slapping each other in a frenzy.

'Finn McGrath?'

We jumped up and followed her into a large, high-ceilinged room with views across to the Botanical Gardens. She gestured for us to sit on a long upholstered couch, while she sat opposite us in a big armchair with cushions. Between us was a wooden coffee table, a box of tissues and a bottle of water with glasses. Finn sat back in the couch, but that made his feet stick out, so he wriggled forward and perched on the edge so his shoes could almost reach the ground.

'How can I help you?' she asked, already writing something down.

Finn swivelled towards me requesting I speak, and so I did. I conveyed his reluctance to go in lifts and car parks. She listened, glancing at Finn as I spoke. Then she spoke for about 20 minutes. Marty arrived; she motioned for him to join us on the couch. She began by informing us that fear was a natural emotion. She went on to describe the biochemical responses in the brain and evolutionary development of these responses. She elaborated at length on the effects of adrenaline, panic disorders, phobias, fight-or-flight responses and a checklist of symptoms. Did he get an upset tummy? Rapid heartbeat? Dry mouth? Shivers? Annoyingly, she asked me the questions and then I relayed them to Finn. He sat speechless. Agitated. Clearly uncomfortable, and more than ready to engage the flight response she kept referring to. I stopped listening, having tuned in to his desperation to leave, and wanted nothing more than to cut it short and run. The session ended. We thanked her, made another appointment at her recommendation, paid and descended the stairs. Outside, Marty offered to get the car while we waited on the footpath.

'No,' said Finn, quietly but firmly. 'I'll go in the car park. Just don't make me see her again.'

We walked to the Opera House forecourt, turned into the parking station, pushed the credit card into a machine, retrieved the ticket, took the compact lift down four floors, got in the car, buckled ourselves in and wound all the way up the windy, twisty, helix-shaped, very much underground car park. Finn sat in the back and dealt with his feelings. It had been money well spent.

Seamus was about six years old when we visited a science shop for kids on the north side of the Harbour Bridge. Finn was absorbed by the model volcanoes and small magnifying glasses. Seamus was keener about the heavy sticky-tape holder on the payment counter. We bought a bug catcher and, as I was paying, I asked them if they'd like to choose one thing from the assortment of small, coloured objects lining the counter. They both chose a furry creature resembling an upright mouse. I recall that Seamus's was green and Finn's was blue. Finn always chose blue where he could.

While I was cooking dinner that night, I saw Seamus playing with two furry mouse-like toys, one green and one orange. I crouched down and asked him where the orange mouse had come from.

'The lady gave it to me.'

'When did the lady give it to you, darling?'

'In the shop.'

'Okay. Are you sure she wanted you to have it, or was it that you thought she wanted you to have it?'

Silence. He looked up at me. He realised I knew that he had snuck it out of the shop.

'So, tomorrow we're going to take the orange mouse back and you can say sorry. Okay?'

'Okay.'

We parked outside the science shop. Seamus reluctantly accompanied me inside, clutching the orange mouse.

'Hi, we were in here yesterday,' I announced to a smiling fair-haired woman. 'My son has something he wants to say.'

'Oh. Hi.' She leaned across the counter and looked down at two big eyes.

'I'm sorry I . . .' It was too hard to say.

'My son is very sorry,' I said, and waited for him to continue.

'I took this . . .'

He opened his clenched fist, producing a squashed orange mouse.

'He'd like to pay for it, please,' I added, as he held up a two-dollar coin in his other hand.

The young woman almost wept. 'Oh, that's so, so lovely of you. I know people steal things all the time, but no one ever comes and says sorry. Here—choose something.'

What? I thought. *Don't reward him! I'm trying to teach him crime doesn't pay!*

But she gave him the choice of any other small counter toy, and he chose a small wind-up ladybird.

We arrived home. Finn was lying on the couch. Seamus took me by the hand and we walked into their shared bedroom. From behind the bookshelf, he produced a paper bag. He walked down the long narrow hall and stood alongside Finn's horizontal body.

'Here, Finn, I'm sorry, I took your money.'

Finn looked incredulous. (A couple of days before, Finn had suggested that a friend who had slept over might have taken his birthday money.) Then he responded in the same way the woman had earlier.

'Oh, wow, thanks Seamus. Here, have $20 for giving it back.'

I was standing behind Seamus, waving my arms and silently mouthing, 'No! No, don't reward him!'

But he did, and they hugged and were happy and I learned once again to back off.

Not everyone likes to celebrate birthdays. For a multitude of reasons, birthdays can be a day of personal acknowledgement of life, time well spent and the expectation of even better days to come but they're also an unpleasant reminder of age and lost opportunities.

I have always loved birthdays—any valid opportunity to celebrate someone seems like a good idea to me.

Our sons were due to be born on the same day, two years apart. A planned caesarean brought Seamus's date forward by a week, but until they were about ten years of age, they had joint birthday parties involving pirates, magicians, bowling alleys and picnics with games. The boys and I prepared by making piñatas, costumes and lolly-filled take-home party bags, and dreaming up crazy cakes.

Finn was turning twelve and had just begun Year 5 at a new school. Finn has one of the most genuinely gentle natures I have ever known. As a small child, although he was naturally strong and physically adventurous, he was placid, quietly observing life from the back seat, patiently waiting his turn and, frankly, quite relieved if his turn didn't come. He has developed extraordinary insights into human nature and society that I find constantly remarkable. As a child in primary school, he was the boy sitting towards the rear of the circle on the floor. I had offered to make mosaics with his class, and was preparing tiles and grouting at the back of the room during lessons. I noticed Finn always sat slightly apart from the other kids. He never volunteered to speak and, if asked, seemed uncomfortable. I assumed it was partly because I was present, but his teachers confirmed, 'No, that's where he always sits.'

He had also lost his two best friends, who had both left to live overseas, and he seemed adrift. Marty and I thought a change might be good, so he moved schools. I decided he should have his own birthday and invited a few of his new friends from his new school. They could enjoy a swim at an outdoor pool, which had a slide, then dinner at a pizza restaurant, followed by a sleepover with movies. Sounded like a good idea.

Finn invited two boys from his new school, Josh and Jasper, although he'd known them from years before, another boy, Colm, who had started the new school the same day he had, and a basketball friend who knew none of the others.

Colm was coeliac, Finn told me. His mother would call me to discuss. *Okay*, I thought as I googled 'coeliac' and its symptoms. Jasper was diabetic, but he was very cool about having it and was expert at dealing with his injections, so there was no need for me to worry. The basketball friend, Felix, whose mother was a dear friend of mine, was desperately sad because his father was extremely ill in hospital. The other boy, Josh, was fun and had no health issues to speak of.

We took two cars to the pool. I packed special gluten-free snacks for Colm and plenty of drinks and sunscreen. It was a hot day in February; the pool was busy and the boys appeared to be having fun. About 5 p.m., we rounded them up. They stuffed wet swimmers into their backpacks as they swatted each other with towels and 'ouched' their way across the baking hot asphalt of the car park. Blaring music, the cars tailed each other to the pizza place. I had called to arrange a table for eight, and had double- and triple-checked that they definitely served gluten-free pizzas.

'Yes, we have a gluten-free menu. Yes, we do.'

Jasper pulled out his syringe and the boys went wild. This party was finally warming up. Nodding to a nearby table of two adults with young twins, I suggested that maybe Jasper inject himself in the bathroom, rather than in full view of the restaurant. The boys all loved the idea and followed Jasper into his lair to watch. They excitedly returned to the table, devoured the pizzas, guzzled the lemonade and gently joked with each other. They looked so clean and shiny, and Marty and I exchanged smiles.

Makeshift beds covered Finn and Seamus' bedroom floor. The boys threw down their backpacks and by the time I reached the kitchen, Josh had flung his fist through the bedroom door's pane of glass. Unharmed, he helped us drag the mattresses down the hallway and into the living room while Marty vacuumed the shards and shook out the sheets.

Colm produced his initial projectile vomit about 10 p.m. By 2 a.m. he was exhausted and many kilos lighter. He sat naked on the toilet, me balancing a bowl in front of him as he emptied what appeared to be his entire life, a 12-year-old boy so unwell that his nakedness with a woman he barely knew didn't even register.

Marty called and texted Colm's parents' mobiles multiple times. He continued to try to make contact with them, while we considered calling an ambulance. Exhausted, Colm eventually fell asleep on our bed.

Once I had cleaned up the vomit and turned off the TV, the other boys had reluctantly fallen asleep. With one boy in our bed and four in the living room, and glass fragments in the boys' bedroom, Marty and I sat in the kitchen and waited for morning. It must have been about 5 a.m. when I went to the bathroom and checked on the boys. I walked into the lounge room, and saw Finn, Josh and Felix sprawled across their mattresses. It was a hot night and they were shirtless and spreadeagled.

Then I saw Jasper. He was lying on the brown leather couch with his upper torso draped off the cushion and the top of his head almost on the floor. His upside-down face looking like a drawing of a face that can be viewed as either happy or sad, depending on how you turned it. He looked contorted but that wasn't the worst of it. His entire face, torso and upper arms were covered in squiggles made in black texta. I couldn't believe what I was seeing. I tried to wake him, but he was out cold. I woke the other boys, demanding to know: 'Who draws on a sleeping person? Who draws on someone?'

The boys woke. Jasper was not waking.

'Find his bag. Find his kit. Now.'

The boys scrambled, threw backpacks around and emptied their contents, but found no item resembling the one that had provided so much entertainment only hours earlier. I called Jasper's father.

'I am so, so sorry for waking you, but Jasper is asleep and I can't seem to wake him. I'm concerned he may not have taken his medication and I can't find his kit. I'm so, so sorry.'

His father was calm. 'No worries. He's a deep sleeper. I've got a spare. I'll come over soon. Shoot me your address.'

I hung up and freaked out. His father was on his way, and not only was his son barely conscious, but he was covered in graffiti. I did the unthinkable, applying make-up remover and warm soapy water to his body. I scrubbed him as gently as I could and ordered the boys to help. Jasper remained relaxed and unconscious. As I covered him with a sheet, I felt like I'd murdered him.

I jumped when the doorbell rang. A tall man with insanely broad shoulders due to his leather jacket, and holding a motorbike helmet, stood on the dark porch with a spare syringe. He didn't seem fazed, which was a relief; however, I anticipated another reaction if he happened to question his son's scrubbed red face, chest and arms.

He followed me down the long hallway and gave Jasper a light shake. 'He'll be fine. Deep sleeper. I'll give him a shot soon.'

'Coffee?' Marty offered.

'Yeah, great.'

The sun was beginning to peek over the ridge of the southern world. My thoughts turned to Colm. As I headed to the bedroom to check on him, the front doorbell rang. I opened the door. Two people, a man and a woman, stood on the welcome mat dressed in white togas.

'Hi. I'm Liz, this is Roger. We're Colm's parents. Is he okay? We were at a toga party and, well, togas don't have pockets, so we left our phones in the car and just got all your messages then. We've been calling you but no answer, so we thought we'd better just come.'

'I'm so, so sorry,' I said for the second time that night to a child's parents. 'Come in. He's fine now.'

I hadn't looked at my phone during the cleansing of the multiple sins applied to Jasper, and wasn't entirely sure Colm was actually fine since I hadn't checked him for a while.

'Coffee?' I chirped, as I escorted them to the kitchen and signalled to Marty to take over. I walked purposefully down the hall, praying Colm would be sleeping soundly and not resembling a mural. He seemed fine.

The five adults drank coffee and chatted, while the boys got up and blearily made their way into the kitchen. Jasper appeared and, although groggy, looked well covered in the high-necked T-shirt I'd encouraged him to put on. His arms were still flushed from the rubbing and faint veinlike marks were horribly visible in the morning light but, to my relief, no one seemed to notice.

Jasper planted his palm on his forehead in a 'D'oh!' gesture. 'Oh damn, I left my kit in the toilets at the pizza place.'

'No worries,' said his dad. 'We'll get it later.'

Marty beautifully diverted attention to Colm and apologised to Liz and Roger about the pizzas, which we had been assured were gluten-free.

'Yeah, they say that,' said Roger. 'The bases are, but the grated cheese they use is from a packet and it's dusted in flour. Happens all the time.'

Wow, I thought, *that's shocking. Last night I thought he was dying.*

We were all beginning to relax and the boys went outside into the backyard to muck around when my phone rang.

'Oh, Heather—' Then heartbreakingly long, deep sobs. 'Bring Felix. Can you tell him, prepare him? His dad's . . .'

I assured Felix's mother we'd be there as soon as we could. I walked out to the boys, and told Felix his mum had just called and would like him to come into the hospital. I kept it as casual as I could, and he high-fived the boys and hugged Finn while I gathered his things.

We drove to St Vincent's in Darlinghurst, where Felix had been many times over the past weeks seeing his dad. He appeared not to suspect that this moment had come. I pulled over and parked. *Do I tell him now? No, wait till he's closer to his mum.*

We got out of the car and walked towards the entrance. With his dad's room in sight, I told him. His mother appeared and enveloped him. I watched them break, fall and dissolve into grief. I walked to the car, drove home, began the clean-up and made a cake.

13

Carry Me

He was stooped; at first, I thought he had dropped something and was bending down to pick it up. He was a good 30 metres from me, about a third of the way across a large bank of vivid green grass, which sloped gently down to the main road. As his hands touched the ground, his body followed. He crumpled like a puppet on strings, each segment of his arms, legs and neck coming apart as he fell.

As I approached him, I confirmed to myself that he was elderly. I stood above him for a moment before crouching down. He was gaunt, wearing a blue woollen checked dressing gown with faded pyjamas underneath. He lay on his back, eyes staring at the sky. I looked around for anyone who may have accompanied him. There was no one. I sat and cradled his head.

His head was cool. I felt for his pulse below his jaw but felt none and asked him if he knew his name. He said nothing, but his mouth was open wide and I could see there was no obstruction. I bent my ear towards his mouth and nose to check for breathing, but there was none. No rise or fall of his chest. I began to wonder if he had passed away as he fell. He wasn't showing any signs of life. Should I get help or stay with him? I waited for someone to come by and help. I sat with him, suddenly aware of where we were and mystified that no one else had seen us, and if they had, had not offered help.

Minutes earlier, I had set off for rehearsals for a production of *Pravda*, written by David Hare and directed by the brilliant John Gaden at the Adelaide Festival Centre. I enjoyed my morning strolls in the city of churches, beautiful parks and pleasing walks. When I left the North Adelaide house I was sharing with the wonderful Merridy Eastman, it was a glorious day with expansive blue skies and a warmth that gently bathed the skin before the onslaught of the midday heat. Now, I had an unknown man in my arms.

It had happened so fast. He was standing almost upright one moment and was now crumpled, apparently lifeless. His collapse seemed painless. And final.

My urgent need for help subsided as I waited. 'Someone will come soon,' I told him.

Looking up, I saw a woman walking briskly towards the city. She seemed to register a sound from my direction, but continued on unaware. I watched her recede, wondering what all-absorbing business was taking her away from us.

A man appeared over the crest of the hill. There was no need to call out. He ran towards us with an alarmed expression.

'Fuck . . . what's happened?'

'This man . . .' I began.

'What happened?' he repeated, as if he might keep asking this same question for some time. He seemed in shock.

'I think he might be dead,' I answered. 'Why, do you know him?'

'Yep, it's Frank. Shit. He did a runner.'

He crouched and felt Frank's pulse.

'They're all looking for him.' The young man pointed towards the hill he had come from. I wondered who 'they' were.

I held Frank while the young man went for help, taking his panic with him. A couple of small, dark grey birds with white throats and eyebrows came right up and cheep-cheeped beside us. The sun began to intensify, so I shielded Frank's face with mine and, touching his translucent skin, closed his eyes with my palms, as I'd seen done in the movies. I felt useful, needed; I was suddenly thankful to be here.

Frank: he had a name, and with the name, a history. I wondered why Frank had run, who or what from, how he had found the energy, and whether he had tried before and failed. I chose to believe that this was how he hoped to die, in the sunshine on the green grass under a cloudless sky. I thought of one of my favourite kids' books, *A Fly Went By,* by Mike McClintock. A young boy asks a frantic fly where it's going, and the fly explains that it's fleeing from a frog. The boy reprimands the frog, who explains that it's being pursued by a cat, the cat by a dog, and on it goes, with each animal that passes the boy running from another until, eventually, a man runs by who is being pursued by an unseen monster. The fearless boy discovers that the monster is simply a lamb with its leg caught in a tin can. The rattling of the can and the bleating of the lamb had initiated the chase, and so the boy shouts 'STOP!!!' He frees the lamb, reveals the truth and calm is restored.

Frank lay in my arms, not breathing. He had shaken off whatever pursued him.

I remembered hearing about a well-known Australian director, who was greatly loved by a devoted group of actors, who had also tried to run. The group of friends had visited him in palliative care, believing he was in his final moments. With a force they recounted as 'mighty and unstoppable', he had elevated himself from the bed and run around the entire ward, ripping tubes and clothing from his body. It was traumatic for the friends and, understandably, not much fun for the director either.

I recognised the incredible privilege of holding a person at the end of their life, and thought about the mystery of energy, where it comes from and where it goes.

My attention was taken by the scattering of small grey birds hopping nearby, the faint scent of gardenias and cut grass, and the touch of a light breeze that carried the sound of humming traffic and a buzzing fly.

I felt an onrush of gratitude for being alive and thought of my mother's death, and all the millions of people who had died since. I remembered my mother's note to me, saying how tired she had been and that death would be a relief. As I held Frank, I thanked my mother for making the experience of death an uplifting one, of wonder even, at a time when my emotions were full and extreme and my senses hyper-keen. A memory flashed into my mind of my mother telling me that, when my brother was in primary school, he had expressed his frustration to her: 'The teacher told us at school today that we have five senses. I know I have them . . . but who is going to teach me how to really get the utmost out of them?'

I reassured Frank he was not alone as I stroked his fine hair and waited.

Vera came with the beautiful French provincial single-storey cottage we rented in Simpson Street, Bondi, from a woman called Susan. Through the friendship, we met her best friend Sharon and Sharon's daughter Emily. Sharon and Emily helped us with looking after the boys, and we all sort of adopted each other.

Vera lived three doors down from us on the corner of Simpson and Edward streets. Early every morning, Vera, who was eighty-something, would meander down to Bondi beach in her tiny old Volkswagen to swim in the surf. During the day, she would educate herself at the University of the Third Age.

Vera had been a teacher, and her sharp, quick mind was matched by a take-me-as-you-find-me attitude. She read widely and had lived alone since her son, a talented dancer, had moved out more than 30 years earlier.

Vera's door was mostly open and she would toddle up to our place wearing her thin cotton nightie. Sitting on a tall stool at the kitchen island, legs akimbo and sipping black tea, she wouldn't move when I casually reminded her that the boys could see right up her you-know-what. She adored Marty because he had fixed her tray table, which she used to read in bed, and together they discussed their shared love of the literary classics.

Vera developed cancer; eventually, she went to hospital only a short time after her beautiful son had died from an AIDS-related illness. She lay in her hospital bed, never complaining or self-pitying, but always interested and engaged.

One day, while rehearsing *Neighbourhood Watch* at Belvoir Street, I received a text to say that Vera was going. At lunchtime, I arrived at St Vincent's Hospital, walked into her airy room and sat on the chair by her bed. Her cheeks were hollow and her lips were parted. I leaned towards her and whispered my thanks. I could feel no breath escape her mouth or see any rise in her chest. She was deathly still. I was unsure whether I had just experienced her passing, or whether she had died before I'd arrived. I was looking at her, exploring her fine skin and contemplating the little I really knew of her life, when she sat bolt upright, gasped a huge breath of air and asked, clear as a teacher in front of a class, 'Read any good books lately?'

My father Red developed Alzheimer's in 1997, which altered him in ways that were out of character. And that's how I chose to see it. His character was changing. The thoughts he regularly relied on were sometimes missing. The images he interpreted were morphing and fading including, eventually, his recognition of me. By accepting that he was delving into different facets of his character, ones that had been unexplored, I was able to enter into his reality and reconcile my need to keep him as he once was.

Red was cared for by his wife Elizabeth in the Blue Mountains for years, with frequent visits and respite from my sister and me. Red and Elizabeth met many years after my mother's death; they married and based themselves in Springwood. I was thrilled he had someone to love, and who would love him and travel with him and share experiences with him. Elizabeth was considerably younger than Red and his Alzheimer's diagnosis was a blow for her. She remained emotionally connected, but clearly needed her own relief from the pressures dementia can bring. On one occasion, Marty and I rented a small wooden shack in Blackheath, so Red could come and stay in familiar surroundings, and be close enough for Elizabeth to see him whenever she wanted to.

Marty was shooting a film in Kangaroo Valley in 1997. It was mid-winter and the film involved weeks of night shoots. Red and I spent days rugged up against the biting cold, taking short walks, collecting small rocks and twigs, and drinking hot chocolate on the couch by the window. The tiny rustic house reminded me of the old jails and post offices Red had painted in oils on his field trips and, because it was surrounded by pillars of eucalypts, red cedar and the sweet smells of wattle and gum leaves, I thought he'd love the shack and it would make him feel secure and comforted.

It did not. The shack did bring back his past, but many of the associations upset him. He didn't seem to recognise the tall red cedar that he spent his life planting and protecting. His watercolours frustrated him and the brushes were difficult to control. The few he attempted were dark and foreboding, and distressed him. I tried swatting a fly one morning with a rolled-up paper. Red erupted, 'Don't hurt it. Don't do that.

Stop it! Stop it!' Once again, my beloved childhood book came to mind.

I felt ashamed. I considered that he was identifying with the fly, whose life was being stalked and threatened by the hand of death.

The actress Brenda Blethyn, who was working with Marty at the time, confided in him that she was disappointed she had been given accommodation in a glamorous hotel overlooking the mountains, when she'd have preferred a farmhouse. He invited her to our shack. She loved it. She connected with Red and her visits ignited him; sometimes, I wondered whether what he really needed was new company, not people from his past. Maybe spending long days alone with me was only intensifying his frustration at being unable to place me.

Alongside the house, under an awning, was a woodpile. The wood was neatly stacked in large blocks ready to burn in the kitchen stove, the house's only heat source. This meant waking at intervals throughout the night to stoke the embers and dampen the severity of the bone-chilling mornings.

Red loved trees. He had spent his life caring for, tending to, writing about, carving out and lying under glorious trees. Protecting them. He had taken great satisfaction in his field work, and loved sleeping out, boiling the billy and rising early. He knew that what he did was useful, and I think he hoped that helping people recognise and understand the importance of our relationship with the soil and trees would contribute to preserving our precious environment. He spent hours every day at the woodpile, sorting and rearranging the pieces like a complex jigsaw puzzle, pulling splinters from his fingers and occasionally sitting on a rock, stroking a lump of rough bark and grain.

The pile diminished as the first week progressed, so I called the wood delivery service and placed an order for more. The truck arrived early and reversed beeping down the gentle slope. It opened its tray and wood spilled out, tumbling, thumping, rolling towards the exterior wall of the house.

Red rushed out, alarmed, into the frosty air. Seeing the avalanche of chaos, the scattered mayhem, the rough-hewn landscape, he held the roots of his hair and rocked on his feet. 'How will I be able to learn all their names?' His voice was strained, not in anger but anguish. 'It took me so long to remember the others!'

Marty had given Red one of his warmest jackets to wear. It was a puffy zippered number, which Marty had been given by Kodak after a shoot. Marty had never worn it despite its superior quality, because it had 'Martin McGrath ACS, [the accreditation for members of the Australian Cinematographers Society] Director of Photography' with a list of credits, some of which he'd rather forget, embossed in shiny gold across its right side below a Kodak logo. A tad pretentious to be seen in, Marty had thought, but Red looked happy in it. Even proud. Red was found one afternoon wandering around a mall, clearly disoriented, and a woman had alerted the local one-hour Kodak shop. They in turn had called the head of Kodak Motion Pictures to warn that Martin McGrath ACS, Director of Photography, was lost and unsure of who he was.

Red always removed his shoes indoors. Now at dinnertime, he began scraping the contents of his meal carefully into one of them. It gave him the advantage of not needing to sit down at the table; he could walk around with it easily and sit where he wished. I purchased two pairs of super lightweight men's velcro-opening shoes from Target and lined them with plastic. Together, we ate harmoniously from our left and right feet. No washing up, just a scrunched-up piece of plastic and contented peace.

One night, he opened the front door and ran, still barefoot. I grabbed a torch and ran, too, chasing his silhouette down the deserted street. Bush loomed around him and then he vanished. He scrambled down an embankment, tumbled and stopped. The night was silent except for rock bouncing off rock. I slid down, scraping my hands, and stopped behind him with my legs straddling him on either side like we were playing piggyback. I wrapped my arms around him, and he didn't flinch. The torch was off. It was dark. We slumped together like tobogganers at the bottom of a hill, the adrenaline leaving our bodies. His back muscles were still strong, despite him being eighty-two. His scratchy beard and soft fine hair smelled of the bush. I remembered all the times I'd cried, 'Carry me! Carry me!' as a child. With a single motion, he'd lift me onto his shoulders, and I'd wrap my arms around the crown of his head and bounce up and down, feeling invincible. Or clinging to his back as he swam into the deep water at Morgan's Harbour in Jamaica, where we would dive and resurface again, laughing and spluttering. Or carrying me from the car at night after the ignition was turned off, as I waited in a half-sleep for footsteps and the squeak of the car door.

These hands had lifted me and carried me along paths and through doorways, along hallways into rooms, and laid me on my bed and tucked me in. I reached for his right hand, and he accepted mine. His hand was rough and warm. I squeezed it. He squeezed back. All the times he had held my hand, guiding me, protecting me, soothing me, proud of me. I wanted to stay like this forever. I didn't know if I was strong enough to go back, to continue watching him, not as the man I knew but someone else. I doubted he would come with me, anyway. Was he done with living this life? I felt crushed for being unable to provide him with the feelings of safety and love he had always given me. *Did he want to be free*, I wondered? Was he trying to run away from himself, from death, or maybe towards it? Either way, he was on the move; returning to the house may not have been part of his vision of the future. The heart-wrenching agony of making someone you love do something they may not want to do is awful. To force a parent to act against their will is sickening.

I wanted him to tell me what he wanted. Was I going to have to choose right now between losing him to the dark bush, explaining it to Elizabeth and my family and living with it, or dragging him back to a house he didn't know and people he didn't remember? What did he want?

It hit me how many choices he'd had to make on my behalf as I was growing up, as every parent does. What a burden that can be. What a responsibility. How does one choose for someone else?

He began to shiver. I had forgotten how cold I was. The cold returned suddenly and ferociously. We clung to each other, not speaking or moving. I began to feel prickles in my feet, a stinging on my skin, a numbness in my legs and the dry dirt in my mouth. Marty would be home soon; he'd be worried. As I began to feel concerned about Marty, Red shifted as though in response and we struggled to our feet. His agitation returned. I could only think of using words to reassure him. We scrambled hopelessly up the slope, slipping backwards, grabbing for traction, eventually making it back to the shack.

We lay on his bed side by side in the quiet. A branch scraped the roof with its spindly fingers. Fizzes from the fire spat. The whole house seemed to groan, mourning its past. The last time we had lain side by side on a bed was a few nights after my mother died, and he cried in my arms. I felt so much love for him it was almost unbearable.

When people say, 'Live every day like it's your last,' it fills me not with energy but with a semblance of despair. *Last day* means saying goodbye to everyone I love, and being tormented by all the 'what ifs' that haven't even occurred to me yet, and the business I've yet to realise is unfinished. It means looking back, joining all the dots and neatening things up. I prefer to say, 'Live every day as if it's your first,' which offers an invitation to be curious and wonder. It means I can rediscover things. See, hear and touch them for the first time. Appreciate things afresh and wonder how they came to be. I would rather look only at the present with awe. I rarely enjoy talking about 'old times'.

Deep within me is a strong memory of 'last days'. Ever since my aunts' and my mother's deaths, I've been acutely aware that life will end, sometimes without warning. When I became a parent and developed breast cancer, which triggered my deep subconscious belief that I was going to die once I had kids, I had to consciously re-train my brain to not believe it.

I recall the moment that belief left me. It actually evaporated. Before that moment, I sometimes overcompensated and helped Finn and Seamus too much, concerned that my time with them was limited. I wanted them to remember me as someone who was always there to fulfil their every need. Another mother may have instilled a stronger independence in her children if she knew she would be leaving them. In time, I realised that I did not want to continue this approach to parenting, unconsciously feeling that every day with my children could be my last. I fought strongly against this and replaced it in my mind with *firsts*. When it happens, my death will be my *first* and I want to feel excited about it, if that's possible, and for my boys to feel content for me and accept that my leaving them is part of the journey. Occasionally, it amazes me that I'm still here. I feel so grateful, and every single day knowing them is utter joy.

Last days can hurt. I think of my dear friend Nick Enright. When he wrote his first play, he did a reading of it and was understandably nervous. I loved it, I said. And that's all it took to further enthuse Nick. Kindness and loyalty were all he asked for.

For several years, Nick wrote with the knowledge that he was dying. He could never forget this. I had invited him for tea one day with our friend, the actress Linda Cropper, and he arrived in a taxi. When he arrived, we both wondered why we had thought it was a good idea. I poured tea but could see it wasn't going to be drunk.

'I need to go,' he said. 'This is a mistake.' He rose to his feet and walked swiftly, agitatedly, towards the front door.

I grabbed my keys and asked him where he wanted to go.

'Drop me at the hospital. I want to go to the hospital.'

'Okay, I'll park and come in.'

'No. Please don't. Just drop me.'

Two nights later, we had booked tickets to see a play at the NIDA theatre in Kensington. I arrived as the bells were ringing and saw Nick hanging back, waiting for me. I misinterpreted his anxiety and apologised for keeping him waiting.

He turned to me with the tickets and grabbed my hands. 'I can't be here. What was I thinking? I must finish my script. I'll never get it finished. I have to go.'

Although we watched the play, I knew he was struggling the entire time. It must have been excruciating for him to consider that his work, his art, his communication, his love may be left incomplete. And every moment he spent not doing it was tearing him apart. He wanted to be completely immersed in his art form. Communicating his ideas in the present. Creating until the very end. Making something out of nothing.

When Finn was only a few months old, Red stayed with Marty and me in Rockwall Crescent. It was midwinter. The open fire in our below-ground floor living room was glowing in Red's face as he held a coffee cup and stared into the fire's flaming majesty. I had put a fire grille around it but, even so, I wouldn't leave him alone. When I needed to cook or make calls, I enticed him to the kitchen with freshly made chocolate cookies. Finn was upstairs asleep. So far, it had worked out well that, when Finn woke from his naps, Red would accompany me upstairs; as I got Finn up, Red would lie down and take his nap.

This day, Finn began crying moments after I'd put him down. I invited Red to join me upstairs to find where the noise was coming from, but Red wouldn't budge. I considered my options and ran up the spiral staircase to either settle Finn or bring him down. He settled. Four steps from the bottom, I froze. Red was no longer in his chair. He was not in the kitchen, nor the dining room or the back courtyard. The front door was open. He was gone.

Shit. What have I done? I made the potentially dangerous choice to go find him. I left a sleeping baby alone in a cot, but if I looked right now, I thought, Red wouldn't have got far; he might be just out the front. I stood on the street with the gates to St Vincent's College only doors away. I checked; the gates were locked. I looked down the back laneway and into shop windows. I asked people if they had seen an older man with red hair, and was either told 'no' or ignored. I ran much further than I intended. I ran with dread, not only for Red but also for Finn.

I was midway along Darlinghurst Road, where Springfield Avenue intersects it, when I saw his shoes. They were attached to legs that were splayed on the ground, his body obscured by the entrance to a building. People were stepping over his protruding feet as though he were just 'sleeping it off' and best left alone. He was slumped on a shallow step, leaning against a glass-paned foyer door, breathless. He must have run fast to have got so far.

He looked like he had been there for days, not minutes. He looked abandoned and unloved, when only 10 minutes before he was secure and adored. How shocking, I thought, the assumptions we make about people. A person lying in a doorway in

Kings Cross can only mean one thing. Whatever has happened to them, they somehow had it coming, and it was best to avoid them and not interfere.

I gathered him up. Without protest, he allowed me to guide him home. We descended the stairs into the house. I sat him in his chair, removed his shoes and checked on Finn, who to my relief was still sleeping. The house had not burned down or flooded, no one had broken in, Finn had not noticed my absence, and all was well.

I reflected on Frank from years before in Adelaide. I'd met his son and daughter for coffee in the Rundle Mall one morning a few days after his funeral. They filled in a rich picture for me. It was so wonderful to hear about Frank's life and their love for him, and how thankful they were that he had not died alone.

Red spent his last few months in a nursing home. It was old yet spacious, and the carers were kind. At about 9 p.m. on a stormy night, I received the call that he was dying. I drove in pouring rain, talking to Marty on the car phone. I was crying so hard. Marty, who was interstate working, let me sob, reminding me to watch the road or pull over. He talked to me for the entire journey, keeping me focused and sane.

As soon as I arrived, everything changed. Red had been put in a room on his own, which was cosy and dark. My sister Rosemary was with him, as was his wife Elizabeth. I whispered to him that I'd found out that morning I was pregnant with our second child, and that it was great timing for him to go because a new life would carry him forward. Red died about an hour later, on the night of his and my mother Shirley's wedding anniversary, the shortest day of the year.

Any fear I felt for Red, his life and his safety vanished when he died. In fact, I felt elated. When he went, Rosemary and I laughed—the kind of laughter that comes after a fright when you know everything will be okay and there is nothing to be scared of. I felt certain that he would love wherever he was going as much as he loved his life here. He had always existed on two levels: in the present but with his eye on eternity.

It was not until a few years after Red's death that Elizabeth, Rosemary and I could all get together. We drove up to Govetts Leap in the Blue Mountains. We followed a track that led to a smaller track, which led to an even smaller one, which opened up to a magnificent clifftop view. We scattered him in a light drizzling rain. The dust didn't travel far and some of it fell in small clumps where we stood. A few curious birds came and pecked, and we all smiled and hugged and thought how fitting it was.

Marty and I drove up there to show the boys when they were older. I tried to retrace our tracks. I'm not entirely certain I found the exact spot, but it was beautiful. As we were leaving to head back to the car, a blue fairy wren appeared. It hopped alongside us for at least a kilometre and whenever we stopped it did, too.

'Is that you, Red?' Seamus and I asked. It accompanied us as far as the car park, and as soon as we hit the asphalt, it flew off.

14

The Gift

I played a spaewife recently in Kate Mulvaney's beautiful adaptation of Ruth Parks' *Playing Beatie Bow*, directed by Kip Williams at the STC in 2021. A spaewife is a prophetess or fortune teller, a woman with the magic to communicate across space and time. In the show, I played 'Granny', an Orkney woman who possesses the 'Gift'. This Gift gives her the ability to call out to women unrestricted by time and space, encouraging them to keep going in the face of hardship, loss and struggle. The Gift connects women and unites them by sharing their insights and stories, and offers a guiding force ensuring that, as we grow older, we become wiser versions of ourselves. Sadly, many people still associate ageing with feelings of failure. The failure to remain desirable. The failure to attract work, relationships and adventure. I find these feelings are only useful when they encourage me to ask for help from other women. Why do we rarely encourage wisdom in one another, and make growth a priority but accept too readily that age is a time to settle, a time to wind down and recede and accept our lot? Why do we fail to really listen? To listen to each other and ourselves? Listen to the voices within us? Not only our own, but the multitude we carry from those we have known. Those we have met and listened to and dreamed of and read about.

My mother Shirley still calls to me. She encourages me to wade into unknown waters, and helps me to swim in them even on the coldest days. Other women in my life offer insights from their past or revelations about the future. Some have given me warnings, some confused signals and some have literally saved my life. Women call across time, and speak to and through me. My mother, her sisters Audree and Rosemary, and their unofficially adopted sister Joan. My grandmothers Rose and Hattie, and my mother-in-law Kathleen. My sister Rosemary, and my sisters-in-law Madelin and Carmen. Vera, who lived four doors down in Bondi, Jean who is currently in palliative care, my girlfriends, my fellow actresses, roles I've played and those I'm hopefully yet to play, as well as doctors, nurses, cleaners, shop owners, Uber drivers and strangers. Women I always look to for questions to ask and answers to be pondered. We are all speaking together and listening to each other.

I think about the stories that are important to me. I think about the vast differences in everyone's stories and their intimate similarities. I keep coming back to *feelings*, and the importance of recognising that every single person has them. Not everyone is good at expressing them. Not everyone feels comfortable having them. Not everyone wants to share them, but we are very good at carrying feelings whether we are aware of it or not. I want to carry the feelings that make me feel good about things. I like to carry the feelings that remind me of people who have impacted me and taught me things—the pleasant things and tough things. I want to carry the love that people have given to me. People kind enough to tell me the truth and those too scared to do so.

In 2006, I opened the letterbox and found a hand-addressed envelope inside. This was strange; usually, we only got bills or advertising material in the mail. The note was from a Mr Anon and started: 'Dear Ms Mitchell. You do not know me but I am writing to you because over the years I have so much enjoyed your performances.' The letter went on to say that she knew actors were poorly paid, and that it gave her great pleasure to thank me in a tangible way. Within the folded paper was a bank cheque for $30,000.

I stared at the cheque, disbelieving. I showed it to Marty, and we both stared at it. I called the bank, I spoke to people who I thought might possibly have done such a thing, but the woman remained unidentified, no matter how hard I searched for her. Her unstinting generosity meant we slept and woke without financial worry. Receiving an unexpected amount of money was an enormous gift. Mr Anon's reason for offering the money was a gift, I hoped, even to herself.

Anonymous and generous acts of kindness bring me to tears. They are everywhere. I have been offered work by people without having to audition because they have faith in me. I have looked after other people's children, who trusted me enough, and I have entrusted them with my children. I have met women who decided they wanted to help my sons and went way beyond their professional requirements. I have a girlfriend who invests in my ideas, because we are connected by history and she believes in me. I have friends, or 'angels', who recently provided a cleaner and food supplies for me during a period of personal difficulty. Women who cook meals for me and insist I use their holiday homes to repair in. I share dressing rooms with women who have become my playmates. They not only challenge me to 'act better', but have fun with me and drink post-show wine with me late into the night. I have my 'Pilates Girls', who exercise with me and with whom I discuss my daily ups and downs. My 'Gang' of girls, who make me laugh and party harder than I should. My Bookclub, who offer me conversation and broader perspectives. Edwina, who offers meditation and care to me and others on a regular basis. Mary, who has helped me more than she will ever know. My individual treasured relationships, which fill me up. My family, who remind me of the love we all share and of how fortunate we are.

Generations continue to pass by, and we keep making up and telling stories. We continue to try to make sense of family and life, and what is before us and behind us. We still want to communicate our ideas with others in the hope that someone will listen. We maintain the need to create something out of nothing.

The creative spirit is in everyone; some people have nurtured and developed it, while others have assumed it belongs only to people with 'talent' or to their childhood, and have dismissed it long ago as futile. Whatever their reason for developing or dismissing it, I like to think that everyone has IT. If someone was robbed of it in childhood, then I see even more reason for it to be cultivated in adulthood. Creating something from nothing, whether it be a child, garden, dinner or idea, and recognising it as a creative achievement, enriches the soul. The need to create can be so strong and powerful, it's no wonder some people feel they are driven to madness by it.

I am constantly amazed and heartened by people who are not practitioners in the arts and sciences, but are supporters and admirers. The people who sit in the dark of a theatre, who wander through galleries, who queue for movie releases, who attend concerts, who sit on couches watching movies and series, and who stargaze. I am indebted to the individuals who donate their money and time and strategic thinking to developing the arts, ensuring its survival. Because without these people, without their passion and vision, artforms would diminish even more than they have. I believe the arts will always survive; stories will always be told, raw materials will be made into objects of pleasure and the need to communicate will continue. Unless we consider our own personal value for these things, however, I fear we may neglect the things we love. And many may watch them die, not even realising they loved it.

One of the things I like most is to peek between the theatre curtains, or look around a cinema, and see people waiting. Waiting for an adventure. Waiting for something to happen. Something unexpected. Something from nothing. It requires us to take a leap of faith. To leave, for a moment, our lives and abandon ourselves.

We are in the dark together. A light goes on. The world is shaken. And snow falls.

Epilogue

Last night at 7.10 p.m., my oncologist Michael rang.

'I'm afraid it *is* cancer.'

A week ago, seventeen years since his last phone call, I discovered a lump in my right breast directly below my first cancer scar. I was sitting in bed reading Joan Didion's book *Blue Nights,* eating pieces of apple. As I picked up a slice that had fallen onto my chest, I felt it.

'I'm so glad I found it,' I said.

Michael offered to call my surgeon, Andrew, to arrange a mastectomy. Within the hour, he had called back to say Andrew's rooms would call tomorrow to make an appointment.

I was in the kitchen when I got the call, a knife in my right hand. A halved avocado lay on the benchtop before me, about to have its seed removed. I reminded myself that nothing had changed in the moments between picking up the phone and putting it down, that I was in no more danger now than I was before the call. Even with this thought, I felt a heat spreading in the rear of my skull and in my stomach. My legs felt wobbly and my hands were clammy. It was not an unpleasant feeling; it fascinated me that my body could react to a perceived danger even though my mind was telling me I was fine. I finished making dinner and served Seamus his, and walked to the bedroom to call Marty. Marty and Finn were on the Gold Coast, shooting the series *Young Rock.* Marty answered.

'You can do this,' he said. He remained calm, and I tried to imagine what his body was telling him as he stood in a small apartment on Main Beach with Finn drawing story boards at the table behind him. He walked onto the balcony, and we managed to talk about his day, which felt good.

How far we had come since the last time, when all we could focus on was the fear of the unknown. We assured each other that we were up for it. I told him how important it was to me for him to remain working this time. Especially because he was loving the work and had job offers that took him through to September. The sticky part was that all his work would be in the USA and Tasmania, but we would always be in contact. What made me falter was the realisation that we were still in Covid times. I would need to protect myself, because the worst part for me would be to get Covid and have my treatment delayed.

It's so hard to fathom that cancer cells could be reproducing in my body when I myself feel so well and happy and relatively stress free, with so much to look forward to. In the next room, a painter is removing damp from the walls of the boys' rooms in the apartment we rent. A leaf blower is screaming intermittently across the road. Seamus is reading a Stephen King book on my bed. A light rain is falling. I'm going to wash my hair, have a cup of tea and make some phone calls. The rest will unfold day by day.

For months now, I have been reading every book on Ruth Bader Ginsberg (RBG) and listening to all her speeches and judgements on record, because I'm due to play her in a production with the STC in a matter of months. Suzie Miller, my dear friend and a gifted writer, has written a phenomenal script. I'm to be directed by the uber-talented Priscilla Jackman, who I did the Catherine McGregor story with. Catherine McGregor is an inspiring trans woman and friend who Priscilla had interviewed and created a wonderful show about based on Catherine's courageous and complex life. We had performed it for the STC in 2018 to enthusiastic audiences.

Similarly, RBG is a project I feel passionate about and Ruth and her rich and impactful life are consuming me. I consider our similarities for a moment. On a private and personal level, we have a few. Both our mothers were Jewish. Both of us have American citizenship (I have Australian as well). Both have husbands called Marty. Both of our mothers died at the end of our final year of school, and were not there to see us graduate. We had two children each and developed cancer and had cancer return almost two decades later. I laughed to myself, adding, *And I've played a judge so know the weight of the robe.* I feel gutted that this production, scheduled to start in four months' time, may not be part of my future.

Today, I cried. I felt all the losses. For a moment, grief overcame me. I am not a crier; it takes a lot for me to feel the need. It felt so wonderful to cry. I momentarily observed myself, trying to identify the impulse that triggered it. It was simply the feeling of losing control. The realisation that I would need to let go and fall for a while, and not assume that every step had a clear destination. The tears were essential for me to experience the calm that comes after a good storm. When all the water subsides, the wet pavements glisten, birds fly from the branches and people venture out to walk their dogs. That wonderful settling as the breath regulates and creates an emptiness in which anything can happen. The expulsion of feeling that allows new space to be filled. New feelings to grow. Choosing those feelings is everything. Choosing carefully, wisely, consciously.

I called my agent Trent and he, El and Aimee began the difficult task of alerting the people I was about to work with that my availability might be in question. I called the STC and told them I wouldn't be able to perform in June due to treatment. Kip, Danielle, Anne and Alex were magnificent, telling me they would push the production back. Helen Bowden, a close friend and producer, assured me that she would manage the schedule and work around me in season two of *The Secret She Keeps,* the television drama based on Michael Robotham's novel, and not to worry. I tell the gorgeous Tim Minchin, who is an executive producer, writer and star of the TV series *Upright*, season 2. He and the team rearrange the date for my single but stunning scene. I fly up to Queensland, wear a skullcap and play his mother, dying of cancer, days before my surgery. I anticipate the conversation about *Love Me* season 2, a beautiful series I am deeply committed to and am hoping they may excitedly incorporate my cancer into the storyline if need be. To me, this feels like a great opportunity to further explore ideas of loss and love in relationships. I seesaw between feelings of excitement and sadness. Wholeness and emptiness. Hamish and Nicole, two of the producers of *Love Me,* and great friends, reassure me that all will be done to make it work.

I resist the temptation to seek sympathy, to call people and tell them, in case I lean towards the desire for mutual feelings of dismay and sadness: the trap of self-pity, which I loathe. I decide to only tell those who need to know, and do it gradually. I ask people I love to keep it private; they all do and I feel protected. Last time, I wore my cancer like a garment. I never really removed it; over time, it wore thinner along with my own decreasing size and, together, we came dangerously close to vanishing. This time, I would keep it in a beautiful box wrapped in tissue paper, on a shelf in the cupboard. I would open it when I needed to inspect it and care for it, but I would choose when to look at it and when to put it away. It would be moments in my life, not my whole life.

Suzie accompanied me for PET scans and an MRI. She waited in the reception for three hours and wrote while I lay in whirring, beeping, superhuman-sized tubes. We ate rice paper rolls in haste at the hospital cafeteria and crossed the road to my surgeon Andrew's rooms for the results. To our joy, the cancer hadn't spread. I announced that I would like to get rid of both breasts, whereupon Andrew's eyes showed alarm. He proceeded to gently explain the opportunity for reconstruction and recommended a plastic surgeon, Dr Fred Clarke, to discuss it with me before I made any decisions. Another Suzie, at the front desk, kindly arranged an appointment for me to see Fred.

Edwina, an amazing meditation teacher and a beautiful friend, drove me to the appointment. Dr Fred Clarke was impressive and kind. His explanation of the procedure and the expected results was thorough and thoughtful. He expressed no doubts that I would be a candidate for breast reconstruction depending on a test to check the vessels that would need to be removed from my abdomen to create blood flow into my breasts. Flesh from my tummy, stretching from hip to hip down to the pubic line and up to the belly button, would be removed. After the breast was scooped out, it would be filled with fat from my tummy, hooked up to blood vessels attached to my heart and I'd be sewn up. I could choose to have the new breast at the same height as the old breast (as if), or it could sit higher. Later, I could come back for a second surgery, which would seek to match the left breast with the right and make a nipple from saved flesh that was origamied into shape. I was dumbfounded. I was so impressed with his plan, expertise and availability, yet I could feel myself forcing down an invading unease. I felt conflicted. He was offering me a beautiful new breast and a tummy tuck, something most women would probably gag for. He showed us photos of before and after. Incredible shots of women, who were once carrying rolls of extra flesh, suddenly looking svelte and wearing six packs. Their once naturally low breasts were now perkier and seamless. It was an impressive and tempting offer. I looked down at my lap and tried to imagine my already small tummy no longer existing, and wondered how I would ever stand upright again if I had it removed.

We thanked him and walked to the car. We had 30 minutes before the next test, which measured blood flow. I panicked. It all felt wrong. I didn't know why. I cancelled the tests. Edwina drove as I opened my computer, paired it with my phone and listened in to an STC board meeting though headphones. Edwina drove the hour and a half to her beach house a little way north, as I tried to concentrate on the discussion happening in a faraway room.

Four days later, I sat in Dr Spillane's rooms with my close friend Joanne, who had been there for me throughout my first cancer, and who now picked me up in her little black Fiat. We chatted about our kids as we travelled, arriving early to scan the Covid QR code and do the temp check. Joanne remained accommodating and calm as I changed my mind twice about where to park, a clear indication that I was anxious.

Andrew looked at me.

'I've decided not to do the reconstruction,' I said breezily.

Andrew waited.

'I feel good about it. I don't need the breast and I don't have a great cleavage anyway, and Marty and my sons are fine about it, and they love me no matter how I look.'

'Who doesn't?' Andrew said.

This little comment, even though said in jest, reassured me.

'Well, I can do it the day after tomorrow or in a month's time,' he said calmly.

My certainty wavered, and he could see it. I wasn't ready to have it done in two days. I had a day's filming to finish, and wanted Marty and Finn home to be with Seamus so he wasn't alone.

Andrew remained steady. 'I don't think you're ready. Take your time. I'm taking a holiday. The ninth of March, I can book you in.'

'A month? I don't want to wait a month!' *I want to do it next week. I want to do it and get back to all the things that make me feel great.*

Joanne had been listening. Gently and succinctly, she offered: 'Maybe waiting is a good thing. You are on medication that has stopped the cancer growing, and you can finish your work, have the boys' birthdays and give yourself time to be certain.'

I heard her words and Andrew's. Although unconvinced, I balanced them with my low-lying panic and thanked them.

Andrew booked me in, and we headed out.

I decided to fact-check, to do all the tests and weigh things up. I proceeded to do the vessel test, which checks whether there is blood flow necessary for reconstruction. The results were good but a spot on my liver was of concern, so another MRI was arranged and, two days later, that too was clear. I had undergone every test available and, on the whole, my body was performing damn well. It was only this lump, this collection of cancer cells, that was of concern. It had to go. The decision to make was, what goes with it?

I called Sally, who I'd only known for three weeks. Sally is a life coach and I decided to work with her to help me clarify what I was seeking during this time in my life. She answered my call and listened to my concerns. She sent me a worksheet. I answered the questions and things became clearer. I thought about what things make me happy. Where I find joy. What is important to me. What my values are. I talked them over with Edwina, who, I must add, has now had breast cancer twice and had a bilateral mastectomy. Edwina listened and asked questions, but steered clear of advice except to say, 'But you don't have a tummy. Where the hell would they get it from?'

I felt sure that my breasts did not, and had never, defined me. I did not 'need' them for child rearing or sexual satisfaction. I wasn't likely to wear low-cut tops and reach across tables and press my chest in anyone's face for any reason. I wondered why my focus had shifted from saving my life from cancer to whether my tummy and breasts would look good.

I had to consider that losing a breast would leave me without symmetry. How did I feel about this? Symmetry lies at the centre of the concept of beauty. Symmetry is what women in particular spend thousands of dollars to achieve. Symmetry pleases both the viewer and the owner. However, my breast symmetry would only really be appreciated, or not, by people who saw me naked. Marty was most likely the only person who would get that benefit, and he simply wanted me alive in any shape. A prosthesis in a bra would create symmetry for public appearances. I could, of course, also take pleasure in daring to go 'side saddle', swinging only on one side, and discover whether a woman in her sixties can still turn heads.

One of my answers to the questionnaire, regarding joy, was the pleasure I derive from making something from nothing, or turning an adverse situation into a positive one. These challenges always make me feel alive, and here I was, standing immediately before a wonderful challenge. In my heart, I could begin to feel a tingle of potential.

I told Seamus, who was to turn twenty-one in a week's time, about the two options for surgery while we ate dinner.

'So, I can have my breast removed and remain flat, or I can have a reconstruction made from my tummy.'

He didn't falter. 'Well, I suggest you ask Siri to flip a coin and she'll decide your fate. Or you could do an Option 3 and create a ritual, and transfer your cancer over to someone you don't like.' We laughed and continued to eat our fish.

I rang Marty, who was still in Queensland with Finn. 'How would you feel if I had only one breast?'

'I'd love you,' he said.

I spoke to Finn, now twenty-three. He asked me if I was not telling him everything. I answered that, when I'd originally had breast cancer, he was only five years old and I had tried to protect him. But now he was an adult, I would share everything with him. He could ask me anything and I would answer honestly. I explained to him my options, described the processes and asked him what he thought. He listened and said, 'I think you should do whatever is safest and has the fastest recovery time.'

'How would you feel if I only had one breast?'

'Fine,' he said.

'What about a new breast made from my tummy? If I did that, would you design a tattoo for me, to adorn it with?'

'Yes, that would be great.'

I hung up.

I made a vow to myself: 'I will keep a sense of humour. I will remind myself that I'm loved. I will carry my heart under one breast and my son's art on the other.'

I made my decision and I felt great.

The ten-hour surgery was carried out masterfully and my recovery, aided by enormous support, felt reasonably effortless. Within three months I was walking upright and ready to work. STC arranged for a rehearsal space in the Wharf 2 theatre for Priscilla, where the creative team and I could rehearse *RBG: Of Many One.* After a warm welcome from Anne Dunne, the STC's new executive director, and the company, we immersed ourselves in the world of Ruth Bader Ginsburg. The stage management team plastered the walls with images of Ruth throughout her ages and her meetings with Presidents Clinton and Obama.

Priscilla had confided in me that she and her husband Mark were expecting their first child just before our opening date. Paige Rattray, an associate director at STC, had the inspired idea to bring in Sharon Millerchip as assistant to Priscilla and the phenomenal David Fleischer, Paul Charlier, Alex Berlage, Katie Hankin and Jennifer White were all on board. Suzie Miller had just returned from the UK after the massive success of her play *Prima Facie* at the Harold Pinter Theatre in London's West End.

We rehearsed for four weeks, with Suzie offering suggestions for cuts and rewrites. The final three days were spent drilling scenes between Ruth and Obama, which my brain was struggling to retain. We left the rehearsal room knowing that we would not return to the script for five weeks and I knew that the work we had done was still sitting on and around me, not yet *in* me, and that during the precious days leading up to the opening of *RBG* I would need to make the demanding but essential transition from conscious knowledge to unconscious knowing.

I flew to Melbourne and filmed the second season of *Love Me,* directed by the beautiful Bonnie Moir (the extraordinary

Emma Freeman had directed the first series). Hugo Weaving and I shared a flu and shot all our scenes in three weeks and once more I learned from him and loved every moment with him.

I returned to Sydney and moved into the small rehearsal room, taking time out of rehearsals only when I needed to sleep. Priscilla gave birth to a divine baby girl and Zoomed in to me daily. Less than five days later she was back at work guiding the technical rehearsals as we cooed over her daughter. Sharon Millerchip had caught Covid, but never missed a beat and Zoomed into the rehearsal room for long days, helping me run through the play, prompting me with lines whenever I dried. Suzie kept suggesting adjustments and lending support from meetings she was conducting overseas. Throughout this whole journey our male partners were encouraging and supporting us and the male creatives on the show, David, Paul and Alex, were deeply committed.

Another man who was in my heart daily was the painter Nicholas Harding. Nicholas had expressed interest in coming to a dress rehearsal and sketching me as Ruth. For years Nicholas captured remarkable theatrical moments in characters' lives. With the simplest of lines he illuminated behaviours and revealed new insights into a role, which melded with and transcended the actors' experience. For many months Nicholas had been undergoing treatments for cancer. We spent many joyous morning and afternoon teas in his studio, surrounded by glorious canvases he was working on. In late 2022, Nicholas's devoted partner and wife Lynne invited me over to see him. Nicholas was lying on the couch and Lynne and I had tea and a slice of cake at the table. Nicholas rose and went to the bathroom and on his return said, 'I'll draw now.'

Lynne deftly gathered his tools and put a beautiful green-covered bound book on the table. Nicholas sat with his back to the light and I sat across from him in a black coat and a crocheted white collar. As I murmured lines from the play, he sketched with a quiet determination and deep absorption. My heart was doing somersaults. I was amazed that he had the strength, the means of concentration, the energy. He drew for over an hour. I could sense Lynne's excitement and we both knew we were being transported by him, his passion, his need to create, his light, his life.

I am performing in *RBG* as I write this, and the memory of that intimate hour with Nicholas and Lynne carries me and I draw on his energy, his beauty, his talent. Nicholas passed away on 2 November 2022.

Today, I am well. I am working. I am surrounded by friends and family I love and I have a wealth of past experiences to draw on.

I hope when my time comes, I will echo Suzie Miller's words at the culmination of *RBG*:

> My heart soars and I breathe in this world one more time;
> Infused with a merging, a one-ness with everything [and nothing].

Acknowledgements

My thanks first to my beautiful family, Marty, Finn and Seamus. To my sister and brother Rosemary and Steven, the Mitchells, McGraths, Stevensons, Berricks. In particular Elizabeth Mitchell, Suzanne and Katherine Kelley, Ricky and Gary Mitchell, and Keira Lockyear.

To Malcolm Knox, who asked me to write a short story and then encouraged me to continue and supported me throughout the entire process.

To Joanne Corrigan, who was my first reader and great supporter, and Lulu Pinkus and Katrina Foster, who also championed me. To Robyn Backen, Victoria Hill and Edwina Parsons for their constant support.

My agents El, Trent, Aimee, Jennifer, Brittany and Jackie.

My brilliant editors, Samantha Kent, Tessa Feggans, Jessica Cox, and all at Allen & Unwin.

My heartfelt thanks to all the many friends who have been beside me throughout my life.

heathermitchell.com.au